The Power of Mindfulness

Amy Baltzell • Joshua Summers

The Power of Mindfulness

Mindfulness Meditation Training
in Sport (MMTS)

 Springer

Amy Baltzell
Counseling Psychology and Applied
Human Development
Boston University
Boston, MA, USA

Joshua Summers
Boston, MA, USA

ISBN 978-3-319-70409-8   ISBN 978-3-319-70410-4   (eBook)
https://doi.org/10.1007/978-3-319-70410-4

Library of Congress Control Number: 2017963052

Printed on acid-free paper

This Springer imprint is published by Springer Nature
The registered company is Springer International Publishing AG
The registered company address is: Gewerbestrasse 11, 6330 Cham, Switzerland

Kate Richardson-Walsh's keynote speech at the International Council for Coaching Excellence (ICCE) Conference, Liverpool, England (August 2017), after being asked what she learned most from her coach.

What do you need to function at your highest level? She responded,
It is not about what you want, but about what you need.

It felt selfish to be mindful.
(Yet) being present and in the moment helped me in Rio.
I could almost see things before they happened.
My mind was not so jam packed with thoughts.
I realized that it [being mindful] was not selfish.
It was the right thing to do.

Kate Richardson-Walsh,
English field hockey player
Olympic Gold (Rio)
and Bronze (London) Medal winner

Preface

I invited Josh to teach a class on mindfulness in a graduate level Positive Psychology course about 10 years ago. The students and I were fascinated by Josh's adept way of sharing a clear understanding of mindfulness. Mindfulness does not only include having a quiet, peaceful mind. It is not about chronically remaining calm and unphazed by the life around you. Mindfulness, in contrast, is being able to remain a witness and experiencer of *everything* that arises in your life with acceptance (or tolerance)! And then when you cultivate a mindful approach you are also developing poise, you can be much more at choice and wise in terms of how you respond to life challenges and opportunities and where you place your attention.

I began to understand the perhaps radical implications of bringing mindfulness to performance psychology: a mindful approach would mean that athletes I worked with would not have to work to block bad thoughts or manifest good ones. They instead could learn to change their relationship to thoughts and feelings that emerged *and* have the choice of where to place their attention. Cultivating mindfulness means strengthening the skill of awareness and acceptance of whatever occurs in life. In this mindful space, you are empowered to make wise and, if you wish, courageous choices about what actions you take (e.g., keep pushing hard even when being passed in a foot race).

Soon after having Josh to class, an opportunity arose for Josh to offer a mindfulness intervention for a collegiate sport team and a chance for me to study the impact of the mindfulness intervention. In response to this opportunity, Josh developed Mindfulness Meditation Training in Sport (MMTS), a mindfulness meditation program. In the first version MMTS was essentially a mindfulness, meditation training intervention with an educational component, tailored to help athletes with concentration and attention on the field.

We revised the program, after its initial run, and renamed it as MMTS 2.0. Since its first offering, we have integrated the concept of self-compassion throughout the program. We believe that offering an appropriate level of kindness in sports can be essential to dislodge you from intense performance anxiety or harsh self-criticism (more on this, throughout the book.). Since this initial intervention, research practitioners have run MMTS 2.0 for a range of sports athletes including collegiate golf teams, collegiate tennis teams, an Olympic badminton team, Army Rangers, a collegiate basketball team, and injured collegiate athletes.

MMTS 2.0 has been organized into six modules. The program is 6-hours long (1 hour per week over 6 weeks or two ½ hour segments per week over 6 weeks) with the addition of recommended daily 10-minute mindfulness practice throughout the program. Each 30-minute segment includes about 10 minutes of instruction, 10 minutes of practice, and 10 minutes of discussion. Sessions are offered to groups of athletes or to an individual sport team. The purpose of each module, the main concepts offered, and the exercises recommended for implementation are offered at the end of the book (see the Protocol of MMTS 2.0 in Appendix A).

The goals of MMTS 2.0 are to help you improve:

1. Attention: Helps increase your ability to focus attention (i.e., concentrate).
2. Poise: Helps increase your ability to cope with the experience of negative thoughts and emotions (change the relationship with aversive emotions, thoughts and sensations) that may be present due to the pressures of competition. You can learn to stop trying to change what arises, but instead learn to accept and work with it.
3. Adapt (with Clarity): Help your ability to be fully present and able to adjust during performance so you can be freed up to pay attention to what is happening moment to moment on the athletic field.

Through the MMTS 2.0 practices, you can improve your ability to perform optimally (given physical, time, and other constraints), via an adaptive and enhanced ability to notice cues in the sport environment (that may have been ignored before).

We wrote *The Power of Mindfulness* to help mentally prime you for excellence in practice and competition. The ideas offered in this book are transferrable to any area of performance. We wanted to share the ideas we brought together in the development of MMTS 2.0. Athletes no longer have to be restricted by erratic emotions or limited mindsets. They can learn to tap their true potential: diligent physical training does not need to be compromised by aversive emotions, boredom, or distraction. With mindfulness training, athletes' minds can become an invaluable ally in their pursuit of athletic excellence.

The Power of Mindfulness is one of the first books on the market to offer clear, practical strategies about how to use mindfulness practices to improve sport performance. The strategies offered throughout the book are the same ones used in Mindfulness Meditation Training in Sport (MMTS) 2.0, an intervention for sport created by the authors.

The structure of *The Power of Mindfulness* aligns directly with the six modules of MMTS 2.0. Part I includes Chapters 1 through 3 which provide an introduction to mindfulness and the purpose of developing MMTS 2.0. Part II includes Chapters 4 through 13 (which mirror MMTS 2.0, Modules 1 through 6). These chapters focus on introducing mindfulness to the world of performance, the value of tolerating difficult thoughts and emotions (versus avoiding or getting tangled up in the difficulty), self-compassion (particularly useful in times when athletes suffer from performance anxiety and harsh self-criticism), and self-regulation. The last chapters offer ways to create inspirational performance values and apply them on the field (whether you feel like doing what needs to be done or not) and on being fully present when practicing and competing. All chapters include explanation of core ideas, examples from private practice working with competitive athletes, as well as clear guidance about how to apply mindfulness and self-compassion to performance. At the end of each chapter, the mindfulness meditation exercises used in MMTS 2.0 are offered.

Part III offers specific ideas to those who want to run MMTS 2.0 as an instructor. Those who have run MMTS 2.0 were interviewed and their challenges and suggestions about running the program are offered. We end with future directions of mindfulness meditation based training in sport and performance.

Please use this book in the way that best works for you. For some of you, simply reading through and learning about how to mentally approach distraction and regulating your attention differently can offer the impact you are seeking. For others, this book can be a wonderful starting point for implementing mindfulness and compassion practices within and outside sport to help with performance. And, of course, we offer the book to those of you who would either want to run MMTS 2.0 or use some of its elements in your own professional services. If you use MMTS 2.0 for such purposes, we only ask that you stay true by about 90% to the program if you opt to call it MMTS 2.0 and, if not, to cite the ideas you have drawn from the book

Thank you for picking up this book. We deeply hope that this is of value to you.

Boston, MA, USA   Amy Baltzell

Acknowledgments

I (Josh) want to extend my deepest appreciation to all the students (Trevor Cote, Bob Diehl, Jake Cooper, Lani Silversides and Kyle Mcbrierty) for their help and thoughtful feedback in editing and reading through this manuscript. I'd also like to thank all the people who participated in our studies, putting MMTS 2.0 to the test, and for helping us evolve our vision of the application of mindfulness to sport. Finally, I'd like to express my enormous gratitude to Dr. Amy Baltzell for her support, vision, and heart throughout our many years of working together.

When I (Amy) do any project, I am always surprised at how much effort many contribute to make it happen. None of my work in mindfulness and sport would have happened without Josh. I will never forget the awe and wonder I felt when I first heard him lecture on the concept and practice of mindfulness. Teaching a course on this topic over the past years with him at Boston University has been a joy, an honor, and a continuous learning experience. I am forever grateful and indebted to him for bringing most of the ideas in this book to me for the first time. Thank you to my sister Lola (Laura) Baltzell for her consistent, inspirational mindfulness meditation practice. She has been a devoted practitioner for over a decade before I became open to the idea (and thank you for introducing me to Josh!).

I offer deep thanks to Bob Diehl. He urged me to continue developing and studying MMTS during our first research meeting during his doctoral studies and helped me in editing this book. His contribution and tireless collaborative support has been invaluable. I also thank Trevor Cote for his steadfast, excellent editing support. Thank you for your encouragement and high standards. Thanks to Jake Cooper as well for stepping in and offering excellent editorial feedback toward the finish line. Your enthusiasm, willingness to be a member of the team, and magnificent heart were very welcome at the end of the editing process. Also, I offer special thanks to Lani Silversides and Kyle Mcbrierty who each offered a last careful read-through of the manuscript. Thank you for sharing your energy and precision. With appreciation, I thank John McCarthy for sticking by me through this project and the many others. I thank my three children – Shayna Daisy, Luke Henry, and Zoey Violet – for their innocent, open-hearted love that keeps me going and feeling like what I can offer matters.

Boston, MA, USA   Joshua Summers
                                                                                             Amy Baltzell

Contents

Part III   Research and Future Directions

14   Lessons from the Field: MMTS 2.0 Instructors' Insights Gained......   131

About the Authors

Amy Baltzell is President of the Association of Applied Sport Psychology (2017-2018), Director of the Sport Psychology Specialization at Boston University within the Counseling Psychology Program, and an Olympian. She also is a Reiki Master Teacher, Men Chhö Rei Kei certified practitioner. She teaches a graduate course entitled *Mindfulness and Performance* along with a range of courses in Sport and Positive Psychology. She taught the first Sport Psychology course offered at Harvard University.

She is the editor for the book, *Mindfulness and Performance* (2016, Cambridge University Press) and author of *Living in the Sweet Spot: Preparing for Performance in Sport and Life* (2011, FIT). She has extensive experience personally and professionally in sport. She was a member of the 1989–1991 U.S. National Rowing Teams, the 1992 US Olympic Rowing Team, and the 1995 America's Cup All-Women's Sailing Team, A³. She served as the Radcliffe Head Varsity lightweight rowing coach (1998-99). As a sport psychologist she has a private consulting practice in which she has been providing one-on-one sport psychology services to collegiate, Olympic level, and professional athletes. She also provides educational workshops and talks to coaches, sport teams, and clubs.

Joshua Summers is an internationally respected yoga and mindfulness teacher. He is the founder of Sati Solutions, a mindfulness-based consultancy in Boston, MA. For twenty years, Joshua has trained extensively in yoga and mindfulness meditation both in Asia and the United States, with two months of intensive training in a Burmese monastery. He now teaches yoga and meditation internationally and consults with performers and athletes on mindfulness skill-sets for optimal performance. Josh also holds a masters degree in Oriental Medicine and has a private acupuncture practice in Boston, MA.

He earned his BA from Columbia University. He (2009) is the author of *The Buddha's Playbook, Strategies for Enlightened Living*. Highlights of his mindfulness-based teaching include serving as Insight mediation teacher for 7 years; Director of Contemplative Practices at Back Bay Yoga Studio 2004-2008; Northeastern University Spiritual Center: Retreat Leadership Facilitator;

International Meditation and Yoga Teacher and Leader (Ireland, Amsterdam, Switzerland and Germany in 2010, 2011); Leader of Yin Yoga and Mindfulness Meditation Teacher Trainings 2005-Present; Mindfulness and self-awareness facilitator with medical residents at Mass General Hospital, 2009; and Meditation Teacher for a Women's Division I Soccer Team, 2010.

List of Figures

List of Tables

Part I
An Introduction to Mindfulness and Sport

Chapter 1
The Power of Mindfulness in Performance: Mindful Meditation Training for Sport 2.0

Mindfulness is essentially awareness and acceptance of what is occurring. This simple idea has profound implications when you apply it to the sport and performance context. How could mindfulness education and training matter in sport? Aren't you always aware? And isn't acceptance precisely what you *do not* want to do in performance? Doesn't acceptance lead to complacency and laziness? And how in the world would sitting down, meditating, help you score more baskets or run faster on the track? How could the practice of doing nothing and practicing not reacting help on the athletic field? These are all good questions and will be addressed throughout *The Power of Mindfulness.*

I (Amy) had similar initial reactions to the idea of mindfulness. I thought that the idea of meditating was interesting, but certainly not something I could do or would want to do. And yet over the past 10 years I have discovered that helping athletes cultivate a mindful approach is precisely what is sorely needed within the performance world. Over the past decade I have come to discover the power of being mindful: Learning to be more mindful – yes, simply just noticing and accepting what is happening – gives you the power to choose how you want to respond versus react. In fact, this simple idea of cultivating a mindful approach can have a profound impact on performance, such as empowering you to be:

- More at choice in how you want to act versus being reactive (i.e., having a choice not to throw a racket or break a hockey stick in a moment of sport rage),
- Better able to handle intense negative feelings like anxiety or fear,
- Better able to focus and concentrate when feeling performance pressure, and
- Better able to adapt and adjust within performance.

The use of mindfulness to become more present, balanced, and able to respond effectively to life challenges is not new. The concept of mindfulness is an essential element of Buddhist meditation training, which encompasses intentionally bringing awareness to the contents of the mind while practicing formal meditation. Cultivating mindfulness is also central to Jon Kabat-Zinn's Mindfulness Based Stress Reduction program, the dominant mindfulness intervention across the western world and has

© Springer International Publishing AG 2017
A. Baltzell, J. Summers, *The Power of Mindfulness,*
https://doi.org/10.1007/978-3-319-70410-4_1

been the forerunning intervention in mindfulness research. Mindfulness has been used in many psychologically based interventions and quite recently, over the past decade, the effort to help cultivate a mindfulness approach has made its way to sport and performance interventions.

What Is Mindfulness?

Mindfulness refers to *being aware of what's happening in the present moment,* which is a fundamental ability that we all share. If you are aware of these very words you are reading, the sensations of this book in your hands, or the sounds of a neighbor's dog barking, then you are successfully using your innate capacity to be mindful. Mindfulness is not magical or mystical. It is the simple awareness of what is unfolding in real time, *right now*, just as it is. There is nothing more, nothing less.

While the ability to be mindful is a very natural function of the mind, we'd like to address some of its key characteristics and functions that make it such a vital capacity for performing at your best. First we'll introduce three key characteristics of mindfulness:

1. **Non-judgmental**. Being mindful means being non-judgmental (or accepting to tolerating what has already happened). This means when you are mindful you are able to acknowledge *just* what is happening. You opt to acknowledge the reality before you take action. You may not prefer what is happening. You may prefer to go back to sleep versus get up at 6:00 am for the morning workout. But instead of chronically and reactively judging an experience as being 'good' or 'bad,' you are able to accept or tolerate that it is what it is – for the moment. And with this skill of first noticing, you give yourself a bit of space to respond in a wise way versus reacting based on past experience. So, for example, when the athlete is woken up at 6:00 am for practice she can notice the tiredness, notice her aversion to getting up and then in a balanced way decide whether or not it is wise to get up or go back to sleep. Another example is rain. You may prefer that it never rains, but the fact is that sometimes it does rain, and even pours. So instead of judging that the rain is "bad" and getting caught up in irritation, it can be much more productive to simply notice the rain and perhaps notice irritation as well. And then with a mindfulness approach accept (or tolerate) the rain and the irritation in order to respond in a wise way, such as putting on a raincoat and carrying on with the day or opting to wait the rain out.

On the face of it, being non-judgmental might seem like a really odd quality to try and cultivate for athletes and performers, in general. After all, don't you want to judge how you are doing so you can improve and achieve more? The answer is a resounding, *Yes!* However, you must *first* be able to be mindful (aware of what is happening) before you move on to making wiser and better choices. First, you have to learn to be present to what is occurring: when you judge, you limit noticing all that may be happening in the moment. Once you can be fully present, then you can be more open, more creative, more proactive in competition and in training. Developing a non-judgmental attitude can be a radical shift in how athletes typically relate to competition. After all, you have been well trained to judge everything. You think about whether or not our last play was "good" or "bad." You think about whether our workout is going "well" or "poorly."

In short, you are always interpreting your experience in a self-focused way, based on what you want to happen or what you don't want to happen. Here, 'self-focused' points to the psychological manner in which you habitually filter our present-moment experience through our self-oriented *ideas* about that experience. These ideas are conditioned by our past experiences. For example, imagine a game situation where an opponent on defense blocks your shot in basketball. As a result of this you might, in the moment, feel angry. Your self-image as a competent player is under threat. A self-focused response would be, *"Damn! I shouldn't have let that happen. What is wrong with me?"* Here, the mental reaction includes not only the initial anger at your shot being blocked, but also the subsequent reaction to this anger in the form of self-blame.

With mindfulness practice, you strengthen your awareness to recognize the presence of both what just happened (e.g., a shot being blocked) and the resulting emotions (e.g., anger), without judging them. Or more frequently, you might notice judging arising and learn to tolerate this normal occurrence. Another way of saying this is you can learn to tolerate what happens and your emotional responses. No one likes to get a shot blocked, and the shooter experiencing a reactive surge of anger is a typical response. But with a mindfulness practice – you can learn to notice such patterns of emotional reaction and notice how your typical response might get in the way of performance. In such moments of noticing, you can learn to choose to respond differently (e.g., accept the rush of anger and still stay focused on the next play).

Playing mindfully, the athlete may still get their shot blocked, may still experience a surge of anger. Yet with mindfulness, they can choose to change how they respond to expected emotional reactions and urges to behave in ways that hurt performance, such as give up or try too hard. Instead, even when feeling such uncomfortable feelings, the athlete can learn to stay engaged in performance, in the metaphorical next play (instead of giving up).

Another way to think about the power of mindfulness is that one's awareness of an ineffective response is like stopping the domino effect of upset. Getting a shot blocked and being washed over with emotion is enough to deal with when you have to focus back on the performance demands in front of you. However, the real damage (for performance) comes with staying locked into the upset. Continuing to be upset by your frustration or anger drains your energy, becomes counterproductive, and ultimately hurts performance. In this example, the athlete could become mindful by bringing to mind the thought, "there is anger" and "there is self-blame," which can result in acceptance and a re-focus on play (though the negative emotions may still be alive and strong in their system). Rather than mindlessly ruminating, "I'm angry, I hate this!," or "This is not my day, I always fail when it counts!" and shutting down or mentally giving up, you have another option, another way to respond to the inevitable disappointments, frustrations or self-critical busy mind.

Mindfulness gives you a way out. You can opt to be aware of the difficult thoughts and emotions and opt to respond differently to them (e.g., tolerance and focus back on the performance at hand). While this awareness, the power of mindfulness, might seem like a slight shift in perception, it leads to a *radical reorientation* towards how athletes can learn to respond differently in the moment and to subsequent experiences (instead of just automatically reacting). When reactions are judgmental and self-focused, and you get caught up in this, it is easy to find yourself in any number of negative tailspins or downward spirals, ever lost in *self-defeating reactivity*. The same holds true for intense positive emotions. In certain circumstances even positive emotions can distract you from focusing on the task at hand.

Through cultivating mindfulness, you can cut that chain of the reaction and engage with the experience in a free and direct way. You can notice a missed play, the typical emotional reactions to missing, and then notice your next opportunity on the field. With this poised awareness (or less reactive awareness) of what is occurring in the moment, you can empower yourself to get much more out of each training bout and competition.

An important point needs to be made clear: being mindful and non-judgmental does not mean you stop caring about outcomes, or that you just become indifferent to results, goals, and success. "Oh we scored? Oh we lost? I'm non-judgmental so I don't care." No, that's not it. Not, at all!

Of course winning still matters, in every instance possible. The aim remains high. Maybe even higher, because with a mindfulness approach you can more easily tolerate the highs and lows with competing on the edge, thus more empowered to push your limits. Your fears and worries around what is actually happening and *attachments* to what is happening in the moment are reduced. In other words, when you are mindful, your self-reflexive reactions to situations no longer cloud and limit your ability to perform at our best. You can learn to let go of the distractions that can cause significant emotional swings and blur essential awareness.

2. **Bare Attention.** As you release yourself from the tendency to automatically react or judge your experience and yourself, a mindful approach then allows you to meet your experience with *bare attention*. Bare attention as a factor of awareness means that you can see very clearly just what is happening with minimal distortion. The distortion is usually from habits of how you have always seen the world (e.g., they are better than we are) or how you *always* respond (e.g., when someone passes me in a foot race, I slow down).

There is a famous Japanese poem that beautifully illustrates this quality of bare attention: "The old pond; the frog jumped in; plop." Here the experience is just as it is, without any additional distortion from the observer. Nothing is added to the pond, to the frog, or to the sound of contact between the two.

In sport this could look like a basketball, a shot, and two-points. Nothing else. Under normal circumstances, most people tend to filter their experience through lenses of desire, fear, craving, aversion, or dislike – they can become so tangled up in their emotions and thoughts that they can't see what is right in front of them. This normal tendency to filter inhibits your ability to see clearly just what is actually happening. And clearly seeing with bare attention is the essential basis for skillful action in any performance because you are responding to the task at hand *as it actually is,* not as you distort it to be in your mind. Essentially you are freed up from believing thoughts like, "today just isn't my day," or "I can never win in this pool."

The distortion often comes from extreme emotions or habits of you "know" it will be. With mindfulness, you experience the immediacy of the moment with crystal clarity. And when you see just what is happening, more frequently, the 'right thing to do' spontaneously flows out of that pure lens (and from the Buddhist tradition, "clear seeing"). For example, in the previous example the basketball player's shot got blocked and the wise response is to get back to defend the basket as quickly as possible (versus being embarrassed and missing the opportunity to stop the easy layup by the opponent).

Another example, without the overlay of negative emotions, is mindfully playing a tennis match. The tennis player might be aware of the sensations of how the racket feels in his hands. He might consciously notice the movement of the ball back and forth across the court. He might feel the temperature of the day or notice patterns of movement in his opponent. He probably would not notice the sound of traffic and birds because these cues would not help optimize performance. He might be mindful of a sense of 'doing well' or "not playing my best." But all these experiences would be known just as they were. Most of the feedback could serve as information about how to best take the next swing or where to place the ball on his opponents' side. But the bare attention aspect is just the sensations. Just a thought. Just a sound. And as he plays with such bare awareness he would be able to flexibly adapt to the moment-to-moment conditions of the match, without being burdened by oppressive opinions and ideas about the match.

In many ways practicing mindfulness can prepare you for the experience known as 'flow' (a state of being fully engaged in what you are doing for as many moments as possible – more on this later in the book). With such bare attention you can actually become much wiser in how you respond in real time to any competitive condition because all of your attention can move to cues, your competitor's moves or environmental changes, to give you the best chance at optimizing performance in the given moment. When you are fully in each moment, you are more empowered to know just what to do in that given moment.

3. **Intentional**. The third factor of mindfulness is that it is intentional. This simply means that the quality of our awareness is fueled by your intention to be mindful. Without this core intention, it is very difficult to strengthen the quality of the mind's awareness. Under normal circumstances, the habitual energy of the mind is tipped so far towards the tendency of absent-mindedness or mindlessness (i.e., relying on how you know it will be, how it has always been), that unless you intentionally value and respect the importance of mindfulness, itself, it will be near impossible to develop this skill. When not mindful, you can easily react and think in habituated ways and not attend to what might warrant a different response.

As you'll see when you start intentional mindfulness practice, you often can't control when you're going to be mindful and when you're going to space out. As will be confirmed time and again by your own direct experience, you'll see the sobering reality that your mind has a mind of its own. Meaning, you can easily be drawn into involuntary thoughts and emotions that arise. We like to think about it by distinguishing between having intentional thoughts (thinking on purpose) and experiencing uninvited thoughts – thoughts that just spontaneously emerge, such as "I can't win," or "you're an idiot."

You can strengthen and support the *intention* to be mindful – and ultimately, to be more mindful. In this way, every time you return to the intention to be awake and aware, you are planting seeds for moments of mindfulness to arise in the future. And the more seeds of intention that you plant right now in your formal practice (meaning doing mindfulness exercises – more on this in the second part of the chapter) and throughout our daily lives, the greater the likelihood that this mindful awareness will arise spontaneously when you need it the most: in the clutch. With practice, your habit of being mindful will strengthen. This fact has been supported by dozens of empirical studies.

Functions of Mindfulness for Best Performance

These *qualitie*s of mindfulness (discussed above)– non-judgmental, bare awareness, and intentional – lead to the actual functions of mindfulness. Joseph Goldstein, an eminent meditation teacher, describes the functions of mindfulness (discussed below) as: (1) increasing concentration, (2) developing clear seeing and perception, (3) guarding the mind, and (4) balancing the mind. This section highlights the value of these functions for athletes both in training and high-pressure performance situations. Essentially there are four invaluable *functions* of mindfulness that are essential to sport performance.

1. Concentration.

Mindfulness improves the ability to concentrate, to "hold something in mind". With enhanced mindfulness skills, you are *better able to purposefully pay attention to what you choose to pay attention to and better able to maintain such attention over time.* Simply put it means you can keep something you care about on your radar, more consistently. You may think that holding something in mind is easy. Yet when you consider the many times a coach will offer the same feedback to an athlete and how the same technical piece of advice seems to quickly dissolve from the athletes' awareness, you can better appreciate the need for the capacity of concentration.

The challenge, of course, is that you have a myriad of things to think about each moment. You get bombarded with what is happening both internally and externally – from the coaching you receive, what your teammates are saying or doing, what your opponents are doing on the field to your own internal judgments and reactions, to all of these. Most of us tend to have very active minds and our minds can be filled with involuntary (i.e., uninvited) thoughts of what has happened, what we'd like to have happen, and some of what happening within our moment-to-moment experience. It takes great practice to purposefully sustain awareness on what you deem to be important (otherwise known as task-relevant cues for performance). Our minds can easily be swayed by our hopes, desires, fears, and input from others. It is extremely normal to have hopes and fears, yet mindfulness helps you determine when it is wise to pay attention to such concerns and when it is best to focus on sport-specific tasks. When practicing and performing, we know that to optimize performance we must direct our attention. The challenge is keeping your attention focused where you choose to focus it and releasing yourself from the judgment, fear, and distortions that cause you to waste your energy and time.

2. Clear seeing

As discussed in the previous section, when you release yourself from your judgments about things and connect with your direct experience through the clear lens of bare attention, you are able to see things as they really are. Your mind's comprehension of what is happening becomes finely tuned with a sharpened accuracy. Jackson and Delehanty (1995) summarizes this quality of clear seeing in his book, *Sacred Hoops*:

> Basketball is a complex dance that requires shifting from one objective to another at lightning speed. To excel, you need to act with a clear mind and be totally focused on what everyone on the floor is doing. Some athletes describe this quality of mind as a "cocoon of concentration." But that implies shutting out the world when what you really need to do is become acutely aware of what's happening right now, this very moment (p. 115-116).

Mindfulness supports this kind of *panoramic specificity* of awareness, where the mind is open and wide awake to exactly what is occurring in real time, free of distortions and at once able to focus on the specific areas of performance that will leverage best performance.

3. Mindfulness guards the mind.

Just as a gatekeeper or guard monitors the kinds of people who are allowed to enter and exit a particular building, the habit of being mindful has the important function of guarding the mind. As you become mindful, our awareness monitors the kinds of thoughts that enter our stream of consciousness, both voluntary and uninvited (i.e., involuntary) thoughts. Some thoughts are helpful and are given free entrance, while other thoughts are quite destructive and unhelpful. Being mindful helps you recognize such thoughts as they arise in our mind and can effectively help neutralize their negative influence. In this way, the mind is protected from the potential harm that can result from negative thinking. Mindfulness does not stop the negative thoughts, but offers each of us a different way to respond to them. It is not just "negative" thoughts that can be problematic. Thoughts like, "I don't need to get up and go to practice; I am the best on the team; and Everyone loves me," can also be quite problematic. As great philosopher and psychologist William James (1842–1910) said, "The greatest weapon against stress is the ability to choose one thought over another." And it is the power of mindfulness that gives you this ability. You can choose which thoughts to engage with, to believe, to value and you also can choose to watch unhelpful, unnecessary thoughts come and go like storm clouds in the sky.

4. Balances the Mind

Related to the last function, mindfulness supports a balanced perspective on what is happening. Without this capacity to bring mindful presence to our thoughts and emotions, the conditioned tendency is to be swept away by a series of domino-like thoughts and feelings. Often a thought arises in consciousness and you tend to get lost in the content of the thought, very easily. You can think of thoughts as inner-advertisements. Imagine what would happen if, every time you heard or saw on advertisement on television, you were to pick up your credit card and buy the very thing being advertised. It might not be long before you were deep in financial debt. This example may feel far from your experience, yet think of a time you have made a mistake and criticized yourself. And think about how that story of feeling badly about yourself, doubting yourself, lasted much longer than the initial disappointment from making the mistake.

This concludes the introduction and background to the basic concept of mindfulness and conceptually how cultivating mindfulness can contribute to sport performance. The following chapter provides an introduction to the practice of mindfulness meditation, a long tested practice that helps cultivate mindfulness.

Chapter 2
Mindfulness Meditation 101

Train the Mind to Be more Present

All of the mindfulness training exercises in this book are inspired by meditation. Just as you train your quads to get stronger through practicing squats we will provide exercises to train your mind to learn to be progressively more present, poised in the face of difficult emotions and ultimately better armed to perform, regardless of your challenge. Given a range of mindfulness-based meditation practices serve as the core tools we will use to help strengthen your habit of mindfulness we would like to consider meditation up front in this book. What is mindful meditation and how do you do it?

Put simply, the word *meditation* refers to a formal approach to training the mind in a particular way. There are literally *thousands* of specific styles of meditations out there. Some meditation styles have you watch the breath, feel the body, repeat a certain word or phrase and others have you create mental visualizations. Some meditation practices are religious practices and others secular.

Most people have some sense of what the word *meditation* means. And often that sense of what it means to meditate refers to one broad category of meditation known as ***concentration*** meditation. You might imagine someone sitting down in a quiet, darkened room, closing their eyes for a (long) period of time. They might watch their breath or repeat a certain word or phrase. And within that period of time, something is supposed to happen. Their mind is *supposed* to clear. Their annoying thoughts are *supposed* to stop. The person *should* feel relaxed and renewed at the end. Anxiety and stress *should* disappear. In other words, the person should feel noticeable beneficial effects after a period of meditation, otherwise why would they waste their time, right?

Well, as it turns out, this popular perception of what it means to meditate represents just one broad category of meditation, and it's not the type that is emphasized in this book. We are not emphasizing such meditation practices because they will not serve you best in effort to optimize performance. There are many historical and

© Springer International Publishing AG 2017
A. Baltzell, J. Summers, *The Power of Mindfulness*,
https://doi.org/10.1007/978-3-319-70410-4_2

cultural reasons that might explain why this popular perception of meditation exists right now. We've all been in the checkout line at a grocery store and seen the covers of new age magazines where a beautiful (air-brushed) model sits on top of a boulder, smiling serenely with inner-contentment. And a caption on the cover often reads something like, "Six Easy Steps to Inner-Ease and Peace." Who wouldn't want that? (OK, maybe you'd want "Six Easy Steps to Inner-Ease and Athletic Excellence." – which we are getting to!) This perception points to some popular confusions about what meditation must be. Meditation is often perceived to be a quiet, peaceful experience that reduces stress. But that's just one type of meditation (concentration meditation). And the truth is, even with concentration meditations, often the mind wanders and is distracted by body sensations, sounds, thoughts and emotions. Concentration meditation is not always quiet and peaceful.

Amidst all these different styles of meditation, there are two broad categories or approaches to meditation. First, there are meditation styles, which emphasize concentration or the ability to stay focused on one thing in particular. With this style of concentration meditation, you would try to shut out all other sensory input and focus only on what you were trying to focus on. And then there are styles of *mindfulness* meditation, which emphasize focusing the mind in the present moment to be aware of everything that is arising in real time. In other words, there are no distractions in mindfulness meditation. Whatever you are noticing, that is what you bring mindfulness to! Our meditation-training program is based on mindfulness meditation, which will help you most with athletic performance.

Many people have the perception that meditation is training in *concentration* but not training in *mindfulness*. They think, "I have to sit down, close my eyes, focus on something, and block everything else out." But that approach is only *concentration* and not *mindfulness* training. In this book, we will use concentration drills as a means towards strengthening mindfulness, but we will not use the concentration as an end unto itself.

The main emphasis in this book is to offer a training for your mind that is based in mindfulness meditation so that you can dynamically engage with the present moment from a space of freedom and spontaneity. So, for example, if feelings of anger in meditation arise – the goal is not to block it out but to acknowledge and accept the feelings. When your mind wanders in mindfulness training and you notice it – this is a moment of success, not another moment of failure. When you are present and aware of what is happening – no matter what is happening, *that* is being mindful.

As this training takes root and develops, you gradually shift your default mental states from random mindlessness to more present and wakeful experiences of mindfulness. This training creates the inner space so that you can respond to whatever is happening in the moment without being overwhelmed by negative thoughts or emotions. With this inner training, you will learn how to 'get out of your own way' and how to, more likely, enter flow (more on flow later). When well trained, the mind will become more adaptive, more resilient, more perceptive, and more creative. Mindfulness meditation is really strength and conditioning training for your 'muscle' of awareness. Just as you train your bodies for performance-specific outcomes on the field, you can train the mind so that it is better able to serve your needs in a game or competition.

Why We Train the Mind

Neuroscientists have now discovered that the brain is capable of re-modeling itself in response to repeated behaviors, actions, and/or thoughts. As Donald Hebb, the father of neuropsychology suggests – and summarized by Siegrid and Löwel (1992), "Neurons that fire together, wire together" (p. 210). Essentially this saying suggests that when the brain is exposed to repetition, it works on the cellular level to make the connection in the brain more efficient. Whether it is building a habit of fear or a habit of *being present to what is occurring* – your brain accommodates you by working hard to engrain your habits on the cellular level. The great news is that you can change our ineffective mind habits – through re-wiring our brains – with appropriate effort!

There has been great interest, on the part of scientists, in researching changes in the brain due to mental practice or experience, which is termed neuroplasticity. Some researchers have explored the impact of *meditation training* on the brain. Richard Davidson and John Kabat-Zinn with their research group were the first to report empirically supported changes in brain functioning as a result of meditation practice. In their 2003 study, twenty-five people participated in the Mindfulness Based Stress Reduction (MBSR) program, which includes a once per week (2.5 to 3 h each week), 8-week mindfulness meditation training program (all participants also attended a 7 h silent retreat during week six of the meditation program.) These meditators, compared to their control group, demonstrated significantly more activity in the left prefrontal cortex of the brain, which is the area of the brain associated with positive emotions and the area, which copes more effectively with stress. These same findings have been demonstrated in a number of subsequent studies.

You may wonder, why does more activity in the left prefrontal cortex matter? Can it help you with performance? In 2010, Antonietta Manna with her research group found empirical data that found, yes indeed, the benefits of meditation could help strengthen essential capacities for top performance. They had novice mediators and Theravada Buddhist monks practice meditation for ten days and then compared differences of the two groups. They found that the monks, again, demonstrated much more activity in the left prefrontal cortex and that these same monks were much better able to purposefully self-regulate their response to sensory experience, thoughts, and emotions. Essentially, their study suggests that the meditation practice created a literal change in brain functioning, lending more support for the phenomenon of neuroplasticity. Due to the meditation practice, the monks were much better at tasks related to focused attention and emotional control – which, as we all know, are both essential for performance under pressure.

Whether you have had deep experience in meditation practices or this is the first time that you have tried it, we invite to begin the MMTS 2.0 experience by engaging in Exercise 2.1, below.

Exercise 2.1: A Quick Exercise in Mindfulness Training

Let's perform a simple exercise in Mindfulness Training. This short experiment will give you a more accurate understanding of the current state of your mind. Here's what you'll do:

1. Get a simple timing device: a stopwatch, a timer, or an alarm on your cell phone.
2. Set the timer to go off in five minutes.
3. Sit comfortably on a chair – with your back straight and feet on the floor – and close your eyes.
4. In a relaxed way, observe the sensations in your body as you breathe in and as you breathe out. Wherever you feel the breath is fine, there is no "right" place to feel it. Try keeping focused on the simple sensations of breath coming in and of breath going out.
5. If, however, from time to time, you notice that your mind starts wandering (involuntary thinking) and you lose the awareness of the breath, ask yourself this question, "Did I intend to think this thought? Or did my mind randomly wander away from the breath?"
6. After you notice this mind wandering, allow your body to relax (or at least go easy on yourself – everyone's mind wanders) and bring your attention back to the breath.
7. Practice this for the 5-minute time period.
8. We'd like you to consider what percentage of your thinking was 'intentional,' meaning that you consciously decided to think about something, and what percentage of your thinking is completely random. And BE HONEST.

Even if you don't have 5 min or an alarm, please give this a try for about 30 s before continuing with the next section.

Developing a Different Relationship with Thoughts

Welcome back! How did you do? When you closed your eyes and watched your breath, what percentage of the thoughts that you noticed was 'intentional'? And what percentage of your thoughts was 'unintentional' or 'uninvited'?

When we ask this question in seminars, some of the more overly confident students will say, "It was 50-50! About half my thoughts were intentional and half were random." But then, someone else will question, "Really? I felt like ALL my thoughts were random." Whereupon a chorus of other participants will chime in, "Yeah, it really seemed like at least 99% of all my thoughts were random." Feeling that they may have been a little too optimistic, the first, overly-confident person generally concedes, "Well, er... hmmm.... I guess it would be more accurate to say 90% of my thoughts were random after all."

Interesting.

In just a short five-minute period of time, we notice that the vast majority of our thinking is utterly random, out of our control, or simply uninvited. For many people, this is a discouraging and even frightening realization. "Wow," they think, "If that's what it's like in just five minutes, what does that mean for the way I live the rest of my life?"

The great news is that in mindfulness training you are not trying to stop your random, involuntary thoughts. You are learning to have a *different relationship* to them. When you are practicing it is 100% OK and expected that the involuntary thoughts and distractions will arise. This is, in fact, part of the meditation process. The mindfulness practice is really about *how you respond* to such involuntary mental and emotional occurrences. Do you notice them with interest? Or do you believe and buy into every desire, criticism, and fantasy of what the mind did or did not say is good or bad?

Many people who start trying mindfulness exercises can feel disheartened by the initial insight that they have streams of random, uninvited thoughts. We all do! Yet, when they first start noticing their busy minds many people prematurely conclude that meditation is not for them. But this is just like a couch potato who one day decides to run a marathon and finds that by the end of the first 200 yards they are winded, cramped, and unable to run another foot. The problem isn't the activity. The real problem is lack of training. And this is where mindfulness training comes in to practice. You can train your minds so that you are better able to choose how you engage with any situation.

Until now, we've been discussing what *mindfulness* is: simple, present-moment awareness of whatever is happening right now, whether it is a sound, a bodily sensation, or a thought. And even though this is a basic faculty or skill of our minds, unless you train this capacity, the forces of *mindlessness* will tend to prevail.

Why Does Mindlessness Matter in Sport?

Mindlessness is defined as acting and reacting in the moment based *only* on experiences and lessons learned from the past. You might wonder, isn't it good to learn, to have habits of reaction in performance? Well, the answer is yes and no! Here are a few examples when mindlessness is *not* a good thing.

- **Fear of Losing**: Imagine an athlete whose team has "always" lost to an opponent and they are preparing to compete against this opponent. Instead of focusing on how to beat them, they could spend the week anxious and imagining about how bad it will be to lose again, to that same team. With this mindset, the team is exercising mindless: they will be quicker to give up and less likely to look for new ways to beat their opponent. And also just think about all the energy and attention wasted that week anticipating the misery of losing. Haigh et al. (2011) note that we all tend to apply previously formed mindsets (i.e., we can't beat them!) to current situations" (p. 12).

- **Bored in Practice**: We have had many clients who go to practice with the intent only to put up with practice, to go through the motions to just get it over with. I (Amy) had one Olympic hopeful who reported when rowing for two hour practices that her main point of awareness was on the anticipation of the turn-around point at the one hour mark, so she could turn around and get off the water as soon as possible. When I asked about what she focused on to improve – like the placement of her oar in the water, the feel of the boat moving with the right pressure from her legs – she replied only with a blank stare. After noting this and talking about how she spent her mental energy in practice we, together, marveled at all the time she now could be present and improve, instead of wasting hours and hours of mindless rowing.

- **Missing key cues in competition**. How about a basketball player who is a great defender but reports that she is "not good on offense." Such a player will be to quick to pass the ball away and predictably will miss out on taking a simple lay-up or shot when open. We have all witnessed basketball players like this – they may not be an 80% 3-point shooter but surely after playing for a few years they could in most instances make an easy two points if they would only look for the open shots.

Ellen Langer, a social psychologist at Harvard, is a respected expert regarding her research on mindfulness. She does an unusually good job at articulating just what you don't want – a mindlessness approach to creativity, performance and living. She refers to mindlessness as an inactive state of mind, a state of mind in which you are not present to what is actually occurring before you in your environment (e.g., the open, easy lay-up). Her summary of a mindless state:

> When in a mindless state, an individual operates much like a robot; thoughts, emotions, and behaviors (hereafter just behaviors) are determined by 'programmed' routines based on distinctions and associations learned in the past. (Bodner and Langer, 2001, p. 1)

This means that if you remain in a mindless state, our past can determine what happens in the present. Ellen Langer often refers to the mindless state as "operating like a robot." This can work well until the environment around our robotic ways has changed. When mindless, you are less able to react wisely to your environment, to learn, or to adapt and adjust. When mindlessness in sport (or any performance realm) you lose out on opportunities to improve or to respond more wisely to what is showing up in front of you or within you.

In the next chapter we offer you an overview of the mind fulness based interventions currently offered in sport and a brief explanation of why we created MMTS 2.0. The big idea is that we have woven the idea of self-compassion (SC) throughout our program. SC helps cultivate courage to stay engaged. Read on!

Chapter 3
Mindfulness Meditation in Sport: Why MMTS 2.0?

Kabat-Zinn et al. (1985) were the first researchers to explore the impact of offering a mindfulness practice to athletes. In their study Jon Kabat-Zinn and his fellow researchers led weekly formal meditation groups with athletes and also offered them audiotapes to listen to in-between the group meditation practices. In these tapes Kabat-Zinn led the listeners through both a traditional mindful awareness practice paired with imagery, rowing in an ideal state.

In this seminal study, collegiate and Olympic rowers participated in 30-min weekly group led formal meditation practice (i.e., sitting quietly observing physical and psychological experience). In addition to Kabat-Zinn led weekly meditation practice the athletes were encouraged to practice meditation for 30 min daily via audio-guided recordings. The intervention was designed to help the athletes accept their internal thoughts, feelings, and physical sensations and to practice being in a state of concentrated engagement while rowing. The athletes reported that the intervention helped them improve speed on the water when racing.

Early in his mindfulness-based intervention research, Kabat-Zinn shifted his attention from athletes to helping those suffering with chronic pain and terminal illness. He designed the now world-respected intervention Mindfulness-Based Stress Reduction (MBSR), which over the past thirty years has been the most empirically researched mindfulness intervention in western medical and psychological research. A myriad of health benefits and reduction of health issues have been documented (Keng et al. 2011).

Though there was a fifteen-year lag, at the turn of the century the interest in mindfulness in sport psychology began again, starting with Gardner and Moore's (2004) Mindfulness- Acceptance-Commitment (MAC) based performance enhancement. This renewed interest on the part of sport psychology researchers and practitioners was in response to looking for new, more impactful wasy to help athletes with the pychological challenges of performance (e.g., responding to sport anxiety; focus on task relevant cues). Mindfulness- and acceptance-based interventions, have emerged as an alternative approach to the traditional cognitive behavioral oriented sport psychology approaches (Sappington and Longshore 2015). Essentially

© Springer International Publishing AG 2017
A. Baltzell, J. Summers, *The Power of Mindfulness*,
https://doi.org/10.1007/978-3-319-70410-4_3

the shift is toward accepting (instead of changing) unwanted thoughts and emotions prior to refocusing one's attention. Though we contend that both approaches can be used skillfully within the performance realm (which we do integrate in the MMTS 2.0 model), conceptually the approaches are distinct.

A little background on this: the mindfulness and acceptance approach posits that optimal mental states are not requisite for best performance but, instead, optimal performance is contingent on awareness and acceptance of moment-to-moment experience; subsequent, intentional focus on task-relevant cues; and committing to actions that are values driven (Gardner and Moore 2007).

This is a BIG idea. This means that athletes don't have to wait to feel *confident*, they do not have to have *the right feeling* or even *feel ready*. With this new approach, it is possible to help athletes optimize performance in spite of how they feel.

What matters most is where you put their attention, not what thoughts, typically in an uninvited fashion, are going through your head or the unpredictable emotions pumping in your veins. With this approach there is no effort to stop or change feelings – but instead to change your response to what is showing up inside your head and heart. We have taken this model to heart and have based MMTS 2.0 on these ideas. (Though we have in addition integrated self-compassion throughout the training – more on that after this overview.)

The paradigm shift, from the traditional cognitive behavioral approach in sport to a mindful approach to sport psychology interventions, has led to the development of a handful of mindfulness interventions for sport. These interventions offer a range of depth, focus, and scope of education and formal mindfulness-based practices. When we consider the research collectively, there is mounting evidence that mindfulness interventions are effective in sport.

Kabat-Zinn's definition of mindfulness has served as the premiere definition of mindfulness over the past 30 years within the empirical study of mindfulness in the United States. He defines mindfulness as "an open-hearted, moment-to-moment nonjudgmental awareness" (Kabat-Zinn 2005, p. 24). A few of studies in sport have also used mindfulness meditation as the main intervention and have resulted in improved performance.

John et al. (2011) did just this. They conducted a controlled study (with an experimental group and a control group) using mindfulness meditation (20 minutes a day, six-days a week over 4 weeks), which resulted in significant improvement of pistol shooter accuracy and reduced cortisol levels (stress hormones). The researchers were studying the salivary gland to see if stress hormones were reduced from the meditation practices. They note that previous research clearly indicates that salivary cortisol (the stress hormones in saliva) is a clear biological marker of precompetitive stress. In the study there were significant changes in both reduction in salivary cortisol and significant changes in performance for the pistol shooters (And in contrast the control group had no change).

When you look at the data, the results are remarkable. The cortisol level in the saliva of the 46 meditators who meditated (versus the 46 controls, with a total of 92 pistol shooters in the study) dropped from 1.3 on the first day of the study to 0.66 on

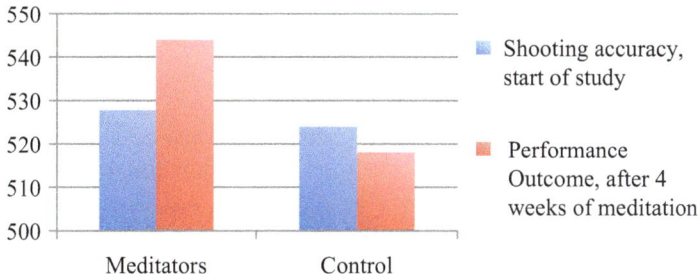

Fig. 3.1 Performance results from the pistol shooter study

Table 3.1 Difference in		Intervention meditators	Control group
Matches Won and Lost,	Matches won	211	99
Tennis Study	Matches lost	120	205

the 29th day. Perhaps more remarkably, the shooting score (or shooting accuracy) at the competition following the intervention greatly improved. The meditating shooters improved their overall score, on average, from 528 to 544 (with the control group – with no intervention – actually doing a bit worse, from a score of 524 to 518 [often with the pressure of competition athletes perform worse]) (Fig. 3.1).

The change in shooting accuracy improvement by the meditating pistol shooters happening by chance is 1 in a 1000 ($p < 0.001$)! This is one of the first RCTs (randomized controlled trials) that demonstrate mindfulness meditation training directly leads to improved performance.

In another RCT study in mindfulness and sport, Stankovic and Baltzell (in preparation) explored the effects of a mindfulness meditation practice using a ten-minute audio-file over an 8-week period with 100 female tennis players and also found a significant improvement in performance. Those who meditated more won more matches and games compared to the control group. (see Table 3.1).

Both of these studies are remarkable, yet it is important to note that they represent most of the research to date that demonstrates a direct link between mindfulness practices and performance.

Keith Kaufman and his research group created a mindfulness meditation based program, Mindful Sport Performance Enhancement (MSPE) (Kaufman et al. 2009, 2016). The program draws heavily on Jon Kabat-Zinn's Mindfulness-Based Stress Reduction (MBSR) program with most of the mindfulness meditation practices coming directly from MBSR. Compared to MBSR, MSPE is shorter in duration (about 10 hours compared to 20 hours for the instructor led portion) and different also in that MSPE makes more direct conceptual links between formal meditation practice and sport engagement. Empirical support for MSPE suggests that the program can help athletes increase mindfulness, increase flow-state experience (Kaufman et al. 2009), and reduce the experience of sport anxiety (De Petrillo et al.

2009), all markers that are related to improved performance. Most of the MSPE research is based on the two-hour, four session version of MSPE, though currently the program has been adapted to a 90-minute 6-session format (Pineau et al. 2014, Kaufman et al. 2017).

The Mindfulness-Acceptance-Commitment (MAC) approach in sport (Gardner and Moore 2004, 2006, 2007) is distinct from the other mindfulness based interventions as well in that it draws heavily on Acceptance and Commitment Therapy (ACT; Hayes 2004). ACT is a form of psychotherapy, which employs acceptance, mindfulness, commitment, and behavior-change strategies. Tailored to athletes, the MAC approach ultimately is focused on helping athletes self-regulate attentional skills for optimal sport performance via accepting potentially aversive internal experience (i.e., thoughts, feelings, and sensations) and, instead of trying to suppress and change them, committing to personally valued actions that support performance (see Gardner 2016; Gardner and Moore 2007, 2012). The MAC approach includes educational information, self-reflective exercises, and discussion as well as mindfulness practices. The majority of MAC based studies use a single case study designs with positive results reported including improved performance of a female power-lifter (Gardner and Moore 2004) and a male springboard diver (Schwanhausser 2009). The intervention is a 7-module intervention that generally takes 10–12 h sessions to complete.

Why MMTS 2.0?

We created MMTS 2.0 because traditional psychological skills training does not meet the needs of all athletes and the existing mindful-acceptance models are time intensive and not necessarily favorable to an athlete's demanding schedule. We wanted a program that was relatively brief and based on a mindful-acceptance model to offer athletes an alternative way to help optimize performance. MMTS 2.0 helps athletes learn to respond differently to sport distress. Instead of only prompting athletes to change their unhelpful thoughts that are fear-based, harshly self-critical, or simply distracting MMTS 2.0 is geared to help athletes accept such thoughts. Our program helps athletes learn to have awareness of such thoughts and then have the strengthened ability to turn their attention toward performance relevant cues. Instead of being distracted by the embarrassment of missing a free-throw or distracted by the fear of failure, athletes learn to accept such experiences and focus on the next play. We also are quite aware of the challenges of athletes dealing with intense anxiety and fear that can result in them being so hard on themselves that they shut down or quit. We see this *performance distress* as a major issue that is calling for new ways to minimize its negative impact on performance.

Performance Dukkha is a Problem

Competitive distress which we refer to it as performance dukkha, we define as, "psychic pain and internal performance distraction that emerges as a function of the performer over engaging with or trying to avoid performance-related, aversive, internal experience" (Baltzell 2016, p. 56). Whatever you want to label this sometimes overwhelming experience, it is becoming a rampant problem in the world of sport and performance. Athletes, and other performers, are given more training at progressively earlier ages. Expectations are ramping up and we offer little effective strategies to help athletes with the emotions and thoughts that often accompany high expectation such as anxiety and harsh self-criticism. We no longer can tell an athlete, "Just don't think, just go do it!". Or, "Just think: Next play!" Yes, of course, we want to help performers build the ability to focus back on the next play, but there remains a chronic challenge of performance dukkha that tempts athletes to quit, slow down, or they get so highly distracted that they are unable to focus on performance.

Teaching athletes to just challenge the thoughts or change the thoughts doesn't always work. And asking athletes to be mindful – such as "be with" the thoughts and accept them just as they are is sometimes like asking an athlete to elect to sit in vat of boiling oil. It is very painful to be fully present to intense anxiety and fear.

Some just can't do it.

In MMTS 2.0 and throughout the remainder of the book we have added a new element – self-compassion – that has turned out to be extremely helpful to athletes when they are experiencing performance dukkha. In the space between realizing that you are being bombarded by unhelpful distress, you are offered a new way to deal with the distress beyond just being told to turn away and refocus your attention. We offer you sport-appropriate ways to offer enough kindness to yourself in such difficult moments so you can muster up the courage to keep going. Via self-compassion in MMTS 2.0 you can learn to offer yourself what you need in the moment to be able to *stay present* such that you can tolerate your negative thoughts and feelings. You can generate enough courage this way to stay engaged and fight to optimize performance (no matter how you are feeling – you don't have to be confident to perform well).

In essence MMTS 2.0 is designed to offer athletes a clear pathway to be more present and accepting of whatever is occurring so they can optimize athletic execution via the connection between mindfulness and performance. In terms of helping with performance sport distress (i.e., performance dukkha) MMTS 2.0 offers athletes new ways to handle such distress. Instead of telling you to just stop thinking, or just focus on the next play, we offer ways to first address the distress so it doesn't keep getting in the way of performance (because trying to ignore it often does not work). Through offering self-compassion exercises and weaving the idea of kindness to self we hope to offer you an efficient way to learn to be poised with all that you might need to deal with and, at once, give you your best chance to optimize performance.

MMTS 2.0 is designed to help you cultivate a mindful and self-compassionate approach to practice and performance. The goal is to help you become better able to handle emotional ups and downs, help you build skills and habits of concentration (and thereby be less distracted), and ultimately to help you perform better! In the next chapter we begin our official introduction to MMTS 2.0. The remainder of the book offers detailed instructions of how to bring such a mindful approach to your practice and performance and, if you would like, how to facilitate the entire program, or segments of your choice. Enjoy!

Part II
Mindful Meditation Training for Sport (MMTS) 2.0

Modules 1-3: Mindfulness, Acceptance & Concentration

Chapter 4
Introducing Mindful Meditation Training for Sport (MMTS) 2.0

MMTS 2.0 was designed based on previous research discoveries in mindfulness as it applies to healing and performance. We all know that mindfulness training, in some mindfulness based interventions, leads to reduced stress, increased ability to concentrate, increased frequency of flow, reduction in negative thoughts – and perhaps the most important -- improved performance. We also designed MMTS 2.0 based on the needs of the twenty-first century athlete and performer. We strove to create a program that is relatively low in time demand and one that makes an ongoing, clear connection between mindfulness and performance.

MMTS 2.0 offers a series of focused mindfulness drills and exercises that will help you establish new habits of attention and regulation of emotion, which we describe in detail throughout this book. The transformative aspect of mindfulness training is that, with repeated practice and training, those initial patterns of practice literally become the basis for new neural circuitry in the brain, increasing the odds that these new habits of your mind arise more effortlessly and spontaneously when you need them most: in the clutch. For example, you can develop more poise in the face of difficulty paired with the ability to pay attention in a flexible manner.

How can a mindful-approach translate, practically, on the athletic field? We and other researchers have begun to conduct studies of the impact of mindfulness training with top athletes, using MMTS 2.0 as the intervention. In our first study, we conducted the MMTS with Division I full-scholarship soccer players. At the conclusion of the program, we interviewed some of the program participants. The following offers an example of how leveraging mindfulness can help with athletic performance.

Kristen

One athlete, we will call her Kristen, described herself like this: *"I am the type of athlete who is really hard on myself. I am very emotional. I wear my emotions on my sleeve, I'm just that kind of person."* (Baltzell et al. 2014, p. 229). Kristen talked

© Springer International Publishing AG 2017
A. Baltzell, J. Summers, *The Power of Mindfulness*,
https://doi.org/10.1007/978-3-319-70410-4_4

about the shift that she experienced after both participating in the six-hour MMTS program with her team and practicing mindfulness meditation. She stated,

> The biggest difference with the meditation was that when I would make a mistake (before the program)… If I would lose the ball, I would sit and be sad that I lost the ball and not even … try to go and get (it) again. So I would be down on myself like that (Baltzell et al. 2014, p. 229).

Kristen, next, offered an example of how her thinking and reaction had changed after participating in the program,

> Ok, that was a mistake. I'm frustrated right now, but it's done and I can move forward from there.' So just being able to relax after the fact, take a deep breath and realize that it's just one mistake. And just not letting it affect my play after that.

This quote from Kristen captures the essence of MMTS and the drive to share this work with others. The idea that a six-hour intervention that can be offered individually or in a group or team setting that can help with both emotional control and concentration on the field is something worth considering.

Alexis

A second player from the study, Alexis, also talked about the changes she experienced from participation in MMTS. The main benefit she reports is a changed response to negative emotions and distractions on the field. Alexis stated:

> I've learned to stop lashing out towards others with my frustration … the program (MMTS) helped me realize this more … I could recognize sooner if I was slipping into a frustrated time period in practice or if I was not focused on what we were doing. I could notice what was happening and think to myself, 'Ok. What are you doing? Why? What's going on? What got you unfocused? Next play—do it right the next play (Baltzell et al. 2014, p. 231).

In essence, Alexis's experience was similar to Kristen's. Alexis was able to tolerate the frustration enough to intentionally become clear headed to get her attention back on sport related task relevant cues. Meaning, she was able to get her head back in the game! Alexis skillfully describes what mindfulness practices help her mind do. When you practice mindfulness, you can learn to be more intentionally present to what is happening. In Alexis's case, she learned to accept or at least tolerate what was happening and, in turn, was empowered to direct her focus (i.e., "next play") and opt out of getting caught up and distracted by the frustration. This space of choice -- of tolerance of what is happening and having the choice in how to respond versus react -- is the heart of MMTS, both versions MMTS and MMTS 2.0.

You might have already noticed that we refer to MMTS in two versions: MMTS and MMTS 2.0. Essentially after the first run of the program, we opted to integrate the idea of self-compassion throughout the program. We believe that when athletes offer self-compassion to themselves, that they are better able to tolerate acute moments of distress and distraction. Self-compassion means being willing to notice one's own suffering and being inspired to do something about it, to help alleviate it. We will offer much more on this later – but we have found that when athletes are really suffering with intense anxiety, dread or self-criticism they tend to either mentally give up, choke or produce a sub-optimal performance. We have found that when you offer yourself some sport appropriate kindness when you are really overwhelmed it can help you stay in the game. We have integrated the ideas of self-compassion to empower courage, to help athletes cope with fear, frustration and self-criticism and still be empowered to keep engaging in their sport, moment-to-moment.

You are welcome to jump to Chap. 10 to learn more about self-compassion. But essentially we found that some athletes, some of the time, needed more than just to be prompted to stay in the moment and accept it. We found that some athletes could not do this when feeling overwhelmed by performance dukkha (e.g., fear of failure, embarrassment, harsh self-criticism). We weave the idea of self-compassion throughout the MMTS 2.0 training to offer performers pathways to cope with such distress such that they can continue to have courage to fight, to perform, to stay engaged when they need it. Some challenges that self-compassion can help most with include intense performance anxiety, harsh self-criticism or debilitating comparison with others.

Mindfulness Serves Athletic Performance

We have found that once the athletes in MMTS 2.0 realize the power of mindfulness (and self-compassion, when necessary) training, they become highly interested in further gaining mindfulness and self-compassion based applied skills to help them with athletic performance. For example, we all know that it is good sometimes for some athletes to "chill out," "calm down," and then "just focus" in performance. Yet it is really hard to get there! If you have not built the relevant skills and, ultimately habits, of navigating distressful emotions and being able to refocus on the performance relevant cues for the given moment, chilling out seems virtually impossible.

Essentially MMTS 2.0 offers practical ways to help athletes gain the ability to control and habituate more effective ways to respond to difficulty emotions. And we believe that cultivating poise, through mindful and self-compassion training, ultimately offers what athletes in distress need when it counts. And, of equal importance, the mindfulness training also helps performers learn how to have more control over where they place their attention as well as being more able to adjust and adapt to what is happening on the field.

All athletes understand the importance of training their bodies in performance-specific drills to maximize their potential in their sport or event. Now, mindfulness meditation training can help guard against those hours of dedication and discipline not going to waste. There is no reason to allow feelings of being overwhelmed by nerves, negative emotions, and jittery focus to take a chip out of your performance success. We were driven to write this book to help reach more athletes. We want to offer new ways to help high level performers cope with such feelings that we know we could have greatly benefited from, and for Amy as an Olympic and professional athlete. We had no answers to such difficulty when we needed them! We want to offer solutions to performance distress, to offer something we wish we had been offered.

Mindfulness Practice Takes Effort

But while mindfulness is *simple*, in some respects, it is by no means *easy* to sustain, which is why it requires training. Everyone knows that a marathon is just a very long succession of strides, one after the other. Each stride in and of itself is no major achievement. Unless impaired, most of us could do that (take one or two strides like a marathoner), just as most of us can notice the weight of this book in our hands. But sustaining that stride over a long period of time takes training as does sustaining our mindfulness over a long period of time takes training.

It's not easy. It takes persistent, disciplined efforts to become more mindful, particularly when under pressure or performance expectations. But over time, the mind's continuity of mindfulness slowly, and, sometimes imperceptibly, increases more and more to the point that it becomes our inner default setting. And that's when the competitive edge becomes etched in your brain. So let's learn a bit more about MMTS 2.0 and then get into some pragmatic ways to train the mind. In the next chapter we begin describing the information and practices in the first session of the program, but for now, an overview.

MMTS 2.0 Overview

MMTS 2.0 is a six-hour intervention that is based on bringing mindfulness and self-compassion to athletes, in a sport-friendly way, to help athletes learn to strengthen their:

1. *Attention & Concentration*: Strengthen their ability to focus on task relevant cues,
2. *Poise*: Deal more effectively with sport distress and distractions,
3. *Adaptability*: Be more engaged, adaptive, and creative while in practice and competition.

We were influenced in the development MMTS 2.0 by traditional Buddhist mindfulness meditation practices, Kabat-Zinn's work with rowers as well as his MBSR program, Frank Gardner & Zella Moore's MAC approach in sport, and Christopher Germer and Kristin Neff's Mindful Self-Compassion program. We have integrated core ideas and some practices from these range of practices and programs and, we believe, created a program that is compelling to the modern day athlete and performer. MMTS 2.0 is for those who experience performance distress, high performance expectations, time constraints, and/or looking for relatively efficient ideas to help with the psychological challenges of performance. MMTS 2.0 offer athletes ways to develop more control over their attention, experience less distraction and ultimately perform better.

MMTS 2.0 is less time intensive than other mindfulness training programs: MMTS still includes typical tools used to teach new meditators mindfulness practices such as focus on breath, counting breaths, and "labeling" difficult thoughts and emotions. Such practices are intended to ultimately help you both increase your ability to concentrate and become more tolerant of negative mind-states, meaning changing your relationship to unhelpful thoughts and emotions such as frustration and anxiety (Sedlmeier et al. 2012). All of these specific mindfulness tools are included in the MMTS 2.0 program as a point of focus while practicing non-judgmental acceptance of thoughts, feelings, and sensations (including acceptance of the natural judgment that occurs!).

MMTS 2.0 is a program that focuses on teaching core mindfulness meditation skills throughout the training as well as offering a straightforward way to practice when not in the group session. In addition to the mindful meditation skills, MMTS 2.0 is designed to consistently provide both conceptual explanations and practical examples of how the mindful and self-compassion skills translate to sport. We offer this same rhythm of information and practice through out this book.

MMTS 2.0 incorporates formal mindfulness meditation practices both in-sessions and between sessions when you (participants) are also invited to meditate daily on you own. MMTS 2.0 participants are asked to meditate 10 min per day on most of the days they are not participating in the instructor-led program. It is important to understand the value and importance of the mind training that can come with formal, mindfulness meditation practices. Because through the formal practice, meaning doing actual mediation practice, a more mindful approach can be cultivated.

See Table 4.1 below for the brief overview of MMTS 2.0. (For the full protocol please see Appendix A.) The program can be used in full, in segments or singular exercises can be selected to either help you or as a sport psychology practitioner. When instructor led, in each session, participants are encouraged to try the offered mindfulness activities (and always encouraged to mentally opt out if need be (e.g., too distressed, distracted, or exhausted), meaning to just stay in the room and sit quietly while their teammates try the exercises.

Table 4.1 Mindful Meditation Training in Sport Overview

Module number and topic	Focus	Exercises
Module 1: Mindfulness Introduction	Introduction to the concept of mindfulness and application to sport including emotional regulation and cultivating courage via self-compassion	Breath awareness
		Compassionate Breathing[a]
Module 2: Labeling and distractions	Explanation of labeling including concepts of de-centering and cognitive fusion – and application to sport.	Mindfulness of sound and body sensation
		Mindfulness and labeling thoughts & emotions as they arise
Module 3 Concentration	Offers overview of the value concentration and ways to cultivate concentration	Breathing ladder exercise
		Pyramid breathing and intentionally integrating kindness to self.
Module 4 Self-compassion	Defines self-compassion and offers clear connection of self-compassion with coping with sport distress.	Sitting with difficulty
		One for me, one for you meditation[a]
Module 5 Self -regulation	Offers an introduction of the importance of self-regulation. In many ways the essence of the program – to learn to accept and tolerate emotions (with self-kindness when necessary) and commit to personal values.	Values in sport exercise
		Soles of the feet meditation[a]
Module 6: Open awareness: Adapt and adjust	Discuss value of being aware of moment-to-moment experience and how this formal meditation practice translates to sport. Ellen Langer version of mindfulness presented.	Open mindfulness meditation practice
		Open awareness to novelty: Accepting and preparing for performance

[a]Exercises inspired by the Mindful Self-Compassion Program

Running MMTS 2.0 Versus Using this Book Just for You

We have set up the structure of the book to meet the needs of both the individual who wants to go through MMTS 2.0 on their own and for practitioners who may want to teach MMTS 2.0.

If MMTS 2.0 Is Just for You

If MMTS 2.0 is just for you, we encourage you to go through the program step-by-step, module-by-module. This means just start with the next chapter and go from there! However, if you prefer, we equally encourage you to pick and choose the sections that most resonate with you now. We also recommend that you keep a journal to track your experience and your insights. After each mindfulness meditation practice, we encourage you to write a few minutes in a journal and reflect on what you are learning and how this can apply to your performance world.

MMTS 2.0 Facilitators

In the next many chapters we offer an explanation of main ideas and offer practices in each module of MMTS 2.0. You can use these chapters to help you lead the MMTS 2.0 modules, as you best see fit. You may just want to skim the overview of the ideas of mindfulness if you are particularly familiar with them (though we suggest reading through the explanations of ideas) and just try the mindfulness meditations exercises for yourself. The more familiar you are with them, the easier it will be for you to share them with others. Please see Chap. 14. It is dedicated to offering insights and suggestions from others who have already run MMTS 2.0. For MMTS 2.0 facilitators, we offer the full protocol in Appendix A. You also are welcome to simply work off of that outline, whatever will work best for you.

Now, finally, onto MMTS 2.0!

Chapter 5
The Power of Mindfulness:
(Module 1, Part A)

We welcome you to a journey of learning a new way of using a mindfulness approach and self-compassion when you need it, to improve your experience in sport and ultimately your performance. We have found over the years that bringing mindfulness, which really is simply being present and accepting of (or tolerating or being interested in) whatever is showing up, can make the difference in performance. With such an approach, you are open to actually being present to what you are doing, instead of being lost in regret of mistakes or lost in anxiety of what the future might hold (e.g., not getting selected; not starting; not making the team).

The basic design of MMTS 2.0 is to (1) introduce you to ideas that can help with performance in some manner and then (2) offer ways to put ideas into practice. For those of you who are engaging in this program through reading this book, we encourage you to keep a journal of your experience and insights that arise after the first time you try each of the mindfulness-based meditations and exercises offered throughout this book. For extra practice, you can check out the scripts we use for the MMTS 2.0 meditations practices. When athletes go through an instructor-led six-week program, they are encouraged to lead themselves through these additional practices (see Appendix D) outside of the organized meetings. For the program, the instructor audio-records these meditations and sometimes tailors them for the needs of their group.

As we begin, we would like to offer a few examples of how a mindfulness approach can help with performance. We have had many athletes (and business executives) who have made significant performance related changes through intentionally integrating a mindfulness approach. Below we offer a few examples of athletes we have worked with, who presented with some significant sport performance challenges, and were able to make personally important changes via a mindfulness acceptance and action approach.

© Springer International Publishing AG 2017
A. Baltzell, J. Summers, *The Power of Mindfulness*,
https://doi.org/10.1007/978-3-319-70410-4_5

Stephanie

Stephanie was a new professional runner and was finding herself frustrated with losing races and obsessed with her inability to "make a move" when it counted in her races. She used to be the one to beat, securing a number of national titles as a collegiate runner. She had no idea how to help herself and (from her perspective) was spiraling out of control, losing race after race and feeling progressively worse about herself as an athlete (and human being).

Things changed when she learned about mindfulness.

Stephanie learned that instead of automatically shutting down in a race and giving up, that she could become more *aware* of what was actually happening and stay present. And when more present, she was more at choice about how she was going to handle the challenge at hand. At first this intentional shift of awareness was very tough. She had to become present and aware of the fact that she was giving up! Right when it counted. Instead of deciding to fight, she would just give into the "caving-in" feeling and run a bit slower as she watched those she had beaten for years crawl past her. It was slow-motion hell for Stephanie.

When Stephanie began to stay present while racing (instead of ignoring how she was really thinking) she became very aware of the fact that she made a decision to give up when she was uncertain of being able to make a move and win. The uncertainty (i.e., not knowing if she would win or lose) was too painful to tolerate, given she had no idea that she had a choice of how to handle that predictable moment a bit differently. She felt stuck in observing her "give-up" reaction.

With mindfulness training, she became aware of her patterns of mindless reaction:

Fear ➡ Urge to give up ➡ Shut down, lose race

With implementing mindfulness practices, she began to understand that she had a *choice* to tolerate the uncertainty (i.e., stay aware instead of going on auto-pilot and giving up) and make a more wise and courageous decision of how to act in race moments of uncertainty. She had a new way of taking moves in the face of uncertainty, something she had never had to do in her past. She was used to dominating raced against. With the mindful approach she was able to tolerate the uncomfortable feeling of not knowing if she could win, stay engaged in the races and began to win some of the races, again.

Xavier

Xavier is a tennis player with a hot temper. He predictably plays well but as the matches heat up, so do his emotions and volatile reactivity. It is particularly hard for him when his opponent makes a bad line call and claims his shot is out (when it was really in – or he thinks so!). Often after a few bad calls, Xavier will smash his racquet on the ground (sometimes shattering his racquet) inevitably losing focus on the point, the game. He thought that this was normal for him (i.e., *It is just how I am*) and could not react in a different manner, until he became exposed to a mindful approach. In MMTS 2.0 training, he learned that if he stayed present in those moments of rage he could choose to NOT smash his racquet. He learned strategies to respond differently (though still feeling the anger and frustration). Throughout the program (and this book) we will offer you many mindfulness-based approaches to handle such performance distress (as well as how to improve concentration and adaptability while performing).

This program is literally about training your brain. Through an understanding of the power of mindfulness and via mindfulness-based exercises, you can change how your mind reacts to stressors, challenges, and opportunities. As Harris (2014) notes, "Your mind is the basis of everything you experience and of every contribution you make to the lives of others. Given this fact, it makes sense to train it." We have found that the very powerful and practical way to train your brain is to begin with mindfulness practices and a mindful approach.

We believe that you can make performance improvements when you simply understand and apply the ideas of a mindfulness approach. Whether via formal meditation or intentionally tolerating difficult emotions and staying engaged in practice (as best you can), a mindful approach takes time to cultivate. No human is 100% mindful all of the time, in all instances. We invite you to practice with a beginner's mind. And this, we know, is not easy to do. Yet, cultivating a mindful approach to competition and training takes time and some open-mindedness. Just like you would not expect to make significant strength improvements after going to the gym for one day, you cannot expect to make significant changes in mindfulness after completing one mindfulness-based exercise. It will take many *mental reps*!

MMTS 2.0 Purpose

The explicit purpose for MMTS 2.0 is for you to gain a heightened ability to have:

Poise
Increase your ability to cope with the experience of negative thoughts and emotions (change relationship with aversive emotions, thoughts, and sensations) that may be present due to competitive pressure. Essentially MMTS 2.0 can help you with distress tolerance and help with emotional regulation. You can learn to be aware of distress or unhelpful emotions and develop a more wise response to them. You will learn to stay more in the present moment instead of worrying about what has already happened (i.e., regret) or worrying about what might happen (i.e., fear). Instead, you will be more empowered to stay in the moment – even if you make a mistake, you can get back and focus on next play, next note, next move.

MMTS 2.0 offers you a new way to deal with challenges, like fear, frustration, and anger. The mindfulness-based approach is probably much different than you have been taught! With a mindful approach, we will encourage you to *change your relationship* with aversive emotions, thoughts, and sensations that have thwarted performance in the past. We will not ask you to stop them from happening! We have found, along with great minds like Stephen Hayes (creator of Acceptance and Commitment Therapy) that in fact it is nearly impossible to STOP intense, spiraling anxiety. The best you can do is tolerate such feelings (and then figure out what you truly value and commit to actions that live out these values – more on that later).

To cultivate poise under pressure is part of the purpose of MMTS 2.0. Poise we think of as grace, balance, or even elegance in the face of distress. Part of the reason Amy became so interested in this topic is that she recalls having no poise and had no idea how to capture such a state when on her Olympic quest (as an Olympic athlete on the US 1992 team). Finding a pathway to help other elite athletes and performers discover a state of poise has been a great joy and brought significant meaning to both of our work.

Xavier (the tennis player, above) is an example of an athlete who was able to regain his poise, even in the face of the frustration of opponents unfairly calling his shots out. Xavier sometimes still suffers from intense frustration – those feelings have not entirely gone away – however, he has learned new strategies about how to handle those feelings. He has taken charge of how he wants to respond (versus allowing his emotions to control him like a puppet). He is developing poise on the court. While tolerating the intense frustration he is able to keep in mind how he wants to play and what he needs to do in the next play to beat his opponent or give himself the best chance to do so.

Essentially cultivating poise in performance is about developing a different relationship to thoughts, emotions, and sensations. Instead of getting tangled up in our made up stories about what is going to happen, what has happened, what others think – you can develop wiser or more skillful responses when these stories, fears, or other distracting emotions and thoughts arise. Such distractions come in the form of thoughts ("I can never beat her!"), feelings ("I am so anxious – I hate this, I want out!"), and physical sensations ("This hurts, I just can't keep going."). You can become wiser, discerning between thoughts that you must attend to (e.g., "If I don't stop, I really will hurt myself") to thoughts that are distracting, (e.g., "Yes, this is physical pain – but I am not hurt and it is a natural part of running a 10K race!"). As sport psychology consultant and Buddhist meditation teacher Mumford (2016) writes, "Think about the eye of the hurricane. No matter how intense the storm or what's swept up in its gale-force winds, that calm, blue center is always there. We have this quiet center with us". And part of the purpose of MMTS 2.0 is to offer a pathway to such poise, particularly when under performance pressures and expectations.

Focus & Concentration

A second purpose of MMTS 2.0 is to help you learn to focus and concentrate more effectively. Why is this important? With an improved ability to focus, you can manage distractions better (you have greater choice where you focus your attention), and you can focus your attention more consistently on task-relevant cues. The improvement of concentration will come from your formal meditation practices, which we offer throughout MMTS 2.0. Hanson and Mendius (2009), leaders in mindfulness meditation, who often highlight associated benefits to changes in brain structure as a result of meditation practice, write that formal meditation practice directly increases one's ability to control their attention. They write, "Having good control over your attention: You can place your attention wherever you want and it stays there: When you want to shift it to something else, you can" (p. 177). You can increase your ability of focus attention (i.e., concentrate) in the MMTS 2.0 meditation practices via noticing distractions and bringing attention back to the present moment.

The formal practice translates perfectly to sport practice and competition/performance. Mindfulness meditation practice strengthens your muscle of attention. Your mind doesn't wander off as much and when it does, you don't get dragged down as fast by negative thinking and criticism. You learn to notice the distraction and, progressively more quickly, focus back on task-relevant cues. In the mindfulness meditation practices you realize that noticing distraction in meditation practice is a good thing because in those moments you *strengthen your response of noticing and choosing to place your attention where you opt to place it*!

Have you ever lost concentration in an important game? In practice? When you lose concentration, what happens to your performance? Maybe, for a while, you can run on automatic pilot. But in most instances you will miss something important your coach says, maybe miss a pass or an opening to take a shot. When you lose concentration you lose out on noticing important (though sometimes subtle) information in the environment that could help you learn and/or improve in some way. The problem isn't losing attention. You just need to have the is have the intention to bring your attention back to what matters when you do notice that your mind is wandering!

Presence & Clarity: Adapt and Adjust!
The third purpose of MMTS 2.0 is to help you develop more presence and clarity when you are practicing and performing. When you become aware of thoughts (and emotions) that arise, including habituated and automatic reactions to events, you can become more nimble in your response to difficulty and opportunity! With being present, you become much more tuned into both internal and external experiences. When you intentionally shift your attention to the present moment (and when it starts happening more naturally as time goes on) you are then able to more easily let go of holding onto what happened (past) and what might happen (projected future). There is simply more attention for what is happening in the moment.

I (Amy) once had a musician client who suffered from a great deal of performance anxiety. One day I asked her how much of her attention was on her music when practicing alone. She reported 60% (the other 40% of her energy was focused on self-criticism and worry). I then asked her how much of her attention was on the music when a teacher was in the room. She reported 30% (the other 70% of her energy was focused on self-criticism and worry). And finally, I asked how much of her attention was on the music when performing before an audience. She reported

10% (and the remaining 90% of her energy was focused on worry, fear, etc.). As the pressure went up, her clarity and presence to her music went down. She was woefully distracted by fear of how others might judge her ability to create music. Unfortunately, she was feeding her fears by paying attention to them, believing them, and getting tangled up in them.

With poise, these same thoughts and feelings can arise (and they often do). The key question is *how do you respond to them?* By cultivating clarity and poise, you can learn to read what is happening and respond as you choose (rather than being on an unwanted autopilot!). Instead of getting caught up in a habitual response, you can develop awareness in action. You can learn to wisely respond to what is showing up moment by moment. You can become more present and intentionally adjust to what is happening (internally and externally) during practice and performance. You simply become more aware of sport or performance-relevant novel stimuli. When athletes cultivate a greater awareness of their experience and are able to notice what is occurring in a balanced way (not ignoring or not getting caught up in) they can most wisely respond to the moment at hand. You simply cannot assume it will be like it has always been in the past is a wise lesson consistently offered by social psychologist Ellen Langer.

Through the MMTS 2.0 practices, you can expect to be able to improve your ability to perform to the best of your abilities (given physical, time, and other constraints) moment to moment, with an adaptive, open and enhanced intention to notice cues in your environment (that may have been missed before). Simply, you can become more present and able to adjust during performance.

Mindfulness Defined

We base our understanding of mindfulness from a range of sources. The first is based on Kabat-Zinn's (2005) concept of mindfulness, "an open-hearted, moment-to-moment non-judgmental awareness" (p. 24). This definition points to the importance of first *being aware* and second being willing to *accept (tolerate…take interest in) whatever is showing up.* We emphasize from the start that mindfulness does not mean you want to become passive. In fact, it often means the opposite!

If you can become present to what is going on, and really see what is happening, you are much more empowered to do something about it! Stephanie's example above is a good example of this. When Stephanie could become aware of the fact that she had the overwhelming desire to give up –and she could accept that this was happening (versus pretend it wasn't there or just react and cave into it) she opened up new ways of responding. She became empowered to respond differently. But first it took her being aware and accepting (tolerating) the urge to mentally give up (though her legs were still moving).

A second way of defining mindfulness is offered by Ellen Langer. She views mindfulness as intentionally noticing novelty (not assuming our experience will be like it has always been in the past). With such an approach you are reminded to come back alive and not respond and react to opponents or competitive situations like you always have in the past (e.g., "We always lose to that team."; "When I feel too much pressure, I just can't play well."; "Practice is so boring, we always do the same drills."). We find Ellen Langer's mindfulness approach quite helpful once you are able to quiet the internal distress. We will talk much more about this approach to mindfulness in module six. But in brief, we see this perspective of mindfulness to be quite valuable when helping athletes learn to adapt and adjust to subtle differences within themselves or their environment to optimize practice and performance.

We offer a definition of mindfulness that captures both the essence of being present, accepting, and noticing novelty. In a more academic way, we define mindfulness like this: "Mindfulness is a quality of awareness that objectifies the contents of experience, internally and externally, promoting greater tolerance, interest, and clarity towards one's experience" (Baltzell and Summers 2016, p.527). Via objectifying what is going on, you are able to take a symbolic step back from things you might otherwise ignore or get tangled up with. Next we offer the first MMTS 2.0 mindfulness-based meditation.

Breath Meditation

This first formal meditation practice can help you strengthen your ability to pay attention. With meditation practices, you begin to remove most distractions with the exception of your own internal experience – thoughts, feelings, and physical sensations. If you can strengthen your ability to pay attention in a quiet meditation practice, this skill can boost your performance – *to pay attention to what you choose to pay attention to* – like the next play or the rhythm of your running.

This first exercise is a "simple" breath meditation (though you must know all of them can be quite challenging!) where you are asked to primarily notice the sensations of your breathing. But know that none of this is easy to sustain for more than a few seconds, even for a few split seconds. Our minds naturally wander.

In fact, it is part of the meditation cycle for your mind to wander. It is normal and happens to all of us. The challenge in meditation is not only holding your attention on the meditation point of focus (e.g., the breath). A great opportunity when meditating includes learning to recover and bring your attention back to the focus of the meditation.

Below is a diagram that offers a visual explanation of the meditation cycle. We hope to help you engage in all of this: focus on your breathing, notice when you mind has wandered (which it will!), relax as best you can, and then bring your attention back to your breath. Most likely your internal verbal chatter will be alive and well. That is OK. And normal. In fact, when almost anyone quiets down to the present moment they often become aware of highly active internal chatter, sometimes referred to as monkey mind in meditation circles. For now, in this meditation, just try committing to keeping your primary attention on your breath (Fig. 5.1).

Fig. 5.1 Meditation cycle

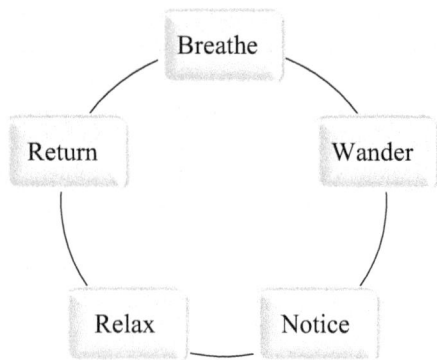

We will ask you to bring your awareness to your experience of breathing. In the exercise you might bring your attention to the length of your breaths. Are your breaths long? Are they short? You might explore the space between inhales and exhales. You might notice the parts of your chest and stomach that are moving, subtly, as you breathe. Do your breaths feel shallow or deep? Is there balance of air flowing through your nostrils? Scientifically, diaphragmatic breathing maximizes the oxygen exchange, which helps the body release tension, reduce muscle stress, and increases emotional control. These are all valuable outcomes. We are most interested in helping strengthen your ability to place and sustain your attention where you choose. With such practice, you can learn to strengthen your habit of mindfulness and weaken your habit of mind*less*ness.

The following practice is designed to be about a ten-minute mindfulness breathing exercise. This will be the first of many MMTS 2.0 exercises offered throughout this book. We encourage you, when possible, to try each exercise as you go. (This is the first practice introduced in MMTS 2.0 program).

Exercise 2: Basic Mindfulness Training: Breathing

The training exercise that follows will form the first part of the Basic Training that establishes the foundation for all the remaining exercises and drills that are found in *MMTS 2.0*. In this part of the training, we invite you to focus your attention on anchoring your awareness in the present moment (which is essential for top performance). You will need a timer or stopwatch and a chair.

1. Set the timer to go off in ten-minutes.
2. Sit comfortably in a chair, but with your seat slightly forward, so that your back is not in contact with the back of the chair. The spine should be upright and relaxed (as Jon Kabat-Zinn says, "*in a regal position*"), shoulders softened, hands in your lap, and your feet resting on the floor. (You can also lie down. Get your body in a comfortable position).

3. For this interval of training, let all thoughts related to the day be set aside. Once the formal training is over, you can plan or think about whatever you need to do, but for now, simply let your worldly 'life' be set aside so that you can focus exclusively on training the mind.

4. Next, close the eyes and relax the muscles of the face, the shoulders, the arms, and the legs.

5. As you relax, bring your awareness to the feeling of the breath coming in and going out of the body. People will experience the sensations of the breath in different areas, but we recommend you bring the attention to whatever physical sensation is most easily noticed. Maybe you opt to focus into the belly and observe the pattern of the breath sensation in the abdomen? When you breathe in, the abdomen will rise or expand. When you breathe out, the abdomen will fall or contract. Simply feel the sensations that accompany each in-breath and each out-breath. Don't force the breath or try to control the breath. Allow yourself to breathe at a pace and depth that is comfortable for you. Just notice the natural breath, moment by moment. Some breaths will be smooth, some a little rough, some deep, and others shallow. We're not trying to make the breath one way or another. We're simply feeling the natural breath as it occurs right now.

Over the course of this ten-minute period, you will see that the mind will wander away from the primary activity of watching the breath. This is not a problem. The mind wandering is very typical and in fact can be a invaluable part of the training. In your practice, like in ours, you are learning to recognize the vital difference between when you are awake and present to this *very* moment versus when you are drifting off into daydreams or into simple mental distractions.

Whenever you see that the mind has slipped away from watching the breath, the most important thing to do is to *relax*. Fully relax at the very moment you see yourself having drifted away. Don't go to war with the thoughts or the 'wandering.' Often times this is the place people think, *I am bad at meditating. I can't do this*. These too are normal, spontaneous thoughts. As best you can, meet these thoughts with interest and acceptance. Another way of saying it is, simply acknowledge that the mind has slipped off and then through the ease of relaxation, allow the breath to re-emerge as the primary object of your attention. And know that this noticing and bringing your mind back from the wandering to where you choose to place your attention is a critical and positive part of the mindfulness training. We view this moment of noticing mind wandering and bringing your attention back to the intended point of focus as a moment of success versus a moment of failure!

The importance of relaxation in the moment, when you shift from noticing your mind wandering back to your chosen point of focus (breathing for now), cannot be overemphasized. Each and every time the mind wanders, it is essential to relax, otherwise you most likely will judge the wandering mind and become easily frustrated. You will be tempted to think, "I'm doing this wrong! I am bad at meditating!"

This response is very common but not true! If you are noticing your distractions and bringing your mind back to your breath, over and over again, you are successfully meditating! And the more you allow the mind to relax, the more it will gain a steadiness and stability of attention.

Please note: It does not matter how many times the mind wanders during this exercise. The whole exercise is about anchoring the awareness with the breath (as best you can) *and* bringing the mind back whenever it has wandered. Many people falsely assume that the objective is to be steadily focused on nothing but the breath. But in fact, the real practice is learning to return to the present moment quickly with ease whenever you see the mind getting lost. Just like on the athletic field, when you make a mistake and start to think about how terrible it is, and how it means you will have a bad game (i.e., like the mind wandering in meditation) – and you notice it – and you get your head back in the game (i.e., like getting your focus back on the breath). That noticing and refocusing is a true moment of success! The more you can do it in meditation, the more you will be able to do it on the field. The sooner you can get your attention away from distracting thoughts and emotions to actually performing, the better.

> *Ultimately, it's that ability to come back (from mind wandering) to the task at hand that will strengthen your mindfulness the most when you are in a game or competition.*

In this exercise, the critical move occurs when you wake up from 'wandering' and realize the mind is with something other than the breath. At that very moment, train yourself to 'relax' first and then let the breath come back to the forefront of your attention. Please, set your timer! Find a quiet place. You can lie down, sit or even stand up – whatever will be most comfortable AND will allow you to stay awake for ten-minutes. Right before you begin, remind yourself that:

1. It is OK that your mind wanders.
2. When you notice it wander, relax and bring your attention back to your breath.
3. You will most likely have other thoughts showing up, uninvited. That is OK! Just let them be there – at a secondary level of attention – and bring your attention to your breath. Think of it like being at a party. Your breath is the thing you are attending to – even though you know that there are lots of other guests at the party who you want your attention (like thoughts, emotions, and physical sensations that arise).
4. The biggest challenge is to sit down, set the timer, and begin.
5. Try to do this in a quiet place where you most likely will not be interrupted.
6. This is hard, but anyone can do it!
7. Begin!! Stop watch, ten-minutes, press start....

Debrief

If you are going through MMTS 2.0 on your own, we encourage you to keep a journal. It can be helpful to think about both what you are learning about how to practice meditation. And, perhaps, more importantly, it can be helpful to think about what you are learning and how it applies to practice and performance. If you are running MMTS 2.0 with a group – please refer to the Appendix protocol for suggested debrief questions for the ten-minute question and answer period.

Recommended Practice Between Sessions or Between Chapters!

We encourage you to practice some type of mindfulness meditation most days for about ten-minutes. It is of course fine to do more, less or none. But when you are just beginning to practice, starting with five or ten minutes will feel like plenty. The meditations (in the Appendix) are about ten minutes each. You can use them in the way that is most helpful to you. Or at this point you may opt instead to practice the breath meditation you just tried instead.

Chapter 6
The Power of Mindfulness With Warmth: (MMTS 2.0, Module 1 Part B)

> *Mindfulness without compassion can be hollow. In fact, the crux of Buddhist philosophy is the combination of these two practices, which together allow one to develop wisdom.*
>
> Jim Doty *(from Newman 2016)*

We have added something new to our mindfulness intervention. Throughout the program we invite you to intentionally bring some kindness toward your experience when needed. Directing kindness toward yourself may sound a bit soft or unnecessary – especially in competitive sport. And, yes, in some instances it is! For example, when you don't feel like going to practice or you don't feel like doing an extra lift, that definitely is NOT the time to be gentle with yourself (unless you are sick or injured). That, instead, is the time to dig in and get inspired by what you want to achieve and go do your training, whether you feel like it or not.

Yet, what we have found that in some instances, offering kindness to yourself is exactly what some athletes need to be able to keep going, the ingredient that they need to fuel their courage to keep trying *even* when feeling terrified of losing, or *even* when harshly criticizing themselves. Top athletes – sometimes – will give up when they are feeling great performance distress. For example, in one of my first studies I (Amy), I interviewed about forty U.S. National Team rowers. I was looking at how elite athletes coped with competitive pressure. One of my research questions was, *"Tell me about a time when you experienced the most competitive pressure and did not cope well."* All interviewees selected a time when they were either trying out for the US team or competing for the team (at the World Championships or Olympics) *and* a time that they were experiencing acute competitive pressure.

Of the athletes in this study 100% experienced great distress when they were not coping well with competitive pressure. For example, one rower recalled, "I just felt horrible, I was a wreck, I was bawling. I couldn't even forgive myself for doing that either. It was this spiral, it was horrible." And of these athletes – feeling such intense negative emotions – about ½ of the rowers (46%) reported also powerful urges and

© Springer International Publishing AG 2017
A. Baltzell, J. Summers, *The Power of Mindfulness*,
https://doi.org/10.1007/978-3-319-70410-4_6

reactively, mentally giving up. One US team athlete commented about his thoughts during racing at an international competition:

> I just want go get the hell out of this boat and I don't want to be here... there is nothing I could have done that could have got me out of that boat faster and just on the plane and out of there... physically I was still rowing and finishing the race but mentally I could care less.

All athletes are exposed to such moments of performance distress, and we want to offer ways for them to cope with such demands. Without the ability to be kind to yourself in such moments, you can get blind-sided by performance distress – which we call *performance dukkha*. Dukkha is a Buddhist term that refers to the pain, suffering, and un-satisfactoriness of many life experiences. We have found that when athletes are in the grips of such sport distress, having the ability to bring kindness to themselves is sometimes, absolutely essential to empower them to garner the courage to keep trying. Instead of shutting down and just going through the motions as described by the rower in the study noted, above.

We have also integrated kindness into MMTS 2.0 because from the Buddhist perspective kindness has long been encouraged as a requisite, integral aspect of mindfulness meditation practices. Certainly, the Buddhist perspective is unarguably the source from which most of what is known about mindfulness and mindful meditations. Integrating compassion into your mindfulness practice, when difficulty arises, is based on this ancient tradition. We have found that the twenty-first century athlete greatly benefits from this added dimension to mindfulness practices.

On a side note, our modern understanding of mindfulness mediation has gotten a bit off track with the loss of including a kindness, gentleness with self. We don't know why for sure, but we suspect that the missing focus on the softer aspect of mindfulness (intentionally including a quality of warmth toward one's experience) is due to lack of understanding of the original intention of mindfulness practice paired with the literal adherence to main definition of mindfulness offered by Jon Kabat-Zinn. Jon Kabat-Zinn was the person to bring mindfulness to the secular, mainstream western audience. His (1994) definition of mindfulness is the one that many researchers use to define the concept: "Paying attention in a particular way: on purpose, in the present moment, and non-judgmentally" (p. 8). We contend that this definition has inspired most researchers to *not* include intentional warmth and kindness in mindfulness-based research. This definition emphasizes the thinking mind – and, as stated, is void of feeling.

Yes, it appears that Kabat-Zinn clearly intended that both *intentional present moment awareness* and *warmth and kindness* within the awareness itself is valued. Another definition of mindfulness that Jon Kabat-Zinn put forward in 2003 emphasizes the value of both what one *thinks* and how one *feels* with the experience of mindfulness. He writes (2003) that "the word *mindfulness* reflects both mind and heart and that the term is the same in Asian languages; *mindfulness* includes an affectionate, compassionate quality within the attending, a sense of openhearted, friendly presences and interest" (Kabat-Zinn 2003, p. 145).

Wandering Mind

Perhaps, for less dramatic reasons, you also need to practice a bit of warmth toward yourself as you embark on trying out a formal meditation practice. Dealing with your naturally wandering mind can be quite challenging (and frustrating, irritating… the list goes on). You may have already noticed with your first practice, that your mind wanders, a lot. Mind wandering is very common, very human. Some research indicates that we all have on average 60,000 thoughts per day and of these thoughts about 95% are recurring (meaning, they show up over and over). Often this high mind activity is below the threshold of awareness. Yet when you start to slow down, sit, and be present to what is occurring in your mind, body, and emotions you might be very surprised at the activity. You also may start to notice how the thoughts that emerge are ones that can be limiting and prevent you from achieving desired goals.

The question is: how can you learn to respond to such thoughts differently? The key is that you don't have to whole-heartedly buy all your unkind, harsh thoughts. You don't have to get tangled up in them! Imagine how things might have gone differently for the rower above if he had been able to hold the intense negative thoughts differently. What if, instead, he had,

1. *Noticed the thoughts of wanting to give up,*
2. *Accepted that the unhelpful thoughts were there,* and
3. *Brought his attention back to racing his boat*? He could have brought to mind – *"OK, there are fearful thoughts. That's OK, back to the next stroke."*

The quality of how you attend to your experience matters. And just telling yourself to accept your thoughts and refocus is really hard to do (and for most people it is impossible, without some guidance). That is why the meditation practices can be a great place to train your mind so you can respond differently when it matters most to you. And for some, just understanding the option of mindfulness (awareness, accepting, and re-focusing) can be a game changer. And why meditation practice? It simply is much easier to practice training your mind when sitting quietly, than when under great performance pressure.

Self-Compassion and Mindfulness

Josh originally designed MMTS. Together, we have revised the program in a way that makes MMTS 2.0 different than other mindfulness-based interventions. We have intentionally integrated the concept and offer practices of self-compassion throughout the program. As you will see, MMTS 2.0 includes typical tools used to teach new meditators mindfulness practices such as focus on the breath and labeling difficult thoughts and emotions while practicing non-judgmental acceptance of thoughts, feelings, and sensations. Traditional mindfulness practices (i.e., awareness and acceptance practices) offer athletes a pathway to respond more wisely to emotional difficulty that arises. We contend that intentionally building self-compassion practices into the mindfulness meditation program is very beneficial. It can offer you a way to tolerate the particularly sticky, intense negative feelings and thoughts that can invade every fiber of your body.

Recall the Olympic rower example. He was thinking, *"I just want go get the hell out of this boat and I don't want to be here."* In such an instance it is tough to tell the athlete to just tolerate and focus back on rowing. Just imagine how badly the athlete must have felt to want to give up in that race. This was not just any race, but a final in a World Championship competition. What could have helped him? We have found over the past few years that when athletes are able to offer themselves some true acceptance... and even kindness in such moments... they are able to keep trying. This athlete did not physically stop but he reports *"I was still rowing and finishing the race but mentally I could care less."* I don't believe that the athlete didn't really care. Instead, he had no tools to deal with the intense feeling of helplessness he felt in that moment. What could have helped him keep fighting? We think one way would have been *mindfulness plus self-compassion.*

What Is Self-Compassion?

Self-compassion is about being kind enough to yourself in an intense moment of suffering to help you better cope with the challenge that you are facing. Two prominent leaders on the topic of self-compassion, Neff and Germer (2013), define self-compassion as "being touched by one's own suffering, generating the desire to alleviate one's suffering and treat oneself with understanding and concern" (p. 28). The three inter-connected dimensions of self-compassion include (We offer a more detailed discussion of self-compassion in Chap. 10):

1. **Mindfulness.** Being able to be aware of your suffering (i.e., making a mistake, failing) without ignoring or getting too caught up in the story of what is happening.
2. **Self-kindness.** Being able to offer yourself what you need in that moment (e.g., recalling a time when you handled a similar challenge well; bringing to mind an empowering image; treating yourself as you would a best friend or loved family member).
3. **Common Humanity.** Holding in perspective that whatever difficult is happening, others also are currently experiencing or have experienced a similar type of suffering.

Initial research on self-compassion in sport has shown that self-compassion helps athletes respond more effectively to emotional difficulty (Ferguson et al. 2014; Reis et al. 2015) and sport related self-criticism and concern of mistakes (Mosewich et al. 2013). Though mindfulness practices are focused on helping athletes learn to accept all experience, including moments of great difficulty, we contend that directly offering ways to help *tolerate* such difficulty may be an essential piece that is missing in most mindfulness-based programs. Self-compassion is not always necessary. But when dealing with feelings of inadequacy, or after making mistakes, failing, or when confronting difficult life situations self-compassion can be incredibly helpful (Germer and Neff 2013). Research in sport indicates that athletes that offer themselves more self-compassion have less catastrophizing thoughts and negative affect (Reis et al. 2015).

Practically, when you suffer you need to learn to take care of yourself. Do athletes in sport suffer? Indeed, yes! After twenty or thirty hours per week of preparation, performance outcomes can mean the world to you. Both of us can recall acute, painful sport moments – and those happened two or three decades ago.

Bring to mind a recent moment when you experienced harsh self-criticism, or intense disappointment from a loss or an embarrassing play. You can learn to care for yourself in such moments, just as you would care for someone you loved. In that moment, what might have you most needed to hear? What did you need most in that moment? You often are waiting for someone else to offer the words of kindness or authentic understanding. Through MMTS 2.0 you will be offered a number of ways to offer self-kindness to be at your best in your sport.

Let's consider the rower, one more time. What if he had offered himself some self-compassion like: "It is OK to feel this intense desire to quit" (i.e., mindfulness); "Others must feel like this too" (i.e., common humanity); and/or "I have felt like this before and still raced well!" (i.e. kindness). Just imagine if you could learn to courageously face these most difficult moments instead of avoiding them (i.e., shutting down or going through the motions).

Warmth and Mindful Meditation Practice

The meditation practices offer a great place to practice responding differently to experience. Having a plan about how to respond to your wandering mind will make a difference in your mindful meditation practices and, much more importantly, can translate directly to the field. The more you can notice and accept what is happening while meditating, the more you will be training to notice and accept what is happening in sport. The big difference in performance is that once you are able to notice and accept something like performance dukkha, you have to act. It won't be enough to just sit back and notice terror or great disappointment. You will have to be ready to accept the reality that is unfolding AND get yourself back in the game, as quickly as possible. Once you notice and accept the unwelcome feelings, you can opt to lean your attention into what it will take to perform well.

The mindful meditation training will continue with the breathing meditation again. You may be more aware of your mind wandering. For this meditation, think of your mind like a puppy on a leash. A puppy can get interested, excited and distracted by just about anything. And your monkey mind is quite similar. When you begin the next meditation and your mind begins to wander, we invite you to gently bring your attention back to your breath. Just like you would gently tug on a leash to bring a puppy back to where you want him to go, we ask you to do the same with your attention. When your mind wanders and you notice it, don't jerk your attention back with criticism of "I can't do this!" or "I'm bad at this!". Instead try to relax your body in that moment and shift your attention to your breath.

In this practice, intentionally be kind to yourself when you notice the mind's contents and wandering. Bring a kindness and curiosity once you notice uninvited thoughts, feelings, or physical sensation pulling your attention away from your focus on the breath. The moment you become aware of your mind wandering, intentionally relax your body and then return to your breath. If harsh self-judgment shows up ("I s*** at this!" or "I'm doing it wrong!") do the same, relax (accept), and gently bring your attention back to your breath.

> Relax and return is a key part of the cycle to strengthen self-compassion.

In this next practice, have your breath serve as your point of focus. When your mind wanders and you become aware of this wandering, it becomes a moment of clarity, of noticing what is really happening. This is a good thing! This moment gives you the chance to practice equanimity, relaxing with a kind intention toward yourself and then returning to the breath. The more you wake up to your mind wandering and opt to return your focus on the meditation in formal practice, the stronger your ability will be to do the same in sport practice and competition. You will be able to more quickly bring your attention back to performance-relevant cues.

Exercise 3: Affectionate Breathing

The next practice is similar to the first meditation and differs in one significant way. The exercise is a modified activity found in the Mindful Self-Compassion Teacher Manual (2015). We ask you to not only notice your breath, but to notice it with the intention of directing self-kindness and warmth toward your breathing and really to yourself. Consider the meditation cycle before you begin (Fig. 6.1).

- Please find a quiet, comfortable place to sit. Position yourself in a way that your bones are supporting the muscles and you can remain in one position for the whole exercise. To do this, try keeping your back straight and gently supported, with your shoulder blades slightly dropped and your chin gently tucked toward your chest.
- Take a few slow easy deep breaths to relax and let go of whatever burdens you're carrying. Then let your eyes gently close, or partially close, which ever makes you more comfortable. Consider putting your hand over your heart, or wherever

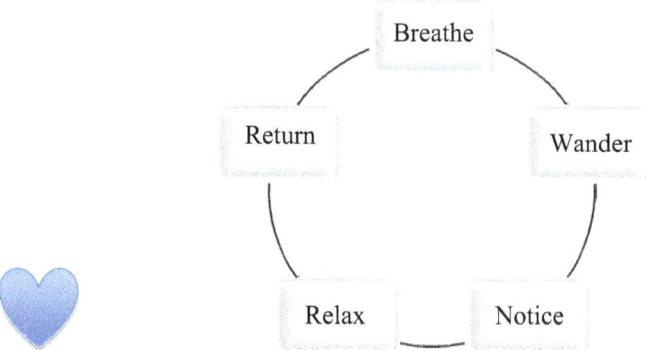

Fig. 6.1 Meditation Cycle, revisited

it is comforting for you, to remind yourself that you are bringing not only attention, but also *kind* attention, to your experience and to yourself.

- Now noticing your breath, wherever you can feel it most easily. Perhaps at the tip of the nose, the belly, or perhaps as a gentle movement of your whole body. Letting yourself notice the simple sensation of breathing. Just feeling your breath for a while.
- Your mind will naturally wander away from the sensation of the breath every few seconds. Don't worry about how often your mind wanders. Gently return to the feeling of your breathing when you notice that your mind has wandered. Be gentle with yourself, as kind as you can be, like guiding a puppy.
- See if you can incline toward your breathing as you might incline toward a child or a beloved pet, with curiosity and tenderness.
- Letting your body breathe you. There is nothing you need to do.
- Noticing how your breath nourishes your body even when you're not paying any attention to it.
- Now feeling your whole body breathe, gently moving with the rising and falling of the breath, like waves gently moving toward and away from the shore
- Or, if you like, allowing your body to be rocked by your breath, back and forth.
- Giving yourself over to your breath, letting yourself become your breath
- Now, take a moment and savor the stillness of your body.
- And slowly and gently open your eyes.

Debrief

If you are going through MMTS 2.0 on your own, please take a few moments to reflect on your experience in your journal. Some things you might write about are: What were your initial thoughts and reactions? Were you able to stay with the breath the whole time? (Generally, no one will be able to!) Did you have any thoughts?

(Everyone will!) Were you aware of physical sensations? (Often people will notice physical sensations and the sensations tend to change.) Did you feel sleepiness? (Many times people will. That is normal. If you fell asleep you might want to try the meditation with your eyes slightly open, sit on a hard chair or even stand up). Did you feel restlessness? (Again, most people will feel this.) Though challenging, we encourage you to keep trying. Learning to be less reactive to challenge is a great initial benefit. The next chapter is on exactly this, learning to be less controlled by unwanted thoughts and feelings. Read on!

Chapter 7
The Power of Acceptance: Labeling (Module 2, Part A)

Life is 10% what happens to you and 90% how you react to it.

Charles R. Swindoll

Joanna

Joanna is a collegiate rower who is highly gifted. She was a contender for the US Rowing National Team before her eighteenth birthday. She was a fierce competitor and able to push herself to extremes, from stadium runs and long runs to grueling lifting sessions. She is the type of athlete others view simply as a "winner." She receives little feedback from coaches about how to improve. She is mentally tough and emotionally steady. What is there to improve? The answer came from a question she asked me: *"Is counting strokes all through a practice a good or bad thing to do?"*

What an interesting question! Is focusing on a point of attention that is *not* rowing specific helpful? As I (Amy) pondered her question, it became clear that sometimes going on automatic pilot is good and sometimes it is not! I could see how being mindful could be of service to Joanna through strengthening her awareness, presence, and clarity. Now back to me trying to directly answer her question.

My response: When you use counting, you are essentially *distracting your thinking-mind and allowing your body to function on automatic pilot*. At times, trusting your body is of course wise — particularly when trying to performance. But if you never thinks about your timing, technique, or even feel for the water – you are essentially committing to not using your thinking mind to improve your rowing technique or strategy during the two to three hours per day that you are *practicing* rowing.

The use of distractions can be good, but only if used skillfully. Sometimes Joanna won't need to purposefully think, perhaps a lot of the time. But sometimes opting to intentionally kick in her thinking mind could be very helpful.

I asked Joanna, "Do you think that you could ever benefit from being fully aware of what was happening moment to moment as you practice, placing all of your attention on the rowing?" A new light flickered. She could see how what she was doing was ignoring the subtleties and learning opportunities.

© Springer International Publishing AG 2017
A. Baltzell, J. Summers, *The Power of Mindfulness*,
https://doi.org/10.1007/978-3-319-70410-4_7

Conceptually, why does paying attention to the moment matter? We think mind-lessness has a lot to do with it. When you consider what happens when you are mindless, tuning into your experience becomes quite compelling. In Ellen Langer's (Langer 1989) article, *The Consequences of Mindlessness*, she offers an explanation of mindlessness (and offers insight into what Joanna was missing):

> *Although people are certainly capable of acting mindfully, they frequently respond in a routinized, mindless way. In much of everyday life, people rely on distinctions drawn from the past; they overly depend on structures of situations, representative of the underlying meaning without making new distinctions. This mindlessness holds the world still and pre-vents an awareness that things could be otherwise* (p. 137).

So while Joanna is counting stroke after stroke, she was losing the chance to see what it might be like to row in those previously mindless moments of counting. The nuances of rowing in varying conditions and how to best adapt and adjust were being lost when she, essentially, was opting to tune out and practice hour after hour – mindlessly, on automatic pilot.

Awareness

Awareness is an essential component of being mindful, being present to what is hap-pening in the *now*. When you are physically awake, you have some level of aware-ness of what is happening around you. Though when awake you could still be lost in worrying about the past and fearing the future. You could be aware of these thoughts – and missing out on what is actually happening in the moment – in those specific unfolding moments of the day. From a mindfulness perspective, we are talking about awareness reflecting intentionally tuning into what is happening in real time.

Clearly at any moment there are countless things that you can hold in your aware-ness. There are myriad thoughts, emotions, and/or physical sensations within your-self and your environment. You are in fact quite used to being aware – present to a whole myriad of small and large experiences, meaningful and not meaningful to us. But there is a difference in just going through the motions and intentionally being present to what you are doing.

In this chapter we will ask you to practice *intentionally* being aware of a range of experiences. Though these practices on some level are quite simple, intentionally being present (and not getting carried away by our regrets and fears) can offer the most challenge to engage in MMTS 2.0. We are not just asking you to go along with business as usual. We are not asking you to follow whatever might draw your atten-tion and subsequently think or daydream about it.

Quite differently, we will be asking you to do almost the opposite, particularly in the formal meditation practices. We will ask you to be still, not intentionally engage in thinking (though thoughts might come and go) and focus on witnessing or observ-ing thoughts, physical sensations, and emotions that arise.

We all know that sport performance takes more – you can't just witness your experience. You have to *do*. You must take action. In sport performance you must be able to choose where you are placing your awareness. Where to place your attention is of upmost importance. Part of the requirement of being successful in sport is being aware of factors within yourself and your environment that will leverage the most learning and wise response to performance-relevant cues. And once whatever is arising is noticed, you may choose to turn away from it (e.g., thinking about going out; comparing yourself to a competitor) and bring your attention to produce better outcomes.

We have found it can be helpful first, though, to *practice being aware – and only that –* in some of the formal practices so you can better tune into what is actually unfolding right before you. And with such formal practice on awareness, you can bring this strengthened skill to notice what is happening from the court, on the field, to in the pool in a poised manner. For example, if Joanna stopped counting through all of her practices and tuned into her rowing, she could become aware of subtle physical sensations and make improvement in her rowing more quickly. Once aware, she could opt to make small adjustments to increase her speed in a range of situations (e.g., slight changes in wind direction; energy available in her body to choices that supported more efficiency of movement). There is an important next step before taking action in the formal meditation practice. Once you become aware – an essential part of mindfulness – in the formal practice is to accept what is showing up (before we get into adapting and adjusting on the athletic field).

Acceptance

We would like to talk about what acceptance is not, before we talk about what it is. There is a big misunderstanding about the idea of acceptance as it pertains to mindfulness. Once you become aware, the power of acceptance is:

• NOT about giving up.
• NOT about giving in.
• NOT about being soft.
• NOT about being complacent.

The power of acceptance is about having the courage to meet reality just as it is. Acceptance is about you facing the actuality of a situation. And when you face what really is happening you can more wisely figure out how to handle it. With acceptance you fuel poise, being able to handle whatever comes at you with a steadiness. Acceptance empowers you to see your options and in turn gives you the chance to make the best choice of how you can move forward. With the reality of acceptance, you then can choose how you opt to respond instead of pretending it is different, making up stories, tuning out, or ignoring reality. To accept, you must first be able to clearly see what really is happening.

The power of acceptance is about having the courage to meet reality just as it is.

On a side note, I commented to my (Amy's) daughter Shayna that she is very good at accepting what shows up from fighting siblings, hours of homework, to receiving a surprise treat. She is able to gracefully, with poise, handle whatever comes her way. When I asked her, *How are you able to accept everything and, especially, not get mad?*, her response was, *Well you can't change it!* And that really is the point of acceptance. Whether you befriend or tolerate what has just happened, it just happened! No matter how much you resist it, it already had occurred. Acceptance is quite distinct from fighting it, being mad about it, or complaining about it. None of responses can change what *already happened.* Of course, you can make choices to make things better from this exact moment forward. But first learning to accept things just as they are is an important piece of the mindfulness training. (In a few pages we will offer the next practice, which is about accepting things just as they are).

Clarity

You may wonder, why we are emphasizing awareness and acceptance? We are doing so because when you are able to be aware and accept, you are much more empowered to see what really is happening. You are not making a short cut and just reacting as you always have (e.g., *practice is so boring*). With acceptance you create an option, a space to decide how you want to respond (think or behave) based on what is actually happening in your current reality (e.g., Wow! *I am feeling so much stronger, today. Let's see how far I can jump today*). With acceptance, facing reality as it is (whether you like it or not) becomes possible.

When you become fully present (or as present as possible) you develop awareness of your thoughts, particularly the uninvited thoughts, and automatic and habituated reactions. You can begin to notice the flow of self-criticism, or hopelessness, or of simply not paying attention. You can begin to notice how you interact with your external experience. You might notice that when you get angry and explode, you might also notice how teammates or coaches respond to this. You might notice when you are going through the motions in practice. You might notice that when winning gets out of reach, you tend to shut down, give up. Essentially you start to learn to see your experience, as it is, with some objectivity.

You can learn to notice the magical space between stimulus and response (not just patterned habitual response) and notice the critical moments when you have a choice to respond more effectively. Maybe you realize that you *must* take a day off, or that driving yourself into the ground is no longer a good reactive behavior. Maybe you notice a way of acting or re-acting used to work, but no longer does! Or maybe you realize that you have chronic anxiety before big events so instead of having sleepless nights you are inspired to figure out strategies that will help soothe your fears. Maybe you watch film of times you were successful or intentionally bring to mind such moments. Or maybe you bring to mind the reality that such feelings are normal, and maybe even necessary, to get you in the focused, highly energized state you need to be in to perform your best.

Cultivating clarity is not just for moments of difficulty. Actually, when you are able to invest less energy in thoughts and feelings that are not relevant to performance, you can become *awareness in action*. Imagine a snow globe shaken up. That is like your mind when it is jammed full of thoughts, judgments, feelings, physical sensations, and distractions. When you can stop feeding your mind's ruminations, getting caught up in stories of what happened or what might happen, your mind starts to settle down. Your mind settles just like the snowflakes in a snow globe will settle down, when left alone for a bit. And when you get present to what really is happening, most often your mind becomes clearer. And clarity in performance or practice is worth everything.

As veteran USOC Sport Psychologist Haberl (2016) says, "Attention is the psychological currency of performance (p. 222)." You free up your attention by creating some space between your thoughts and reactivity. When you perform at your best, or to the best of your ability in the given moment, your attention is primarily absorbed by the moment-to-moment activity. The more you can cultivate this clarity of present moment experience, the more you can set yourself up for improved performance.

With clarity, you also can become more aware of what is working, what is right and good about your training or how you perform. Sometimes you can miss out on how you have improved or what you are learning. You can miss out witnessing and knowing what you can count on – like your developing strength, flexibility, skill and strategy – what you can rely upon. Clarity is not just for better understanding what is going wrong, it also can be very beneficial to more clearly see what is going right. Just as you are.

Decentering

Once you are aware and accepting of what is happening, you can learn to respond differently to many problematic internal and external challenges *and* opportunities. One place athletes often get challenged is by their thinking. We will offer some strategies to help you deal with your thinking differently, more effectively. The goal of these exercises will be to create some space between the thought and your automatic reaction to them. The academic term in creating such space between a thought and reaction is called *decentering*.

Decentering reflects witnessing your thoughts and experience without automatically responding to them as if they represent reality or are true. Moore (2016) offers a more formal, precise definition of decentering as "the ability to observe one's thoughts and feelings and regard them as transient, objective events of the mind. They do not necessarily reflect truth or reality, and they do not necessitate automatic action" (p. 36). When you have enough where-with-all to label your emotional reactions, you begin to free yourself from having to 'buy' into triggering thoughts or emotions. When you can see what you are thinking and how you are reacting, you begin to be more empowered to choose to respond differently.

Labeling

Labeling is a practical way to decenter from your thinking and feeling. As you become more balanced in your response to such ups and downs in sport, you will start to see the unquestioned tendency to *buy into* your own unhelpful thoughts, just like getting hooked by inner-advertisements. When you allow yourself to get pulled and pushed around by your own thinking, you can easily lose your balance. In training and competition this can quickly translate into losing your wisdom regarding what is most important to focus on to prepare for or to optimize performance.

You may also lose confidence. Such moments often can spiral into deciding that you cannot win or cannot improve. Athletes sometimes decide that their coach doesn't believe in them. Or they might decide someone is better than they are and then subsequently act as if each one of these *decisions about how it is – is true.*

However, as soon as you become aware of an unhelpful thought, you have a choice. And one strategy that can help you respond to them *differently* is to label such thoughts. Yet, labeling thoughts is not a typical thing to do! When labeling, you are intentionally thinking about your thinking (referred to in academia as metacognition). We are not recommending this just for engaging in fun mental gymnastics, or just to offer a clever activity.

The practice of labeling one's thoughts is a many centuries old tradition within Buddhist mindful meditations. There is a good reason that the Buddhist monks practiced intentionally watching their thoughts (in meditation) and not doing anything about them. The task is to be aware of thoughts, feelings, and physical sensations and do nothing BUT accept them.

Here is an example of using labeling to decenter in sport. If a coach unfairly yells at you for not trying hard enough you might experience a burst of anger. When angry you might reactively throw a racquet, walk out of practice, or shut down. But with labeling, you could note, *This is what anger feels like.* You could allow, just for a moment for the feelings to wash over you. And in that space – between stimulus and response – you could *decide* to respond differently (instead of reacting like you always have in such instances). Maybe in that moment you opt not to move, nor to say anything. Maybe you opt to keep trying just a hard as you had before – no more, no less.

Sounds easy, right? It turns out that it really is not. Why? You, if like most others, so easily can get caught up in your thoughts, meaning you easily believe your thoughts. Of course, sometimes what you are thinking is true. But the problem is that the true thoughts get mixed up with thoughts like, *You'll never make it; Coach hates me; I am not big enough; I am not quick enough; I'll never be that good; They are so strong; They are so much better than I am.* If you are like most performers, you have had thoughts like this.

But are such thoughts true? If so, does that mean that they will always hold true in the future? Much of the problem is our minds getting in the way. You can so easily believe such thoughts in sport. You can buy those thoughts that are running through

Fig. 7.1 Decentering
through Labeling

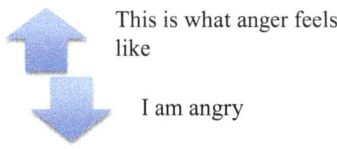

This is what anger feels
like

I am angry

your heads – hook, line, and sinker. When you start watching the thoughts that spontaneously arise in your awareness, which we like to call uninvited thoughts, you might start to think twice about believing all of them.

In the next exercise you can practice a way to first observe your thoughts, accept that they are arising yet NOT buy (i.e., believe) them!

You will be asked only to witness what shows up in your mind and to allow the thoughts to come and go. Try not to stop them. But also try not to engage back with them. This practice is key to having mindfulness help you with performance. Just imagine if you were able to simply notice the wide variety of harsh self-criticism, accept (give no power to) these thoughts, and get back to business of throwing, running… competing.

Regardless of what you end up deciding to do about the thoughts, the idea of *labeling* in a meditation practice is to objectively label the feeling or thought that arise. Of course, you wouldn't want to label your experience all of the time, but this labeling exercise can be a very helpful strategy to use to help dampen typically unproductive reactions. With labeling, instead of thinking, *I am angry*, it can be helpful to note instead *There is anger* or *This is what anger feels like*. When you take the "I" statement out of the equation, there tends to be an easier movement away from over-identifying with or allowing the feeling to take over and dominate your response or reaction (Fig. 7.1).

Thus when you label your experience (e.g., *this is anger, this is embarrassment,* or *this is fear*), your identification with that thought can be loosened and you can eventually learn to naturally reclaim a sense of psychological balance. It is generally not a smooth or easy thing to do, to shift away from the negative thoughts and feelings that can rush in on you. Even when you label such thoughts, often it still can feel badly, emotionally.

With decentering, via labeling, you can stop the negative domino effect. Such mental balance from mindfulness training can truly help you better ride the inevitable ups and downs that come with top-level performance, facilitating (ultimately) almost immediate renewal in your mental balance in the face of adversity and challenge.

These next meditations are labeling practices. We will ask you to pay attention to thoughts, feelings, and physical sensations. You will be asked to label what arises. Before you begin, remember to bring warmth, curiosity, and kindness to what is happening. Also, we would like to normalize a bit about what will tend to show up in others' minds when they practice any of the meditations. Here is a short list:

- mind wandering;
- unexpected thoughts arising;

- thinking about what happens next;
- difficult uninvited images arising;
- sleepiness;
- falling asleep;
- irritation;
- intense desire to move, to stop;
- quiet mind;
- sense of comfort and ease;
- wanting to do something else;
- *not* wanting the exercise to stop.

It is normal for any of this to happen. Please remember, if you simply try to participate in this exercise, it will be a success! If you become aware of wandering mind, and that is all, that is a start to a meditation practice. If your mind wanders and you bring your awareness back to the focus of the exercise, you are also successfully meditating! And, yes, this will take some effort.

Anything worthwhile takes effort.

Labeling (Sound and Body Experience) Meditation Practice (ten-minutes)

One practical way that you can learn to create some space between your awareness (observing mind) and the thoughts (and emotions) you are experiencing is through the *labeling* of experience. In this labeling meditation practice, please set a timer for ten-minutes or you can set it for five-minutes and re-set during the second half of the meditation.

Sound (five-minutes)

We would like you to note, by silently labeling, any *sound* occurrence that appears in your awareness. In this first five minutes we would like you to notice sounds as they come and go. Please simply attend to the sound that most easily draws your attention. Allow your attention to rest with this sound until it either fades away or some other, more dominant sound draws your attention. For example, as I (Amy) write this section *I am aware of the sound of a car engine running. I stay with that sound. My attention just shifted to a car door slam.... next, to a rumble of a car driving by... next, to a rumble of an engine, not identifiable.*

In addition to noticing each sound occurrence, please notice the experience as it is being observed. You can note things like the sound getting stronger, more intense, less obvious, or fading away. During this exercise, in between noticing sound occurrences, just bring your attention back to your breath. Meaning, if no sound is showing up, just go back and rest with gentle attention on your breath. Keep your primary emphasis on allowing your awareness to remain open to *any sound* that arises. (Please do not to give your breathing preferential attention.)

In this exercise, you are practicing being in the space between stimulus and response.

You will be practicing what it is like to notice experience, strengthen your awareness of what is occurring moment-to-moment... and do nothing about it but just notice (For now. But, eventually, you can use that space to make wise decisions when practicing and performing). After five minutes has passed, please shift your attention to physical sensations.

Physical Sensations (five-minutes)

We now ask you to shift your attention, bringing the same awareness practice to physical sensations. You might notice a multitude of physical sensations such as "pressure," "itching," "tension," "tingling," "hot," or "cold." And now for the labeling, which is inspired by the Mahasi Method of the Vipassana style of meditation in Burma. We ask that you label the physical sensations you experience. You can either note, "thought," if thinking of the precise sensation is frustrating or distracting. But, if you can, try to note the actual physical sensation that is arising (i.e., pressure, itching, hot, cold). As an example, we would like you to say silently in your mind "cool" if you become aware of a part of your body that feels cool.

Try to just label the actual experience (e.g., tingling, burning, pressure) versus an overarching concept (e.g. This hurts!). Another example, if the experience is for example comfortable, we ask you to note the actual physical sensations of the comfort like warmth, pressure, and tingling. In this exercise, you may be aware of other experiences like "thinking," "hearing," and "(day) dreaming." If these show up in your experience, which they most likely will, once you are aware of them gently bring your attention back to noticing and labeling physical sensations that arise.

> This entire process of paying attention to physical sensation, labeling a few sensations, losing focus – planning dinner or a date, becoming aware of distraction, relaxing, and intentionally focusing back on the body – ALL – include successfully meditating.

In this practice, we invite you to notice experiences that are relatively easy to accept (sounds, physical sensations). This practice is about *awareness, **acceptance**, and decentering* from experience. This is also a practice of attention, attending to what you choose to notice. When you can do this, it will strengthen your ability to see what is going on. And with such clarity brings power. You can begin to make more clear choices in how you want to adjust your effort or what you are paying attention to, once you are tuned into what you are actually doing. Make sure that before you begin, you intentionally also bring a kindness, acceptance, and warmth to yourself as you bring your attention back to the sounds or your physical sensations.

The mindfulness practices we offer will help with such issues on the court, on the field, in the pool… wherever you compete. As you are better able to focus your attention where you want it to go in meditation practice, you will be empowered do the same in practice or performance. For example, in practice you might get *distracted* (just like mind wandering in meditation) about making a mistake, being yelled at by a coach, or having thoughts of a date later that night. Once you become aware that the mind is wandering you can gently (and more quickly) bring attention back to practice.

Now, we invite you to set your timer and begin! Just as a reminder: Try labeling sound for five-minutes and then transition directly to labeling physical sensation for five-minutes. Ten minutes total…. Begin!

Debrief

If you are going through MMTS 2.0 on your own, please take a few moments to reflect on your experience in your journal. Some things you might write about are:

- What was it like to try to keep your attention on what was arising? Were you able to accept (i.e., not-judge) the judgments that were naturally arising?
- Did you label the sounds? Did you label the physical sensations?
- How was it different, in this meditation, when you labeled your experience versus just noticing what was arising?
- Were you able to be kind/gentle with self when you refocused on either the sounds or labeling physical sensations?

This practice can help you when you are trying to keep your attention on what matters, like when the play is unfolding. For example, a golfer could notice fearful thoughts or his mind calculating standings between shots. The golfer could create some space by thinking "planning" or "just thinking." After the intensity of these distracting thoughts begins to dissolve through the decentering effort, the golfer could bring his mind back to golf. We encourage you to keep practicing some type of mindfulness meditation for most days for about ten-minutes per day. It is of course fine to do more (or less!).

Chapter 8
The Power of Acceptance & Tolerance (Module 2, Part B)

The goal of meditation practice: Be gentle, tolerant and interested

– Joshua Summers

This chapter is dedicated to those athletes or performers who get side tracked by negative thinking or suffer from performance dukkha. While teaching MMTS 2.0, it has become abundantly clear to us that many twenty-first century athletes suffer from such distress. It can be invaluable to learn a bit about how to tolerate such distress so you can prepare how to handle such debilitating thoughts and emotions. We offer you a clear pathway to contend with such difficulty. You will be equipped to change your response to such experience and thus *not* let the thoughts and feeling get in the way of *your* performance. We do not promise that such thoughts and feelings will dissolve, completely. Though your overall expeirence can certainly get much better, quickly.

Olivia

Olivia had trained for the U.S. Olympic Rowing team for five years post-college, full time. She lived, breathed, and dreamt only of rowing. She became one of the top performers, physiologically demonstrated by earning some of the country's top ergometer scores (that is the in-door rowing machine you might see in most sport clubs across the country). She was one of the physically strongest athletes (as measured by specific lifting, tolerance training that simulated rowing). Yet, when it came down to the final push, the final set of races for the Olympic Team – she fell apart, psychologically. She had all the tools to be successful technically and yet physically she had no idea how to handle performance distress – *performance dukkha*. When the fearful thoughts of losing, of failing arrived, she became

© Springer International Publishing AG 2017
A. Baltzell, J. Summers, *The Power of Mindfulness*,
https://doi.org/10.1007/978-3-319-70410-4_8

overwrought and fully tangled up in what her future failure would mean. And with full focus on failure, this intention set the domino effect of thoughts, choices, and action to failure. She did not end up racing for Team USA.

Olivia had never been taught nor had she ever come in contact with ideas that would offer insight into how to handle such unexpected fears and distress. When she was hit by intense fear of failure, she had no idea where to turn. Her teammates seemed to indicate that they were tough, simply champions. So what did that mean about Olivia? And worse, where could she turn for help? She wondered, *Perhaps only the true winners could succeed*? Now consider T.J., who experienced similar challenges, but was also offered some ways to handle the sport distress.

T.J.

One of our (Amy's) clients, T.J., is a full scholarship basketball player. His biggest challenge comes with the first few shots of the game. If he makes his first few shots, he decides that it will be a great game and in most cases he will be the highest scorer and his team will win. However, if he misses the first few shots, he predictably thinks, *It is just going to be one of those games.* He then proceeds to have an emotional explosion and quickly mentally shuts down. He thinks it is just luck, having an on or off night. Predictably in the games his shot is off at the start, he will give up and just go through the motions of playing, have a poor performance, which usually results in his team losing.

T.J.'s experience is 100% controlled from the initial thought, *It is just one of those games.* He allows this thought to snowball into bad feelings, he gets distracted, he keeps missing, and then he gives up. It is one thing to be washed over with disappointment after missing a shot – a very normal, human response. It is another to allow these thoughts to dominate the next two hours of play and be the reason for giving up, poor performance, and ultimately losing which unfortunately is more common than any of us would like to admit.

In a sport psychology session, when I asked T.J. to slow down the story and tell me step by step, what happens in his mind. He was shocked by what he learned. The conversation went something like this:

A: *Can you recall a game when you shut down, the way coach describes.*
TJ: *Yes*
A: *What is happening?*
TJ: *It is just one of those games. Nothing.*
A: *Well, OK. Can you tell me about the last time it happened?*
TJ: *Yeah.... I went down and took a couple of shots and missed.*
A: *OK, then what happened.*
TJ: (Now irritation starts) *I went down, took another shot, missed... Coach took me out* (he says with a flash of anger). *I go to the end of the bench and sit down, It was just one of those games!*

A: Ok, and then what happened.

TJ: (Silence. And then he says slowly) *I didn't play well the rest of the game....*
        (In this moment he saw that his belief in his initial thoughts – judgment of the
        game – shut him down for the remainder of the game.)

At this point he began to realize that it was his thinking about missing, his emotional and mental reaction that was truly causing the performance problem for him. With this insight TJ began to be freed up from only reacting when things were going poorly, which was mentally giving up. With his insight he shattered the belief that he 100% would have to have a bad game because he missed his first three attempts at a basket. And more generally he freed himself from always believing his doubting thoughts. He was now able to begin to choose how he wanted to handle such key performance decisions in the future when his doubt was strong. This required him to be aware of his thoughts, accept them as they were and be willing to choose differently. He had the new option of staying in the game, mentally, no matter what his doubting mind was saying.

When T.J. became aware of what he was doing, at first he was shocked, almost in disbelief. It was hard for him to take responsibility for his reaction of quitting AND accept that he had the option to choose differently. He realized that he could opt to allow the feelings of disappointment and embarrassment to wash over him and STILL fight, stay in the game, and lead. Staying in it, in the moment, can be emotionally harder than quitting. But most athletes – if they knew that they had a choice – would prefer to take such heat if it meant that they would be more successful.

In the last chapter we spoke of awareness, acceptance, and de-centering. This is not too hard to do unless you are dealing with distress – like T.J. and Olivia, above. It is easy to label distracting thoughts – just thoughts – and to focus back on the game. But it becomes much more difficult when the thoughts and emotions include aversive, uncomfortable emotions like embarrassment, fear, self-doubt, or harsh self-criticism. In this chapter we offer another labeling practice to address such performance dukkha to help you de-center so you are not led around like a puppet by your intense, aversive thoughts and feelings. But first, we'd like to talk a bit more about a way of thinking about the space between the initial experience (e.g., doubt, fear, anger, to frustration) and our typical reaction (e.g., trying too hard, not trying hard enough).

Stimulus and Response

There is a difference between your automatic reactions to things (e.g., like T.J. giving up when he missed too many shots in a row at the start of the game) and being willing to accept (tolerate) the negative emotion in the "space" between the stimulus (e.g., anxiety, fear, self-doubt) and your response. In this space of noticing and choosing, you can respond based on current information or react as you have in the past (e.g., for T.J., his reaction was to mentally giving up).

Fig. 8.1 Stimulus, response and choice

Often you don't feel like you have a choice. Yet, you do. You can learn to choose to respond differently to a whole range of typical, habitual thoughts and physical reactions (Fig. 8.1).

> Between stimulus and response there is a space. In that space is our power to choose our response. In our response lies our growth and our freedom. *Victor Frankl*

Typical reactions we have seen in sport are things like a frustrated tennis player throwing his racquet, giving up when an athlete or team realizes (*really just believes*) that they cannot win, or emotionally shutting down when an athlete feels highly criticized by a coach. These are just a few examples of the countless moments when you can have uninvited thoughts, emotions, or factors in your environment that can trigger you to react, spontaneously, in sub-optimal ways. Being mindful includes living in that space. You can remain awake in the moments between stimulus and response and opt to accept reality and *not* automatically react. In that space of acceptance you have choice, just like T.J.

Yet, it can be quite difficult to be mindful of, to remain in contact with, unpleasant experience. Athletes often would rather quit or mentally give up than have to put up with the feelings associated with hopelessness or anticipated looming defeat. Often in the mindfulness training, you are told that you need to be able to accept the unpleasant to be able to face it. Yes, you have to be able to face the monster to be able to do something about the monster, which might include to understand it. When experiencing distress, we prefer the word *tolerance* instead of the word *accept* because sometimes it does feel like you have to face a monster, which is not easy to just accept.

Acceptance Continuum

When being mindful of unpleasant experience it takes effort not to close down or avoid the unpleasantness. Christopher Germer (2009), a world leader in the area of mindfulness and self-compassion, offers an even more expansive way to consider

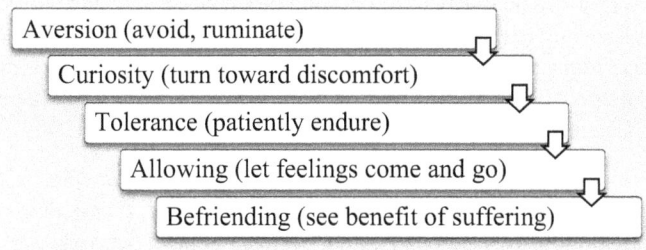

Fig. 8.2 Acceptance continuum (Christopher Germer 2009)

acceptance. He views acceptance of one's experience on a continuum from aversion to befriending (Fig. 8.2).

Aversion. Aversion is when you resist, avoid, and ruminate. This is when you are actually being almost mindless, meaning tending toward avoiding (like T.J. giving up) or over-engaging (like Olivia, overwhelmed with anxiety). Aversion is an absence of being mindful.

Curiosity. The next level is *curiosity,* when you are willing to turn toward the discomfort. Perhaps in such instances you are willing to face unusual soreness in your legs; the hurt that emerges from a teammate betraying your trust; or the intense anxiety you sometimes feel before you perform.

Tolerance. Next, with *tolerance* you can safely endure, which means to be able to suffer through something patiently. And with tolerance, you are not running away or quitting. When falling behind in a race, you are able to tolerate the frustration and embarrassment and keep running. For an athlete who gets a bad call from a referee, she is able to feel the anger, suffer, but still make wise choices in how to continue playing her game to the best of her ability.

Allowing. *Allowing* is the next step where you don't hold onto the feelings tightly, such as anger, frustration, or irritation, instead you can let the feelings come and go. You don't fan the fire of negativity. When thoughts of self-doubt or uncertainty arise, you notice them and keep your attention on what you are doing. When the feelings or thoughts are aversive, it is like having to share space with someone who you don't like. Perhaps someone you really don't like, like Uncle Joe, shows up to your family party. You may not spend time with him. Yet you know that he is there and you know that you cannot make him leave.

Befriend. And finally, you can befriend or have *friendship* with what is occurring, even if it is unpleasant. You can simply embrace the feelings of being alive and being human, regardless of whether the emotions are pleasant or unpleasant. And perhaps in the best of moments you can even see the hidden value in difficulty. For example, you might learn to see that the anxiety you feel is driven by your wish that you are successful, that all of your hard work pays off. Or you could see that the fear is coming from the good place of you wishing yourself safety and comfort. We offer this range of ways that people accept what is happening under the umbrella of the mindful *acceptance* so you may have a better understanding of the range in ways that you can accept: sometimes you have curiosity about what is happening and other times you are called to stoically endure what is occurring.

It won't mean you will always like what shows up, but acceptance does mean that you won't resist reality and thereby make it worse. Consistent with Victor Frankl's idea, Buddhist teacher and author Shinzen Young summarizes this idea into a simple formula: $S = P \times R$. In written form, this formula states that suffering equals pain times resistance. The pain (or anxiety, or frustration) will be there but the idea of resisting it (e.g., ruminating on how bad it is; anger at the unfairness of a situation) just makes the suffering worse. And an ideal scenario would be one in which the pain or anxiety emerges and with no resistance; therefore, no real suffering occurs (because zero multiplied by anything equals zero).

Suffering = Pain x Resistance

How does this idea translate to sport? Imagine T.J. noticing thoughts of, *it is just one of those games* and having awareness of the emotions of intense frustration and embarrassment. Consider what might have gone differently if he had the understanding and practice to notice automatic, uninvited thoughts and accept them by noting, *just thoughts* or *It is normal to think that, but next play!* The suffering comes not from the missed shots but the reaction to what missing the big shot means: For T.J. missing a few in a row in front of a big crowd might mean to him that he is not living up to the expectations of being the super star. But if there was no resistance (i.e., it is OK to have those thoughts and feelings) than the suffering T.J. would experience would shrink (and eventually evaporate) and he would be empowered to get his head back in the game.

We know it is a rhetorical question, but have you ever experienced automatically reacting to difficulty and then regretted how you reacted or how the upset escalated? Or can you think of a time a time when you got distracted and just went through the motions? Just for a moment, bring such an instance to mind. Perhaps a time you gave up, a time you become anxious and fed your fear with visions of failure. Going back in time, what if you had a choice about how you would have responded, even while feeling the aversive thoughts and feelings? What would you have done differently in that space between stimulus and response? Take a moment to bring such an instance to mind.

When you are upset, filled with thoughts of comparison to competitors, teammates or in some way distracted by thoughts, emotions, or physical sensations it is easy to be told to *just get your head back in the game.* Yet getting back in the game when feeling hopeless is much more difficult to do than to say. Essentially you can get so tangled up in your thoughts and experiences, you react to them as if they are 100% real (e.g., I have had many elite athlete-clients who were so intensely fearful about losing a race that their emotions and thoughts *before* the race were consistent with someone who had already lost!).

Uninvited Thoughts vs. Intentional Thoughts

Intentional Thinking

Intentional thinking, thinking on-purpose, you do countless times per day. For example, bring to mind something you want to make sure you get done in the next 24 hours. Purposefully use your mind to think about what you want to do and when you will complete the task. Pause now for just a moment. Think about it. The thoughts that just occurred were *intentional thoughts.* Just now a thought was created in your mind because you decided to think, to use your thinking mind. Our thinking minds are an invaluable asset, they help us make sense of what has happened and to plan for the future. You often don't separate intentional thinking from uninvited (not-on-purpose) thinking. These two groupings of thoughts, however, are quite distinct and the uninvited thoughts are the ones that tend to be most problematic in practice and performance.

Uninvited Thoughts

Uninvited negative thoughts and feelings are part of the landscape for most, if not all, competitors. What we mean by uninvited thoughts are the thoughts that go through your head that you don't intentionally think, on purpose. It is easiest to demonstrate an uninvited thought. When you are ready, stop reading, shut your eyes, and don't think on purpose. Really. Try it. See how long it takes for a thought to pop up, to come into your awareness. Don't try to think of anything. Just wait to see if a thought arises. Just shut your eyes now and try it....

....
....

How long did it take for a thought to show up? One second? Ten seconds? Whatever it was, at some point a thought will emerge that you did not try to think! *That* is an uninvited thought. Many times a day they occur. In fact, some estimate that people have up to 60,000 thoughts a day and that 95% of these thoughts are recurring, which means they show up over and over. Almost all recurring thoughts are uninvited thoughts. This mind activity of uninvited thinking is very normal. But the question is: Are you going to believe and live by the random, uninvited thoughts that bubble up in your mind?

Sometimes Uninvited Thoughts Are Helpful

Some uninvited thoughts, meaning spontaneous, not on purpose, are actually quite helpful. For example, you could be lifting weights and just at the moment you are not sure you can successfully bench press the last rep, a thought comes into your mind, *I've got this!* Yes, that thought was not created on purpose yet it was motivational and inspiring in the moment, and probably would help you complete that last tough repetition.

You have thoughts all of the time that run through your mind that you are not trying to make happen. That is just the nature of the mind, sometimes it is quite active whether you want it to be or not. Such spontaneous, uninvited thought can be helpful and facilitate performance. Such thoughts can be encouraging; they can help build your belief in your ability to succeed. When they show up and are in fact helpful, you can just be grateful for them and keep your attention on factors that will help with performance.

Sometimes Uninvited Thoughts Are **Not** *Helpful*

At other times, uninvited thoughts are not helpful. And in fact, harsh, self-critical uninvited thoughts are a pervasive, destructive force. In our examples at the start of the chapter with Olivia and T.J., they both had thoughts that got in the way of performance. A list of uninvited, unhelpful thoughts that do not help could be endless: *I can't do it; I can't beat her; It doesn't feel right today; I will never be as good, as fast, as strong; I am too tall; I am too short; I am too tired. I cannot endure the pain like they can.* Uninvited negative thoughts emerge frequently. Often such thoughts are under our radar of awareness, yet they can have devastating effects on performance – if you allow them to. Often with clients, if we ask them what they were thinking, they often say, I don't know. But if we ask, what were you feeling – they immediately can re-call their emotional experience. Almost always an athlete can say – *I was dreading playing* or *I felt sick to my stomach.* And with the follow up question I (Amy) often ask, *And with that feeling, what might have you been thinking?* When asked what they *might have been thinking*, then their thoughts will flow. Once these thoughts, connected to negative feelings, are spoken out loud, the athlete then has a chance to look at them with some perspective (i.e., de-center).

One great value of MMTS 2.0 is to see that when you build awareness of your thought patterns and emotional reactions, you have a choice in terms of how you want to empower (or not) the thoughts and feelings that have been debilitative in the past. You can learn to de-activate typical patterns of emotional response, especially when they get in the way of performance. You can be aware of your thinking and *label* thoughts, particularly the sticky (mean, harsh to unhelpful) thoughts. Of course, sometimes uninvited thoughts that emerge can be helpful (e.g. *I better call my mother; I really should get dressed and go work out*). With awareness training of your thoughts, you can decide which thoughts you will agree with and which ones you will notice and not feed.

Avoiding or Over-Engaging with Aversive Experience

If you buy into your uninvited thoughts they can lead to problems, particularly the ones that are harsh, self-critical, and obsessive. You can both over-engage with your thoughts (and get lost in thought) and opt to avoid situations that tend to be filled with such unsavory thoughts and associated painful emotions. Steven Hayes, in his Acceptance Commitment Therapy (ACT), offers these ideas of *cognitive fusion* (i.e., over-engaging with our thoughts) and experiential avoidance (i.e., avoiding experiences where these type of awful thoughts show up), respectively, as ways to explain how people often poorly cope with emotional distress. These ideas are very helpful in explaining what can go wrong when you believe (i.e., swear by or give weight to) your uninvited thoughts, particularly the ones that are aligned with deciding you will fail for some reason in the most challenging moments of performance.

Cognitive Fusion

Consider Rachel, an elite athlete with Olympic aspirations. She is a triple jumper in track and field. Before competitions, she becomes predictably, intensely anxious before it is her turn to compete, to take the run and triple jump. She has thoughts like, *I won't be able to beat my record*; *I will over-step the line again*; *I am not as powerful as she is*; or *I just don't want to jump*. These thoughts are recurring and create great angst for Rachel. In Hayes' work in ACT, he would refer to Rachel's experience as cognitive fusion. She is so aligned with her thinking, that she experiences the thoughts as if they are true. Her attention pivoted into these thoughts and unfounded beliefs in her mind. And, when this happens, she is unable to notice what is happening in her body, with her five senses. She is no longer the Rachel warming up her body and thinking through her upcoming jump. Instead she is preparing for the failure that her uninvited thoughts are feeding her.

Cognitive Defusion

When caught up in cognitive fusion, people will often make decisions based on the thoughts that are emerging (i.e., images, memories, beliefs, and assumptions) instead of what is actually happening in their world at the moment. In Rachel's pre-jump moments, the truth is that she is well prepared to jump, that she has all the strength and skill to successfully compete. In such moments it would help Rachel to work on *cognitive defusion,* meaning distancing from thoughts and feelings and having the ability to see what is (and is not) true. In the Acceptance Commitment Intervention, clients are encourage to "stop, step-back and observe." Labeling can help with this. Rachel could practice observing her thoughts and objectively consider thoughts like, *I won't be able to beat my record.* She might be able to notice that this thought was inspired by fear and see that her thought just may not be true and certainly not worth her time and energy to stay locked onto. Yes, she may or may be able to beat her record. Yet thinking exclusively about this does not help her prepare for her jump. And with defusion comes seeing that your thoughts may or may not be true. You don't have to make behavioral choices based on them. Thoughts are not actually happening but just images in your mind. If you allow them, such thoughts will float in and float out of our awareness. Simply put, cognitive defusion is a result of you releasing yourself from believing your thoughts. Through doing this, you can help you avoid setting off a negative domino effect in your sport performance.

Experiential Avoidance

When the negative feelings are predictably powerful, sometimes athletes will simply avoid the situations in which they have to tolerate such difficult internal emotional states. Rachel often would balk and not jump. She would begin her run down the strip and then instead of taking the jump she would hesitate and stop. In such an instance Rachel was more focused on trying to avoid potential painful thoughts and feelings by not taking the jump: If she did not jump she would not have to endure the harsh self-criticism of not doing well enough or obsessing over how she should have jumped. Of course, she was not aware of all this underlying explanation. She didn't know that she was just seeking temporary relief from the suffering, by not taking the jump. All that she knew was that she was miserable and embarrassed by her balking and stopping. Until we talked about it, she had never considered the (very) temporary relief that *not jumping* offered her.

This example may seem extreme. Yet athletes very frequently exercise experiential avoidance. Think of the runner who gets passed in a foot race. They often slow down. Why? Being present to one's internal state, one's heart and mind, can become acutely uncomfortable when strongly tied to uninvited thoughts that scream: *Loser!, I hate this!,* or *I don't care!* And in such instances, unfortunately, it is more common than any of us would like to admit that all of us (sometimes) will opt for the temporary relief of quitting, not having to feel badly (due to buying our thoughts) in exchange for taking actions that are deeply important to us. Yes, performers opt to quit instead of fight because in the moment of quitting they experience a very brief sense of relief. Athletes opt to quit instead of fighting when behind in a basketball game, swimming hard in a race or continuing to sprint after being passed.

When you stand up to such emotions, you then become willing to continue to train hard even when not put in the starting lineup. Most people love giving full effort when they feel good and are dominant. The trick is to figure out how to give such full-hearted effort, no matter how you feel or no matter what lines our uninvited thoughts are offering us. When you can do this, you have no need for experiential avoidance. You can get back to the business of being the joyful, tenacious athlete.

Suppressing Thoughts

Why do you have to tolerate such awful thoughts and feelings? Why not just ignore them? A very common request coaches make of their athletes is, *Just stop thinking and go out there and play!* The strategy coaches are encouraging at this point is referred to in academia, in the sport psychology world, as thought stopping. Shutting down your thoughts and going out and play can work, sometimes. If, for example, you are daydreaming and unengaged, it might help to tell yourself *knock it off, get your head back in the game.* Yet, when it comes to harsh self-talk or thoughts provoked by intense dread or anxiety such thought-suppressing strategies simply don't work. Our thoughts become too powerful. When your mind has become flooded with negativity, can you just stop it using just your will and determination? Sometimes it works. But most frequently the best you can do is to learn to tolerate our uninvited negative thoughts.

A mindfulness strategy that can help tremendously with such think is labeling. Labeling is a readily available strategy that you can use to de-center. Specifically, labeling can be a pathway toward creating some space from such difficulty: Labeling can help create space between our uninvited thoughts and behavioral choices.

Labeling Thoughts: Spider Web (ten-minutes)

This practice can be incredibly helpful when you notice your mind is having thoughts that are distracting you from focusing on what you need to focus on (e.g., a high jumper thinking about how bad it will be if she misses her next jump [distraction] vs. productively thinking about the rhythm of her approach and sensation that will occur when she has a good take off). This practice, of labeling thoughts and emotions as they arise, will help you learn how to create some space between your awareness and the thoughts that emerge in your mind (particularly the thoughts that arise on their own, which we refer to as uninvited thoughts).

When doing the exercise, we encourage you to do the following: Do not try to change your thoughts or feelings. Just allow yourself to observe what is going on. Often when athletes bring awareness to their thinking they are very surprised by the volume of thoughts that show up. And though we ask you very directly not to intentionally use your mind to respond to spontaneous thoughts that arise, it is very hard to stop interacting with the spontaneous thoughts that show up.

Here are a few things athletes have done when trying the following exercise: They will visualize calming scenes; they will count and visualize numbers; they will almost do anything to try to stop their thoughts from showing up. We ask you to try

Fig. 8.3 Spider web

to NOT bring anything new to mind. Thoughts will emerge like the words going across a CNN television news screen. That is typical. We just ask that you *try* not to intentionally engage in thinking or respond to thoughts that emerge in your mind. Just watch and observe to see what shows up.

Before you begin, we ask you again to bring a kindness, acceptance, even warmth to yourself as you bring your attention (again and again) to the uninvited thoughts that show up in your awareness. We ask you to do this in an effort to practice, intentionally, shining self-compassion toward yourself. Just trust us in that uninvited thoughts and feelings are a very normal experience. It is just not as common to slow down enough and make the time to fully take in the thoughts and feelings that are showing up.

So as you get ready to begin, as best you can get comfortable in a quiet space. Start your 10 min timer, gently close your eyes, and rest back in awareness until a thought emerges. Hold that thought in awareness until the thought fades or another emerges. Do the best you can to not get caught up in intentionally thinking about whatever shows up. Try not to solve some problem that your mind starts to focus on or try not to plan what is next. If thinking, problem solving, and planning shows up – that is OK – just witness that as well. Try not to intentionally – on purpose – keep thinking about what is showing up in your awareness. Let the thoughts come and go. Just observe (Fig. 8.3).

We offer you the spider web metaphor. Think of your quiet mind as a spider and your open awareness as its web. Imagine the spider sitting quietly in the middle of the web. Allow your awareness to rest with your breath in the center of your experience. When a thought arises simply allow your awareness to observe that thought. That is like when the spider scurries over to a fly that lands in the web. Try not to allow your awareness to get caught up in, capture, your thoughts. Just let your to bring mindfulness to the thoughts that are arising. Just notice. When a thought passes, you can return to your breath, like the spider returning to the center of the web after it has wrapped the fly. Rest in awareness until something draws your attention. Again, do not try to change anything. Unwelcome thoughts and feelings are very normal. It is important to keep this perspective before you begin. And once the fly is dealt with, the spider returns back to the center of the web.

When thoughts do show up, simply label them, to help de-center. It is fine to just use the word *thought* when anything shows up in your mind. If you like, you can be more specific using words like *planning, worrying*, or *story*. If at any point you start having a hard time figuring out the right label for what is showing up just return to using the word *thinking*. We certainly don't want you to get focused on picking out the precise word and get lost in the frustration of not being able to! This is a common challenge when people first try this meditation practice. This round is a bit more challenging to keep an accepting, interested mind. It is much easier to do so when listening to sound or even noticing body sensations. Most of the time these senses are not good or bad, they are just arising. Try taking the same easy-going approach to noticing and labeling your thoughts.

Now, set your timer for ten minutes and begin when you are ready. Ok, ten-minute timer is ready.... Push start.....Enjoy!

Debrief

This MMTS exercise of *labeling* thoughts is the next step at learning to observe and accept difficult thoughts and emotions, which can carry over to practice and competition. Some benefits in sport that can come with such a practice include:

- *Acceptance/tolerance* of unwelcome thoughts (e.g., *This is so boring!* arises. You notice the thought and re-engage with the training.)
- *De-centering* from unhelpful thoughts and feelings, and
- *Building awareness* of what is happening in the moment.

If you are going through MMTS 2.0 on your own, please take a few moments to reflect on your experience in your journal. Some things you might write about are:

- What was it like to try to keep your attention on what was arising. Your thoughts and feelings?
- Were you able to notice what was arising, without judgment?
- Did you label them?
- Did your mind wander? Were you able to be kind/gentle with self when you refocused on thoughts and emotions?
- You might bring to mind typical thoughts that arise when practicing or competing that are distracting or create unhelpful emotional reactions. What if you could take this exercise and apply it to your sport, what thoughts or feelings would you stop fueling? What would be different about how you practice or train?

This practice can help you when you are trying to keep your attention on what matters, like when the play is unfolding. For example, a golfer could notice fearful thoughts or his mind calculating standings between shots. The golfer could create some space by thinking: *planning,* or *just thinking*. After this labeling, the intensity or distraction of the thinking would begin to dissolve through the de-centering effort and the golfer could bring his mind back to golf.

We encourage you to keep practicing some type of mindfulness meditation for most days for about ten-minutes. It is of course fine to do more (or less)!

Chapter 9
The Power of Concentration (Module 3)

Attention is the psychological currency of performance.

Peter Haberl (2016), Veteran USOC Sport Psychologist.

The ability to concentrate, and flexibly shift concentration, in practice and performance is essential to learning, improvement, and optimal performance. Everyone knows this. When you focus your attention and keep it where it needs be, as well as be nimble and adjustable in where you place your attention. Such flexible attention empowers you to do your best with everything, from training to improving physical abilities and refining strategies. Sport psychology interventions offer a wide range of strategies and skills to help athletes and performers to be freed up focus their attention on task relevant cues when it counts.

The importance of attention is captured by the classic image of two sprinters a few inches from the winning tape at the finish line. One is looking forward and the second is looking sideways at his competitor. The athlete looking forward is most often the winner because he is keeping his attention on his race. Runners look forward to keep their focus on their own race, with an eye of toward the finish line. The winning runner knows instinctively that looking forward keeps his attention where it needs to be versus allowing his attention to be divided and weakened (for performance outcomes) by glancing sideways at his opponent.

Placing your attention where you want it and keeping it where you want, although essential, can be easily lost when competitive pressure increases and the uninvited chatter in our minds magnifies. In such instances you become more easily distracted from adapting and adjusting to what is actually unfolding moment to moment. Typical distractions that predictably lead the mind astray and thwart performance (when you allow yourself to get caught up in the thoughts) include:

- Comparing yourself with competitors,
- Worrying about what a coach, teammate, parent, or opponent thinks,
- Boredom with repetitive or unchallenging drills,
- Anger or embarrassment about a past mistake,
- Worrying about a future performance, and
- Awareness of physical signs that (you think) mean you won't perform well (e.g. racing mind, sweaty palms, tight shoulders).

© Springer International Publishing AG 2017
A. Baltzell, J. Summers, *The Power of Mindfulness*,
https://doi.org/10.1007/978-3-319-70410-4_9

In this chapter, we offer ways to respond differently to such distractions. If you choose to, you can learn to have much more control over what you intentionally pay attention to (though, of course, the uninvited thoughts will be there most of the time, no matter what you do). This chapter is about helping you strengthen your ability to maintain concentration, and a flexibility of attention, in practice and competitive situations. But first, what is concentration?

Defining Concentration

Concentration is a result of *intentionally focusing your attention*. When you concentrate you choose (consciously or unconsciously) where to direct your focus. Concentration requires either habituated or on-purpose mental effort placing and keeping your attention where you choose to place it. And in sport concentration is aligned with being able to place your attention on what is most important in a given situation. The four components of concentration, revised, include (Williams et al. 2015):

Focusing on Relevant Information Essentially this is selective attention. You cannot attend to everything! You can determine and select what you are going to be present with and which to disregard.

Maintaining Your Attentional Focus Once you decide to focus on something, the next undertaking is to sustain your attention on what will help you with performance. These are not obvious, meaning depending on your expertise in a particular sport, you may have quite different needs for attentional focus than a more novice performer. For example, the expert pitcher might focus on the movement of their hip to pitch their best, the movement of their hand as they release the ball or intentionally looking at the target, or the catcher's mitt.

Situational Awareness When thinking of concentration, sometimes athletes mistakenly think that they must keep their attention fixed on one thing, like the meditator's attention on the flame of the candle or their breath. Yet, in every performance endeavor, you actually have to be aware of the situation around you so that you can wisely decide if you should keep your attention locked in or shift it. With situational awareness you must cultivate a flexibility, an openness to what is occurring [within yourself and what is around you] so that you know how best to proceed.

Shifting Attentional Focus It seems like an oxymoron but to be able to concentrate you must be prepared to nimbly shift your attention from cue to cue. Imagine the basketball player in a fast break. She cannot only focus on the basket, but must also be aware of the ever-changing position of her teammates and opponents to be able to make the decision to pass, drive to the basket, or slow down the play. And in the on going sizing up of the situation, she may need to shift her attentional focus each split-second to make her fast break successful.

Concentration: When Things Are Going Well

Concentration is important. Yes, of course. And yet often athletes don't stop to consider what they should be paying attention to. And also they don't think about how to get their attention back, once their minds have (predictably) wandered away. Often athletes will just think that they had a good or bad day, practice or performance – but not think about how they could get more control over the content of their attention. Sometimes you can be lulled into believing that if your body is in motion (e.g., you go to your lifts, runs, or stadiums) that you are doing all needed to improve or perform well. Yet, if you stop to think about it, taking advantage and making good use of your awareness and focus are your most powerful weapons.

One of my (Amy's) clients, Evie, came to me, in my role as sport psychologist, to help her get ready for the speed order trials to make the Olympic rowing team. Evie wanted to focus on racing. In our first meetings I asked Evie what she thought about when she was practicing. Her face went immediately blank. The conversation went something like this,

A: *What do you think about when practicing?*
Evie: *(puzzled look, no response)*
A: *Tell me about a recent work out.*
Evie: *I rowed for an hour. I turned around and rowed home.*
A: Did you focus on anything? Think about anything?
Evie: *No, I just looked forward to turning around so I could get back and get off the water.*
A: Is there anything you could think about during practice – your technique, the feel of the water that would help you improve?
Evie: *Yes, of course...*

This was an ah-ha moment for this elite athlete. Evie realized, in that moment, the amount of wasted time she had spent on the water. She had intentionally tuned out, when she could have been thinking about how it feels to move her boat as efficiently as possible. She realized that she now could intentionally make subtle changes in training to increase the speed of her boat.

At this point in the conversation we had an opportunity to determine specific points of focus for Evie to intentionally concentrate while practicing. For this athlete it turned out that focusing on the feel of her blade when she connected well with the water and the ratio between the time her oar was in and out of the water were important points for concentration and attention. She knew where to place her attention, she just had not doggedly worked on efficiently using her awareness and concentration in practice. She knew that she had been checking out mentally. At that session she reclaimed her power of attention and concentration.

Take a minute to think about what you *know* you should pay attention to during practice and competition. *When things are going well for you,* what is good for you to concentrate on in practice? In competition? Imagine what it might be like to notice your mind wandering in practice or performance and have the ability to notice and quickly bring your attention, intentionally, back to task relevant cues. This is precisely what the following exercise is designed to help you do.

In this next exercise, we invite you to practice putting your attention in a place you choose, and keeping it there, as best you can. You may ask, why does it matter if I pay attention to my breath? It matters because it is a training strategy to train your mind to attend to what you choose to attend to! In the exercise, there are no competing distractions, like being physically tired or a coach yelling at you. The only challenge we are giving you is to focus on your breath and count your breaths. This will help you practice bringing your attention back to what you care about when your mind wanders. So, like Evie, next time she is on the water and her mind wanders, she will be more aware of her choice to bring her attention back to the rowing rhythm and power application.

Breathing Ladders (ten-minutes)

This meditation is a breathing and concentration exercise. Find a quiet place to try this. Eventually you can do this exercise anywhere. It can be great to practice any of these exercises with distractions around you. But if you are new to meditation, set yourself up for success by starting these practices in a quiet environment. That being said, if you do get disturbed by a loud noise, a text ring, or even your dog entering the room remember to practice acceptance. Do your best to respond to all distractions in the same way: bring your attention back to your breath and the count as the point of focus of the meditation exercise. Though, before you start, turn off your phones ringer, alerts and alarm.

- Counting 1 to 10: The focus of this breath exercise is to have you focused on your breathing and count each time you breathe out, on the exhale. For the breathing ladder, you will count silently in your head each time you breathe out. It goes something like this:
- breathe in, breathe out, and silently say *one*.
- breathe in, breathe out, and silently say *two*.
- breathe in, breathe out, and silently say *three*.

   (You continue in this pattern until you reach ten.)

- breathe in, breathe out, and silently say *ten*.
- Once you reach the count of ten, you then count backwards to 1.
- breathe in, breathe out, and silently say *ten*.
- breathe in, breathe out, and silently say *nine*.

You continue in this pattern until your timer goes off. Breathe at a pace and depth that is comfortable for you. We have found some athletes like it better when they can visually see the numbers in front of them, to keep in the count. In MMTS 2.0 training, sometimes we write the numbers on the board.

Distractions Most people who try to this exercise *will* lose count. If you miss a number or lose your place, we ask that you simply return to one. Begin again. For some athletes, starting over can be frustrating. If you can tolerate it, start over at one. This is a good practice in a safe environment to practice working with your frustration – accepting, tolerating or even befriending the frustration – and not getting thrown off by it. But if you just don't want to start over you can take your best guess and continue at the place in the count that you last remember being, before you got lost in distraction. And all of this is successfully practicing the exercise, including having your attention on the count, mind wandering, noticing, bringing your attention back to your breath and the count!

Set your timer for ten minutes. Get in a comfortable position. Trust that even though you are intending to keep your mind on the count, your mind will wander. It might be the case that even with the wandering mind, that you will be able to keep your attention enough on the count to stay with the breathing ladder. This is normal. Just do your best to not intentionally engage in thinking about other things while your primary attention is on your breath and the count. This skill is tranferrable, to sport, to help you keep your attention on task relevant cues. And, in the background or secondary level of awareness, your mind will most likely think about other things (i.e., planning, worrying, regretting, fearing). This also is very common. The goal isn't to stop your uninvited thoughts from flowing. Instead the goal is to keep your primary attention on your breath, the count *and* to gently, kindly bring your attention back to your breath and the count when you get distracted.

It is success when you notice your mind wandering and you bring your attention back to where you want your attention to rest. So instead of thinking maybe you are bad at this mindfulness practice you could instead consider that you are strengthening your ability to concentrate. *Each time* your mind wanders, you become aware of this and bring your attention back, you are strengthening your muscle of attention!

It is time to begin. Set your timer for ten minutes (if this is too much to bear, you can set your timer for five minutes). Ready, begin. Breathe in, breathe out, one.... Breathe in, breathe out... two. Keep going until you go up to ten and back down to one, or until your timer goes off.

Debrief

The *breathing ladder* is a simple way to practice attending to cues that you opt to pay attention to. In addition, it is good training to practice getting your attention back, as soon as possible, once your mind has wandered. Such practice translates well to the practice field or performance. Simply having awareness and more control where you intentionally place your attention can have great positive performance benefits. Essential mental capacities to create best performance in sport include: (1) Directing your attention, (2) noticing when your mind has wandered, and (3) re-focusing your attention and concentration where you want to place it.

If you are going through MMTS 2.0 on your own, please take a few moments to reflect on your experience in your journal. Some things you might write about are:

- What was it like to try to keep your attention on the count?
- Did you lose your place or lose count? If so, were you able to be gentle with yourself when you re-directed your attention? How could this translate to your sport world?
- If you lost count and were harsh with yourself, what could you do differently with this exercise? Within your performance realm?

To help prompt the value of this practice bring to mind a predictable time in practicing or competing when your mind wanders. What if you apply the main idea of this exercise and begin to notice in practice and games when your mind wanders and then intentionally and more nimbly bring your attention back to the points of focus that you trust most facilitates your learning and performance? Just this awareness can bring about a positive change.

This practice also is about helping you keep your attention on what matters. Often your mind wanders and you just accept this as normal (which it is) but you also don't often intentionally bring your attention back to what is of most value, where you know to focus and concentrate. You can empower yourself with a stronger intention about where you focus your mind.

Concentration, When Things Are Not Going Well

It is one thing to bring your mind back, after it wanders, when you are feeling steady. Bringing awareness to your experience with the intention to concentrate is quite a different task when you are being flooded by anxiety, fear, dread to harsh self-criticism. Negative thoughts and emotions can get in the way of effective attentional flexibility. You can get de-railed by your thoughts, by your mind wandering back to your upsetting mental distractions. Once caught in this drain, the distraction, you set yourself up to chip away at your belief in your ability to perform and strengthen a pessimistic viewpoint. We will offer you an example of how distraction can get in the way of your critically important ability to shift your attention where it needs to be while performing.

Katie

Katie is a top female fencer. She came to work with me (Amy) because she would lose concentration. Self-doubt would flood her mind, especially when she would lose a few bouts in a row. When I asked her what she would typically think, when she made a series of errors, this is what she said: *If I lose two bouts, I start to panic. It [the fear and questions] comes rushing at me. How am I going to do the next one? I can't do it!* To help her perform, the ultimate goals were to help her become aware of her distracting thoughts and feelings and get her to focus back on fencing. For Katie, I offered some mental cues of acceptance that would help her regain her attention. The phrases that helped her accept what was happening (the panic) to get her attention back on fencing included the following:

I deserve to be here.
These feelings are necessary and normal.
This isn't going to change the way I fence.

Once she would bring these thoughts to mind, she could accept the panic and get her attention back onto the strip.

For the next practice, we would like you to practice both intentionally concentrating and then coming up with a plan when you will lose concentration. The next exercise, Pyramid Breathing, is a bit more tricky than the breathing ladder. It is much easier to lose count. So before you begin, please come up with a word or phrase that you can say to yourself in the moment you become aware of your mind wandering. It really doesn't matter that you lose count in a meditation practice! It does matter, though, that you get familiar with how you respond to making small errors and figuring out a way to get your attention back to performance as soon as possible (and not get lost in self-criticism or frustration). Though these feelings will predictably show up as well, we invite you to come up with a word or phrase you can say to yourself when you lose your concentration. Some phrases you could consider:

- *It is common to lose count.*
- *Just back to the number.*
- *Ok, no problem.*
- *No worries.*
- *Strengthening concentration.*

If your mind doesn't wander on the first try, our guess is that it will wander on the second! So it is good to be prepared. In this moment, please choose a phrase or word you could say to yourself, when you lose concentration in practice. Now, we shall move onto Pyramid Breathing.

Pyramid Breathing (ten-minutes)

Counting 1 to 10, *in pyramid*: In this concentration-breath exercise we ask that you focus on your breathing and count each time you breathe out, on the exhale. For pyramid breathing, we still invite you to count silently in your head. For most people it is easiest if you count each time you breathe out. With pyramid breathing the count goes up and down the pyramid, which requires a bit more attention. It goes like this:

- breathe in, breathe out, silently say *one to yourself*
- breathe in, breathe out, silently say *two*
- breathe in, breathe out, silently say *one*

Start again from one and go up to three now.

- breathe in, breathe out, silently say *one*
- breathe in, breathe out, silently say *two*
- breathe in, breathe out, silently say *three*
- breathe in, breathe out, silently say *two*
- breathe in, breathe out, silently say *one*

Start again from one and go up to four now. You continue in this pattern until you reach ten, the top of the pyramid (…8–9–10-9-8…). And then, start from the top and count back down (…7–8–9-8-7…). to bottom of pyramid (1–2-1) breath count). If it helps, the visual of the count is below:

```
1            2   1
1            2   3   2   1
1            2   3   4   3   2   1
1            2   3   4   5   4   3   2     1
up to:
1            2   3….  8   9   10  9   8 …  3   2   1
and then back down to
1            2   1
REPEAT
```

A few guidelines to keep in mind for pyramid breathing. If you lose track of your count, please start over, beginning with a count of 1–2 – 1. Please notice if you feel any frustration. As in the ladder breathing, it is common to feel frustrated when you intend to pay attention and you lose count (i.e., if you intend to focus on perfor-mance and you lose track of the play unfolding).

Again, plan to a bring phrase of kindness to yourself. What might be helpful to hear, to bring to mind, in that moment that you notice that you have lost count and you have to begin again? Pyramid breathing is a great place to practice noticing irritation, bringing to mind a word or phrase that could be comforting in some way – something that would allow you to let go and place your attention back into the exercise. This is a practice of attention. The better you get at noticing distraction, offering some kindness toward yourself, the more free you are to focus 100% once again at will.

It is time to begin. Set your timer for ten minutes (if this is too much to bear, you can set your timer for five minutes). Ready begin. Breathe in, breathe out, one….

Breathe in, breathe out… two. Remember to bring a kindness, acceptance, and warmth to self as you bring your attention back to your breath!

Debrief

Pyramid breathing is a useful concentration practice, it can both be soothing and, at once, help you block other things out for the duration of practice. And for many people it can also be a practice of learning to tolerate some discomfort and choosing to bring your attention back to the intention of the practice, strengthening your muscle of attention.

If you are going through MMTS 2.0 on your own, please take a few moments to reflect on your experience in your journal. Some things you might write about in your journal:

- How was Pyramid Breathing similar or different from the Breathing Ladder?
- When your mind wandered, what did you do?
- Did you feel frustration, or a similar emotion? If so, were you able to offer yourself some self-kindness – so you could let go of the negativity and get back to the focus of the exercise?
- How could you apply what you learned to practice or competition? (This is the ultimate goal, to have all of the exercises help you be better in training and performance.)

Keep practicing some type of mindfulness meditation for most days for about ten-minutes. It is of course fine to do more (or less)!

Your Go-to Thought?

Now, let's bring what you are practicing in meditaiton to your sport. We invite you to come up with a go-to thought that might be most helpful to you when you are distracted by the presence of self-doubt or a similar distraction in performance. It is most beneficial to bring to mind a predictably challenging moment in sport. For Katie, if she loses two bouts in a row, her self-doubt mushrooms. What is a predictably difficult situation for you? Distractions that can be disruptive include:

- Focusing on past failures or future potential losses.
- Getting lost in stories of not measuring up (e.g., not being quick enough; having lost to a particular opponent).
- Feelings of exhaustion or lack of motivation.
- Feeling flat, not challenged.

It is important that you bring to mind a typical distraction and then determine where you would ideally place your attention in that moment. Where would you opt to shift your attention? For example, in our recent study of using MMTS 2.0 with tennis players, one player reported getting angry and wanting to throw his racquet in frustration. This awareness is important. The next step is considering what he could bring to mind that would help him get his attention back on tennis. It might be, *Be steady: Let it go;* or *Next Play.* And then the third piece that is just as important is to consider, where to re-focus his attention? It might be on the pressure of his feet as he returns to the baseline; looking to see where he wants to place the next ball; to the body position of his opponent.

We care about you being able to take insights from your mindfulness-based practice and bring them back to your world of performance. In the table below, we offer some parallels between to the pyramid breathing practice and offer a way that it is aligned with performance. Take a moment to consider what distraction in performance you could become aware of, a verbal cue that could help you acknowledge the distraction or to refocus, and then the specific performance cue that would be helpful for you to pay attention to. Consider the table below (Table 9.1).

In a wise, quiet moment, it is helpful to think through times when you are distracted and then where you would optimally place your attention? It can be helpful to consider how to shift your attention away from the distractions, once you are aware that it is happening. What is an important place to shift your focus? Before you get to that heated, emotional (often irrational) moment it can be invaluable to plan in advance for such wise discernment. If you can't think of something you could offer yourself in this moment, consider what a good teammate might say to you, to be of help. Or perhaps you can bring to mind what a trusted coach might say to you. And if it is not their words, you might have an image of their facial expression or tone of their voice you could "hear" to help nudge your concentration back where you know it is most important to rest. The next chapter will dive deep into this, how to bring kindness to yourself in a way that will help you stay in the game and give it your all.

Table 9.1 Connection between breathing pyramid and performance

Task	Distraction	Awareness	Go-to-thought	Re-focus
Mindful breathing	Stories arising	Caught planning	Everyone's minds wander	Back to count
Tennis	Urge to smash racquet	Awareness of urge to smash racquet	Let it go, next play	See the ball
Your performance world?				

Chapter 10
The Power of Self-Compassion:
(MMTS 2.0, Module 4)

The terms self-compassion and sport seem like they do not belong together. Isn't sport only about being tough, being courageous, and passionately (or stoically) investing mind, body, and soul into the moment? Yes, this is what sport and performance is all about. Yet, the question remains, how do you help yourself get into such a focused, engaged, and hopefully passionate state of mind, of being? I (Amy) have spent the past twenty years trying to get better at helping athletes and performers do just this. And I have realized that there is another pathway to dealing with sport distress than just, *Don't think and do it*. Just be mentally tough. Because, truthfully, some athletes some of the time simply cannot do this. Sometimes they can't tough it out, they can get overwhelmed by the unwanted feelings and thoughts. And when they can't handle this, what is the answer?

But first: The traditional idea of mental toughness is generally conceptualized as being resilient and confident. Both important in performance! Resilience is about being able to bounce back from adversity. Yes, important – but how do you do this, mentally? The second part of mental toughness is about self-confidence. There is no question that being self-confident is invaluable. If you are confident, lucky you! It is a great predictor of success. In academia the term is self-efficacy, task-specific self-confidence. And there is quite a bit of data that indicates high self-efficacy is a strong predictor of success.

Yet the question remains: *What is going to get you into the mental state to be able to (eventually) be confident and to bounce back from difficulty if you are experiencing great performance distress?* There are a handful of mental skills offered within sport psychology that can each be very helpful, including the use of imagery, cue words, and establishing goals. Yet, we have found that when athletes are in great distress it takes more than to just say, *Shake it off and get your head back in the game. Or just tell yourself you are a winner or a good shooter and go back in the game and do your thing!*

We need an answer to help athletes deal with distress. We have found that offering some form of self-kindness is essential in such moments. The good news is that offering oneself self-kindness does *not* make you soft or inspire you to give up, but in fact it can offer just the opposite. We have found that helping athletes offer themselves some source of soothing in key moments helps them from giving up, shutting down, or getting caught up in being "the head case." Without such solace, their fear or self-criticism can easily overpower them.

Anecdotally I (Amy) recall a Division I rowing coach of a full scholarship team note that, *There is no room for emotion in sport!*" The Head Coach did not think that it was appropriate for her athletes to allow their emotions to get in the way of performance. She believed that her athletes should function above emotion, that they should be able to act professionally. We agree, to some extent, but the big question is how to get to the place, mentally, to be able to do this. And how do we help those athletes (perhaps millions of performers) who do experience sport related distress? What is the solution for them?

Jean

Jean, a top-ranked New England tennis player came to work with me (Amy) because of her out-of-control anxiety. She would consistently get stomachaches before big matches. Her mind would become filled with thinking about the ability of her opponent, worry about whether or not she would be able to win her match and harsh critical thoughts about her own shortcomings. The physical tightness and pain in Jean's body would get progressively worse throughout most matches. Sometimes is was so bad that Jean's arms were impacted and at the worst the arm that held her racquet could not take full swings. Jean was visibly overwhelmed and felt helpless. She was searching for answers. Jean had tried many interventions: She looked to medical doctors, psychiatrist, and athletic trainers.

Nothing worked until Jean learned to face (accept) and tolerate her anxiety, and doing it kindly. The emotions were intense and very uncomfortable to hold. Her preference was to ignore any emotions or physical sensations that arose. Instead, I asked her to notice the signs of anxiety as they started to arise and to acknowledge them, by labeling them. The phrases of acceptance I suggested, and that she used, align with core mindfulness meditation practice. She came up with the phrases and images that she thought would bring her enough ease that she could continue playing, staying engaged on the court._____,

- *"This is anxiety. This is what it feels like."* (Acceptance), and
- *It is OK that the fear is here* (paired with an image of her coach's face that was instilled with encouragement and belief in her (Self-kindness).
- *Others feel this way too.* (common humanity)

As the sensations of anxiety began to creep into Jean's experience, beginning a week before big matches, she would faithfully bring these phrases and the image to mind. For the few weeks post intervention Jean let me know that her arm stopped freezing up, she was always able to take full swing in her matches even when under tremendous performance pressure. She was performing much better. Jean was still suffering from the sensations of anxiety, but less than before because she was *no longer resisting* the fear. Instead, she faced it and offered herself just enough kindness to allow herself to keep playing, to have courage (feeling the fear and doing what is right, anyway).

What happens when you realize that you have failed in some way? Or times when you predictably suffer (i.e., like Jean's arm freezing up in pressured tennis matches). How do you feel? How do you cope with it? Maybe think back on a difficult moment? Maybe you let in a goal at a critical moment, maybe you were off your time in a key run or maybe you missed a key shot? Bring to mind how you handled this challenge. Did you get your head back in the game? Did you give up? Perhaps you recall going through the motions, no one but you knew that you secretly had given up hope of winning, of being successful? Instead of having to suffer in this way with no solution, we offer perhaps a new way to deal with such distressful sport moments – self-compassion.

When you really suffer with sport distress often athletes either mentally give up or get caught up in the story (believing that whatever they feel means that they cannot succeed). With self-compassion (sport appropriate of course), you can learn to tolerate the distress enough so you can focus back on task/performance relevant cues, on doing your thing well. If you cannot tolerate the distress, you tend to check out or get consumed by it.

Self-Compassion

Self-compassion at first blush can seem indulgent, soft, and maybe even selfish. Kristen Neff (2003), world thought leader on the idea of self-compassion offers her definition: self-compassion, it "involves being touched by one's own suffering, generating the desire to alleviate one's suffering, and treating oneself with understanding and concern" (Neff and Germer 2013, p. 28). Essentially self-compassion is the desire to free oneself from suffering.

> Self-compassion "involves being touched by one's own suffering, generating the desire to alleviate one's suffering, and treating oneself with understanding and concern."

Self-compassion (though seemingly paradoxical) can help with sport performance, specifically when you are distracted by harsh self-criticism or performance anxiety. Typically athletes are taught to ignore or change unwanted thoughts (Wegner 1994), yet we have learned from the work of Stephen Hayes (2004) that suppressing aversive thoughts and feelings can just make them worse. In fact, we see integrating self-compassion into MMTS 2.0 as a revolutionary way to address intense sport anxiety and harsh self-criticism in the sport context.

Self-compassion emphasizes soothing and comforting the "self" when distressing experiences arise. Is self-compassion indulgent? Neff and Germer (2013) note the opposite; in fact, self-compassion in the face of suffering seems to inspire courage: "Self-compassion is associated with intrinsic motivation and greater personal initiative to make needed changes in one's life. Because self-compassionate people do not berate themselves when they fail, they are less afraid of failure and more able to take on new challenges" (p. 31).

We see self-compassion as an act of selflessness. If you are taking care of yourself, your needs, you don't need to look to others to do it for you. You won't need your teammates, your coach, your instructor to figure out what you need to bring your spirits up, to help resolve your anxiety and fear. You can learn to address it head on, yourself. Yes, suffering is hard to take and face. Very hard. But integrating a self-compassionate approach is a tolerable way to face it on your own. So instead of *tough it out*, we say *face your suffering, give yourself what you need, and then tough it out!*

Open-heartedness and warmth toward one's experience, a traditional, integral part of mindfulness meditation practice, is an aspect of mindfulness meditation exercises and practices that are often overlooked in mindfulness-based sport interventions. We have opted to integrate them, with compassion an integral part of a mindfulness approach. Kabat-Zinn (2003) states, "The word *mindfulness* reflects both mind and heart and that the terms are the same in Asian languages; Mindfulness includes an affectionate, compassionate quality within the attending, a sense of openhearted, friendly presence, and interest" (p. 145).

We have taken this idea of bringing warmth and kindness to the athlete's experience, to you. Integrating self-compassion into MMTS 2.0 is a distinguishing aspect of our program. In fact, we have shifted from our original design by purposefully weaving self-compassion throughout the intervention, thus renaming it *MMTS 2.0*. Offering yourself self-compassion is of particular importance when you, the athlete, are experiencing sport distress. In sport, you are far from encouraged to be kind to yourself, especially when in distress. In contrast, you (if in a typical situation) are taught that you should be mentally tough; to keep your feelings from others and essentially ignore them in the service of pretending you are confident. It has become quite apparent that silently suffering and trying to do the right thing can be exhausting, lonely and, eventually, leads to declines in performance. Yet, if you think about it, how is being full of harsh self-criticism or anxiety helping you perform?

With self-compassion you can provide attention, awareness, and kindness in pivotal, distressful moments in sport. The value of freeing yourself from suffering is that when released from the clutches of intense personal distress, when you can offer yourself some kindness, you are subsequently *empowered* to have the courage to get back into jumping, running, competing.

We are expanding our discussion of self-compassion from the initial introduction in Chap 5. We intentionally do this in the MMTS 2.0 program as well. We briefly introduce self-compassion in the beginning and then invest a full module on self-compassion later. Self-compassion is an important idea in the program and takes some time for the idea to resonate, to make sense in the competitive world of sport. It is incredibly helpful and, at once, a challenge to the way you typically think about dealing with distress in sport. Self-compassion is really an alternative to the traditional mental toughness approach. There are three interconnected facets of self-compassion: self-kindness, common humanity, and mindfulness.

1. **(Self-) Kindness**. The kindness piece may be the hardest part of offering yourself self-compassion. In almost all ways, being kind to yourself goes against all messages in the sport culture. Yet when you can soothe yourself enough, it often is just what you need to be able to get yourself back in the game. Neff and Germer (2013) describe this self-kindness as the "tendency to be caring and understanding with oneself rather than being harshly critical" (p. 28).

The value of self-compassion is similar to the need for breath, like being on an airplane when the oxygen masks drop from the ceiling. You are called to put the oxygen mask on. You need it to survive. You put the oxygen mask on first prior to helping anyone else around you. If you don't provide yourself with oxygen, you can be of no help to anyone else. The same often hold true about giving yourself what you need, psychologically, to thrive in the face of distress and performance expectations. What does this look like in sport?

Luke Luke is a nationally ranked fencer. His coach had spent a lot of time working with him on his "mental toughness approach." Luke's coach told him over and over, *Don't think, just do what feels right.* The problem was, as you can guess, that Luke could not stop thinking. To become the mentally tough athlete, by appearances, his coach was demanding that Luke figure out somehow to stop his surges of brutal, negative self-talk. But he had no idea what to do with such thoughts. He often stayed silent and would slowly crumble under the pressure on the strip. He took to self-compassion quickly. He voiced a great sense of relief that there was another answer to his distress than to just, let it go and fence. He could not stop the uninvited thoughts. Once he understood that feeling badly was acceptable and that what he suffered from, performance anxiety, was very common he began to integrate a self-compassionate approach into his fencing.

He learned to bring to mind phrases that would help him deal with the unwanted, uninvited worries about results in future bouts and competitions. Because he was unable to *stop thinking*, he had to find another way to deal with the flood of unwanted thoughts. The phrases that Luke brought to mind that helped free him up that were soothing (and fencing appropriate!) included: *Fencing is my heart, my soul, and my passion,* and *No one is going to hate me based on how I fence here!*

If you don't figure out a way to have a different relationship to thoughts that arise, you tend to become ensnarled by the uninvited, harsh self-critical thoughts about living up to your high expectations or regretting past mistakes. When being self-compassionate, the initial response might be to take a momentary mental break to offer yourself soothing, kindness, or comfort before facing the challenge at hand. In this willingness to be kind, with an eye toward being unconditionally accepting of self, you are willing to first pause and offer yourself what you most need to hear, imagine, recall, or do before facing the next challenge at hand. When Luke could offer himself those kind thoughts (i.e., Fencing is my heart and soul) he was able to get refocused, away from fear and back to fencing. You offer self-kindness in preparation for getting back into the game to compete.

2. **Common Humanity.** The second dimension of self-compassion is common humanity. Common humanity "involves recognizing that all humans are imperfect, that all people fail, make mistakes, and have serious life challenges" (Neff and Germer 2013, p. 29). The main idea is that you are human and thereby you will sometimes fail, suffer, and face difficulty. When embracing the fact that others suffer too, just like you, you can be a bit more understanding of your own failure or embarrassment. You can keep in mind that others (probably a few thousand at least) have suffered just the thing that most easily rattles you. Of course you know this rationally, but to bring this fact to mind that you are not alone, that others suffer similarly, can be freeing particularly when in a distressed state.

One of our clients, Jenny, a returning National Champion of the 24-hour ultra runner circuit recalls how she normalized the experience of high anxiety when having to endure the increased pressure of being a returning champion. She was getting to run for 24-hours, hoping to run a personal best (about 140 miles). She recalls the power of common humanity, as she began her last race to try out to make the Ultra-running U.S. Team.

> One … thing that got me to the starting line of the race. You normalized my stress, and put me in the category of other returning champions who commonly feel much-intensified stress, the second time around. I was feeling (and still often feel) very much like an imposter in the world of ultra-running. Many other top competitors are younger, faster, and pursuing running as a full-time job, whereas I'm just a barely-holding-it-together full-time-working mom who gets dramatically in and out of shape while I try to balance it all. I felt like my race stress was just part of that whole pathology of barely-holding-it-together-imposter. It was so helpful that you pointed out that I could reframe my stress as normal, and as a symptom of being a champion, not a symptom of being an imposter.

3. **Mindfulness.** Mindfulness is the third dimension of self-compassion. A commonly agreed upon definition of mindfulness is offered by Jon Kabat-Zinn (1994): "Paying attention in a particular way, in the present moment, nonjudgmentally" (p. 4). Mindfulness is about being able to be aware of whatever is arising. And in terms of self-compassion, we are talking specifically about paying attention to your own suffering.

The idea is that if you cannot tend to your own suffering, you cannot give yourself what you need. It is kind of like breaking your arm. If you are not willing to acknowledge that your arm is broken, you are not going to make sure that you get the medical help that is warranted: you might not get your arm set and cast. The same holds true for your own psychological distress: If you don't allow yourself to pay attention to it, you are not enabling yourself to give yourself what is needed. This could mean training harder or training less. It could mean bringing to mind images of past or future success. It might mean training with a particular person or team. It might mean leaving a particular training partner or team. You only have the answer of what you need to get your psychological needs met. But being able to do so is contingent on your allowing the truth of any personal suffering to be held in your awareness. You were most likely taught to ignore it. Just like ignoring a broken arm is not a good idea, ignoring your own emotional suffering is also is not a good idea.

We like to think of this as not fighting reality – not resisting what has happened in the past up to the exact moment of awareness. And when you are able to accept reality (from befriending to tolerating reality), you are freed up to wisely interact with the matter at hand. This acceptance of reality does not mean that you like what has happened and does not mean that you are not going to do anything about it. In fact, if you can, you must address your suffering when it is happening. You are called to accept what has happened **so** you can create space to determine how to handle what is showing up with better discernment.

With Luke, being mindful meant being able to be aware of and tolerate his distracting, uninvited thoughts. When he did this he stopped spinning out of control emotionally and shutting down. When mindful, he would be able to witness all of the uninvited thoughts pouring in at him and see them for what they were – habitual thoughts that showed up to try to motivate him or protect him from the potential of losing. Such thoughts, and associated emotions, were quite unpleasant for Luke. But when in a mindful state, such mental antics could no longer dissuade him from focusing on the strip and fencing. With mindfulness, awareness or clear seeing, you are able to maintain some sense of equanimity or balance, no matter what is showing up.

Mindfulness of one's own suffering is an ability to maintain awareness of your suffering in a balanced manner: you neither avoid, shut your eyes to your suffering, nor do you become twisted up with unwanted aspects of yourself or your life. We have offered you an explanation of self-compassion and examples of other athletes. Now it is your turn to *practice* offering self-compassion to yourself. It's a new idea for many people but can quickly become powerful and freeing. If willing, give the next activity a try.

Negative Mind State Fire Drill (Sitting with Sport Difficulty)

Get ready. This exercise can be an emotionally tough one. And, at the same time, this exercise can ultimately be quite freeing. Please bring to mind a difficult moment in sport. We want you to invite a negative mind state and run you through a fire drill. The goal is to help you learn to tolerate unpleasant, difficult mind-states. We suggest that you do not start with recalling the absolute worst moment from your sport. Think about the challenge on a scale of 1 to 10. We don't want you to be bored and also don't want to put you into a truly distressed state. Think of something moderately difficult to have to bring to mind – say a 4 or 5 (moderate) on a scale of 1

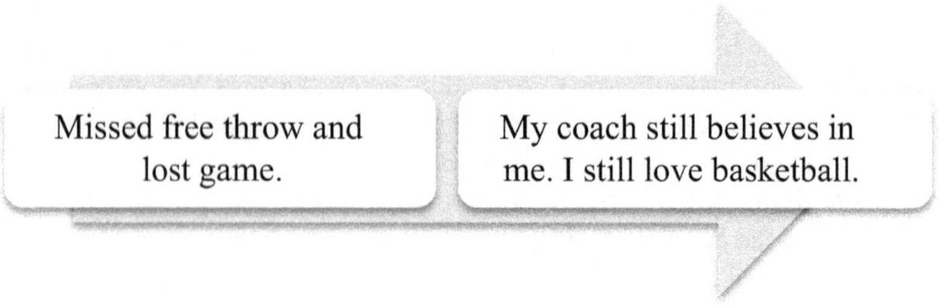

| Missed free throw and lost game. | My coach still believes in me. I still love basketball. |

Fig. 10.1 Phrase of comfort

(nothing memorable) to 10 (awful). Choose something that is a bit hard to recall but not over the top painful!

In few moments we will ask you to visualize this moment. So for now recall as best you can the scene. It is ideal if you can find someone to do this exercise with you, so you can talk about what you experience once complete. If not, you can go through this one on your own. In your difficult sport or performance experience. Take a few moments to recall this situation.

- Who was there?
- What were you physically feeling?
- What emotions were you feeling?
- What thoughts were you having? If you cannot remember the specific thoughts, what thought might you have been thinking?

What Did you Most Need to Hear in that Moment? As best you can, think of a word or phrase that would have been soothing to you at the time that this event occurred. *Before* you begin to visualize this experience, please bring to mind what you most needed to hear in that moment. Get ready to bring this thought to mind when recalling and visualizing your most difficult moment in sport. If you'd like, you can jot down a word or phrase that reminds you of the situation and the phrase or image that you most needed to bring to mind in that moment, a word or phrase that would have given you comfort in that moment of great difficulty (Fig. 10.1).

Other phrases that we have heard others come up with – ideas that they most needed to hear in that moment include:

- *Others suffer like this too.*
- *It is not my fault that I feel like this, I feel like this because I care so much.*
- *Champions feel like this.*
- *I believe in you, always.*
- *You got it, girl! (in the voice and tone of a trusted coach)*

When you use a phrase, from yourself or from someone who cares about you, please include the tone and sound of the voice of that someone who cares about and believes in you. Before you begin, make sure that you have a phrase of self-kindness to work with.

Imagining Difficult Scene (five- to ten-minutes)

Get ready to shut your eyes. When you do, take a few deep breaths and begin to bring to mind via imagery, the identified past negative experience. Here are some reminders you can think about when you try this. Set your timer for ten-minutes.

- Bring to mind the scene. Who was there? What happened? What were you feeling?
- Notice the emotions that are arising.
- Notice in your body where you feel the sensation most strongly.
- Keep your attention with the physical sensation that is strongest. If the feeling gets too strong, you can always opt to bring your full attention back to your breath, for a few breaths, until you are ready to try again.
- Bring to mind your statement of self-kindness (4 or 5 times throughout this activity) about once a minute.

Debrief

Take a few minutes to reflect in your journal:

- What was that activity like for you?
- What were the physical sensations like? Did they change throughout the exercise?
- Is there a typical challenging moment in sport or performance that you know is predictably hard for you. What word or phrase could you bring to mind then? Would the words be coming from you or someone else (e.g., a coach; a team-mate). What would the tone of their voice sound like? Can you bring that to mind now?

This activity is about learning to accept negative thoughts and feelings. It is about learning how to become more comfortable with internal distress. The ultimate goal of the activity is to prevent you from avoiding or getting lost in the stories associated with inevitable negative emotion that shows up, sometimes, in practice or competition. The idea is to help loosen the hold that intense, negative emotions can have on your experience and performance.

Compassion for You and Others (ten-minutes)

The meditation cycle is about you focusing on your meditation of choice. We have offered a number of meditation practices from focusing on the breath, sounds, body sensations, or kind intention toward yourself to this most recent meditation, bringing a difficult performance scene to mind and staying with it. All of these practices

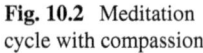

Fig. 10.2 Meditation
cycle with compassion

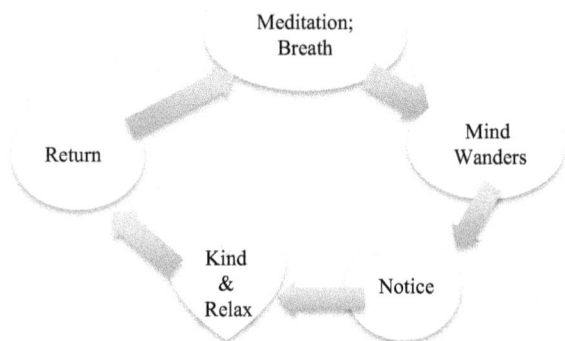

share the same cycle we have presented once before (in below illustration). For almost everyone, with the best of intentions of practicing a meditation (as we have noted before) your mind will wander. This is normal and part of the meditation cycle. Next, you will notice your mind wandering, which can take from a split second to many minutes to notice. What you do with that moment of noticing is crucial to develop your meditation skills. It is important to, as kindly as you can, accept that your mind has wandered. One way to do this is to relax your body. You can also simply practice kindly accepting that your mind has wandered. Next, to stay in the meditation cycle, it is important to decide to return to the practice. Once this decision is made, you are back to focusing on your breath, a sound, your thoughts to a scripted relaxation meditation (Fig. 10.2).

A unique aspect of MMTS 2.0 is the intentional practice of self-compassion. We hope that you will try offering warmth and kindness toward yourself in the meditation practice, particularly when you notice that the mind is wandering. It is possible to relax and return without experiencing harsh self-statements or judgment (e.g., I am bad at this; I am a bad meditator!). And even if such thoughts show up (which they will sometimes) you can still offer balanced, kind awareness to yourself.

It can be helpful to also offer kindness to teammates, coaches, trainers or anyone else in your performance world. Offering care for others also helps solidify the fact that you are not the only one suffering. We all know that this is true but it can feel different (in a good way) to deeply think about someone else who may be going through a hard time and wishing kindness toward them. We have found after the exercise of imagining the difficult scenario, of your own, that it can be helpful to zoom out a bit toward others. So, here we go.

Please read through the following exercise and give it a try. We suggest either just reading through the exercise below, set a timer for ten minutes, and then begin or have someone read it outloud to you. Either way, set your timer, enjoy!

One for me, One for you (ten-minutes)[1]

Please sit or lie down in a comfortable position. Close your eyes of soften your gaze. Put a hand on your heart, on your belly or rest your palms on your knees. Allow the warmth of your hand to act as a reminder to bring loving awareness to your experience, to yourself.

- Taking a few deep, relaxing breaths, noticing how your breath nourishes your body as you inhale and soothes your body as you exhale.
- Let your breathing find its own natural rhythm. Continue feeling the sensation of breathing in and out.

(pause)

- Now focusing your attention on your in-breath, letting yourself savor the sensation of breathing in, noticing how your in-breath nourishes your body, breath after breath… and then releasing your breath.

(pause)

- As you breathe, breathing in something for yourself… whatever you need. Perhaps a quality of warmth, kindness, compassion, or love? Just feel it, or you can use a word or image if you like.
- Now, shifting your focus to your out-breath, feeling your body breathe out, feeling the ease of the exhalation.

(pause)

- Please call to mind (1) someone whom you love or (2) someone who is struggling and needs compassion. Visualize that person clearly in your mind.
- Begin directing your out-breath to this person, offering the ease of breathing out.
- If you wish, intentionally send warmth and kindness – something good – to this person with each out-breath.
- Now begin feeling your body breathes both in and out – breathing in for yourself and breathing out for another. "In for me… and out for you." Savoring the breath. "One for me… and one for you."

(pause)

- If you wish, you can focus a little more on yourself, or the other person – whatever you need.

(pause)

- Allowing your breath to flow in and out, like the gentle movement of the sea, flowing in and flowing out. Letting yourself be a part of this limitless, boundless flow – an ocean of compassion.

(long pause)

---

[1] This exercise was adapted from the Mindful Self-compassion teacher trainer manual.

- Now beginning to release your breath, releasing the meditation, and allowing yourself to feel what you're feeling and be just as you are.

Debrief

Take a few minutes and write or discuss what that activity was like for you in your journal.

- What did you learn that you could take back to practice or your team?
- Did you notice that it was easier to wish yourself or others well?
- How could this practice be related to sport performance?

Research on the value of self-compassion continues to indicate that when you are suffering, offering yourself self-compassion is not a weakness but instead helps you have the courage to face adversity head on. Instead of giving up or avoiding all together (i.e., a triple jumper unwilling to take a jump), offering yourself self-compassion can empower you to take on that which scares you. When self-compassionate you will ruminate less (i.e., less obsessed with your thoughts) and be more able to connect with others. Research indicates that those who are self-compassionate are more optimistic, more grateful, less stressed, and more resilient (more able to bounce back and get into next play). You would be expected to have less fear of failure and more willing to take risks and learn. Perhaps most importantly for sport is that personal standards remain just as high even when implementing self-compassion. Self-compassion is about paying attention to your own suffering and, at once, having the courage to give yourself what you need so you don't get de-railed. When you use self-compassion you will be able to be more balanced and less upset. With self-compassion, when you don't meet your expectations, you are less distracted and have more room to focus on productive, effective, and task (value) relevant options/cues. Overall, with more self-compassion there is a reduction in negative mind states with more room and space to choose how you want to respond in difficult moments or periods of your competitive, performance life.

Chapter 11
The Power of Core Values (MMTS 2.0, Module 5 Part A)

It is easy to control yourself when you are feeling confident. When you are feeling good and want to be there, self-regulation is of no concern. Self-regulation is about being able to make choices about what you think, what you do, and where you place your attention, intentionally. When you have no constraints, no distractions, and a clear desire to perform, it predictably will take you little effort to get yourself locked-in and focused on performance. However, when athletes feel off, physically or emotionally, effortful self-regulation is needed for challenges such as getting distracted by comparing themselves to others and doubting if they are as strong, or fit, or tall, or steady or intense as they ideally should be. It can be easy for athletes to subsequently believe their thoughts (e.g., *I can't win!*) and conclude that their physical signs (e.g., *I just don't feel right today.)* are reliable sources of information indicating that they will not be successful in their upcoming performance.

Sometimes the conclusion, *I just don't have what it takes today*, happens unconsciously and other times you are quite aware of such thoughts. Either way you might have little power to resist the downward spiral of the uninvited thought or hunch that you can not be successful. Almost every performer has had the sickening feeling that they *know* that they are going to fail before the start of a competition or performance, because of physical, emotional, and thought cues (e.g., shaking hands; feelings of dread; or looking around and *knowing* that you cannot win). In such moments performers are aware of having such thoughts and feelings and, in fact, often painfully aware of them. Yet in such instances they often *feel* utterly powerless to do anything about them. It is like beginning a trip of doom. In fact, this challenge is the most common challenge we see with competitive athletes: reported debilitating senses of dread or fear before competition and having no idea how to combat it.

In my (Amy's) research team's recent study, we had tennis players report feeling intense rushes of anger and frustration when a point in a match did not go their way. One athlete reported that his automatic response in such instances of rage was to hurl his tennis racquet to the ground. We have all witnessed such acts of frustration by athletes. The tennis player was being seeminly controlled by his automatic

© Springer International Publishing AG 2017
A. Baltzell, J. Summers, *The Power of Mindfulness*,
https://doi.org/10.1007/978-3-319-70410-4_11

reactions to his anger but felt helpless: he had no hope, no clear pathway that would lead to a different reaction.

The goal in such instances is to exercise self-regulation, having control over directing your attention and behaviors versus being victim to them. But it is much easier, said than done, to understand what you need to do versus executing self-control when under duress. The athlete had heard many times from coaches, teammates, and even his parents, "cool it," and most typically, "Just relax!" And perhaps one of the driving forces for us to write this book is that we both have had life changing events occur in performance (i.e., deep experiences of failure!) because we had no idea that self-regulation was an option and certainly had limited self-regulation skills. But sometimes it is a matter of building awareness, and exercising the various options for developing self-control of your attention. In this chapter we emphasize the importance of hooking into your values, what is deeply authentic and important to you, even when things are quite difficult.

Jenny, the 24-hour Ultra Runner

Jenny the 24-hour Ultra Runner is a 38-year old female, a full time professor of science in one of the top universities in the world, and a mother of three young children. She was reigning two-time national champion and had just recently run a personal record that would have placed her 12th at the previous World Championships. She had qualified for the US team twice before, though she had declined competing due to pregnancy.

When she walked into my office, she had some serious competing demands: training, teaching, research, and parenting. This constellation of demands had never blocked her belief in her ability to win. Jenny's issue was harder to overcome than all of this:

Jenny had stopped loving her 24-hour runs.

The competitions used to be a great outlet, a fun thing for her to do (I can't imagine, either). Yet, she had finally hit the wall. She was tired of being hungry, thin, and physically strained to the very limit. Though she had qualified twice already, she had never competed with the US team, which was an important aspiration. Though it may not be true (there are a few older women on the team), in that moment she felt that the upcoming run that weekend was her last shot to make the team and compete. She had come to the very end and she had lost her motivation. We had an hour to try to turn things around. She asked, "Can you help me?" And my response, "I don't know." To offer the full picture, it is important to also note that I (Amy) had been Jenny's collegiate rowing coach 18 years prior to this discussion. Though we had not been in contact over that time, there was a trust between us that is atypical for a first-time sport psychology session. (She also has given us her permission to use her name and story).

With her seemingly last chance to make the team, she had an additional challenge. Due to an ever-strengthening field of women runners, to qualify, she would likely have to improve her personal best distance. The furthest that she had run before was 138 miles over a 24-hour period. For the upcoming race, her target that would ensure placement on the team was 144 miles!

Her mind was filled with comparisons to younger runners and worse, intense emotional exhaustion paired with no-longer enjoying the process. We talked a lot over that hour, from what she wanted to accomplish (i.e., qualifying for the team) and the thoughts, feelings, and physical sensations that were getting in the way. She was used to feeling confident when running, believing she would win. It became apparent that no go-to past image or mental cue was going to be able to get her back into that confident mental state.

So I offered her a way through: an *inspired value*, a phrase to bring to mind that was deeply important to her and could potentially motivate her in the darkest hours of her 24-hour run. We talked through what still mattered to her, even without the feelings of joy and confidence. I asked her what was worth it about competing, trying to make the US team that weekend, that would empower her to tolerate the anxiety, the comparisons. What were her sport-related personal values? And more specifically, what value would inspire her to keep going even when she did not feel like it. I wanted her to come up with a mantra, a phrase that was an inspired value, one that would include self-kindness plus offer an inspired performance cue. Here it is:

This Is My Lifelong Dream

Jenny reported after the race that she said this to herself hundreds, if not thousands, of times throughout that 24-hour period of running. She reported later, *the mantra got me through the race.* She ran 142+ miles that day-through-the-night, won the National Championship for a 3rd time, and earned an automatic qualifying spot on the US team.

What Do You Value Most?

Knowing what you value, what is important to you, and bringing this truth to mind can be a way to overcome paralyzing thoughts and feelings. Ideally, when you can, it is best to nudge yourself into a state of mind that is optimistic, grateful, and joyful. Yet, sometimes, no matter how hard you try it is not possible to do so – like Jenny's case above.

To thrive, you must value what you're doing if you are not loving it! We hope to help you think about what you value, *why* what you are doing is worth doing based on what is important to you. Regardless of what others think or your emotional temperature in the moment, you can have courage if you have a reason to fight through.

What do you care about in your sport? Why swim, run, jump? Why train so hard? Yes, winning is great. Dominating is thrilling. Yet, how about what is valuable to you, even when you are not feeling the good feelings of confidence, passion, and the knowing that you feel just right? When you are feeling off, it is not your day, your game, or you don't have your stuff, what still matters to you? And ultimately we hope to help you think about an *inspired value*, one that would work in your most dark, negative mind states.

As with Jenny, it is important to come up with what matters to you, even when facing decisions in the midst of emotions that would typically shut you down (e.g., embarrassed, frustrated). What inspired value could get you to keep going, even when you have thoughts that typically would get in the way of doing your best (i.e., *I know that I cannot win this one…*).

For example, if you value fitness, pushing hard physically is tolerable because it will help you work toward something that matters to you (i.e., fitness). However, if you don't value fitness, pushing physically hard is intolerable. One of the inspired values that we have heard many times in a recent run of MMTS 2.0 is, *I am a fighter.* So if you value *being a fighter* on the field, trying hard and *being a fighter* is tolerable, whether you are winning or losing. If you don't value *being a fighter*, trying hard when you are losing is intolerable.

Values Versus Goals?

Though terms can vary in how they are defined, we offer a distinction between goals and values, for the purpose of being clear on the differences between process (values) and outcome (goals). Goals are the outcome you are seeking such as winning, making a team, getting a scholarship. Yes, there are short-term goals, even what you want to accomplish today-goals. And all of these are attaining some planned outcome in the future (whether hours or years into the future). Goals matter. Goals can help inspire you to keep trying, to overcome obstacles, with the external motivation for some important payback for our effort.

But how you aspire *to be* is also essential. What values-of-behavior drive you? Another way of thinking about it is: how would you hope others would view the characteristics of your behavior on the field? What value is most important to you, to put into action? How do you want to communicate, behave – moment-to-moment – on the field? You might want to be the fighter; consistent, steady, determined, focused… the list is long. What matters to you? What would make you proud of how you are in practice and competition, regardless of the outcome?

What matters to you? Bring to mind a phrase that will inspire you to engage, moment to moment. Jenny's example above is really an inspired goal. Her dream was to make and compete for the US team. Her phrase, by definition, was an inspired goal — because it was an achievable outcome (e.g., making the team, winning the race). And yet, for her, when she brought the phrase to mind, she was able to get and stay in a state of high motivation and regain her fighting, determined habit of racing. So technically her inspired value was to stay engaged to come out on top, no matter what. Yet this was not her inspiration. We share this with you – not to confuse – but to encourage you to come up with whatever phrase or mantra that will be authentically motivating to you, whether it falls in line with a value or outcome. For many athletes, they don't need to state their goal as inspiration – because their ultimate sport goal is often quite obvious and a source of distress! Thinking about the goal – the desire to win, to make a team, to making the starting lineup – can put athletes into red alert mode. Whether an inspired value (i.e., a cue word or phrase that would directly guide your action; e.g., I am a fighter) or a goal, we invite you to come up with a phrase that would motivate you and get you focused on what it takes to perform well. But from here out, we will focus on inspired values.

When considering inspired values, how do you want to be playing on the court (in the pool, on the strip, etc.)? We are talking about what inspires your behavior, your actions, win or lose. Some that come to mind include courage (i.e., being willing to face fear and do what you know is the right thing to do, anyway), persistence (i.e., investing in your work ethic in the face of challenges), and steadiness (i.e., having self-control in all instances, possible). Such inspired values help direct our actions. When you live by your inspired values, you are much less likely to be pulled around (and pulled off course) by erratic, unpredictable emotions.

Self-regulation is the basis, an essential aspect, of performance, regardless of external challenge (e.g., big competition, harsh coach, difficult weather) or internal experience (e.g., uninvited thoughts, emotions, and physical sensations). Without some guiding light, some buoys of purpose, it is easy to become pulled down by our emotions tied to our expectations of consistent, top performance. When you exercise this perfectionistic approach, fueled by commonly associated negative thinking, your focus will naturally narrow, shutting down options of thinking and action.

Clear inspired values offer a pathway to wisely respond to distractions (e.g., from fear, low hope, comparison with others to not living up to expectations). Such inspired values offer insight in that mental space between the stimulus and response of life events, and in sport that place is where you decide to either give up or keep engaged. (Fig. 11.1)

Creating Your Sport Career Memory, Now (ten-minutes)

We can all understand the importance of not giving into emotions and playing our best, opting to be that champion in the face of adversity. At some point all of us have been told, *Don't think, just play!* Yet, with all of the best intentions when those negative feelings or beliefs show up, you can so easily react, give-in, and choke, or have sub-par performance. We both have had the experience of the urge to give up, knowing we should not, and somehow feeling powerless over such a key moment in our lives. So how do you change this? One way is to consider how *you* want to remember your own sport career. From the perspective of your future-self, you can think about how your choices and behaviors now will influence how you will remember your sport life.

We invite you to take a few minutes to put yourself in the future, after your career in your sport or performance realm is over. Looking back on your sport career, what would give you deep satisfaction, perhaps even contentment, about how you engaged in your sport? Success, yes. But how would you have to train and compete that would be important to you, regardless of the final win/loss record or your personal record?

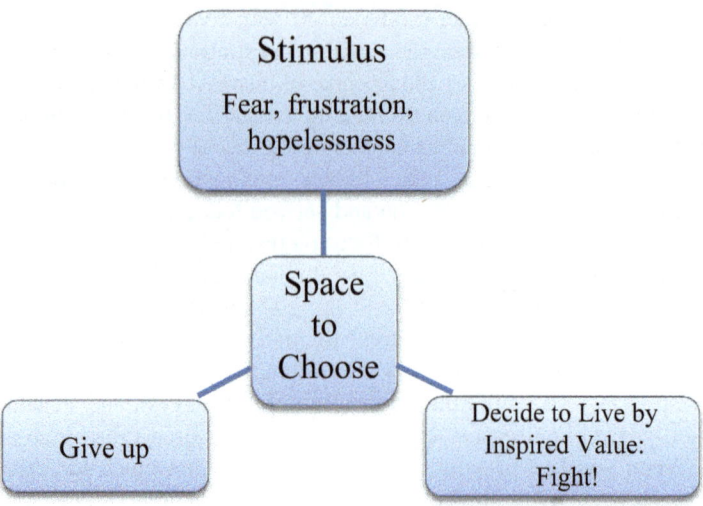

Fig. 11.1 How will you choose?

What would give you deep satisfaction or contentment about how you engaged in your sport regardless of the final win/loss record or your personal record?

How would you like your career (e.g., at your university, on the US team, your professional team) to *be remembered by you*? You might think about someone throwing a big party at the end of your athletic or performance career. (Thank you Lani Silversides for this suggestion). What you would you want them to say about you at that party? You cannot control how important others like coaches, teammates, and fans remember you. However, you can choose to act or conduct yourself in ways that you personally value, no matter what the outcome.

Your Inspired Value

What would inspire you to play the way you want to play, regardless of the temperature of your emotions? What is important enough to you, something that would inspire you to play or compete in a way that would make you proud? What would you want others to say about you? How would you want to look back on your sport career in five, ten, twenty years from now? Some inspired values we have heard are:

- I am a fighter.
- I am a team player.
- I am calm and poised, no matter what.

Take a moment to bring your inspired value to mind. If you can, you can discuss it with someone or you can write down the one or two that resonate most with you. Make sure that you have one in mind before reading the next section. If nothing comes to mind, you can use one of the ones noted above that most resonates with you, as you consider the next steps in this reflective exercise. But do choose some way that you would like to be remembered, or how you want to remember your own effort and presence, before you read the next section. (The next part of the exercise was inspired by the Mindful Self-Compassion teacher trainer manual).

External Obstacles

Your inspired-value, sometimes you live up to it and sometimes you don't. That is just being human. We hope to inspire you to be able to live up to your inspired-values more often. When you think about your inspired-value – let's say it is – *I am a fighter*, what are some of the external obstacles to being able to live your value in practice or competition? Some of the external obstacles could be playing time, clearance from medical staff regarding injury recovery to conditions of the field. There are times you would want to go all out and you are not given the opportunity to do so. You can't be that fighter if you don't have the time and space to fight.

Internal Obstacles

What are some of the internal obstacles – thoughts, emotions, or physical sensations – that can get in the way of being the fighter? Some internal obstacles that get in the way include physical exhaustion, fear, frustration, comparison to competitors (and believing that you don't have what it takes to win), sensations associated with high levels of lactic acid to harsh self-criticism. How do you handle your internal obstacles? In many ways, this book and MMTS 2.0, were partially designed to address just this. How do you handle such moments so that you are not distracted or overwrought and miss the chance to perform in the way that you truly value? How can you handle such experience to afford you the opportunity to live up to your inspired value(s)?

In such instances, how could self-compassion help you live in accord with your true values? For example, when your inner critic is particularly harsh (e.g., *You can never be as good as they are!*), how could self-compassion help you reclaim the ability to fight (instead of shut down, quit, and just run through the motions)? Some things you could bring to mind, to help create the courage to keep engaged, might include:

- *It is normal to feel like this.*
- *I can feel like this and still perform well.*
- *I am not perfect and that is ok.*

When you make choices to live in accordance with your inspired-values, you strengthen your ability to at once perform with poise and concentration in spite of difficult thoughts and emotions. Instead of trying to control your emotions (which really doesn't work) or fight against them (i.e., *I shouldn't feel like this!*) you can allow such feeling and thought to be contemporaneous and still intentionally shift your focus back to engaging in a way that aligns with your inspired-values, regardless of your thoughts and feelings.

Debrief

Take a moment to reflect on this last exercise. Below is a simple table to highlight what you just considered. We invite you to either just think through the table, or fill it in, whatever works best for you.

Your inspired values obstacles and self-compassionate response

Your inspired value	External obstacles to living inspired value	Internal obstacles to living inspired value	How could self-compassion help you live your inspired value?
Example: I am a fighter	Over-training; Coach not playing me; teammates not trying hard enough	Fear; self-criticism; Frustration	It is OK to feel like this; I still love my sport
Yours:			

What did you learn in your reflection on inspired-values? What will you take with you from this chapter? If a phrase of self-compassion came up to help you with your internal distractions, what was the phrase? Can you imagine bringing this phrase of self-compassion to yourself in practice or competition? Could self-compassion help you live in accordance with your true values?

It will be no surprise to you at this point, but we believe that the ability to perform with poise and concentration can be strengthened in spite of difficult thoughts and emotion, by incorporating self-compassion – when you are suffering from performance dukkha. Clearly offering yourself kindness must be doled out in the right amount and at the right time. If you find yourself suffering and you feel close to quitting, slowing down, or are tempted to give up living your inspired value, that is a good indication that some kindness to yourself is in order. This is offered, not to make you soft, but to help you turn down the negativity and turn up the courage you need so that can get back into practice or competition and be the athlete that your future-self will be proud of (and your present self too!).

Chapter 12
The Power of Self-Regulation: (MMTS 2.0, Module 5 Part B)

Awareness is like the sun. When it shines on things, they are transformed.

Thick Nhat Hanh.

There are many ways to strengthen self-regulation, meaning speaking and acting in the way that you value, regardless of the push and pull of your emotions. It sounds easy to choose to focus your attention, where you choose to, until you get challenged by your emotions from distress, boredom to lack of fun. For example, the intense urge to lie down and take a nap sweeps through your body yet it is time to lace up and get to practice, what do you do? A teammate is lazy for a few days of practice leading up to a big competition and gets to start in the game over you, how do you react? You hear about a big party but have loads of work to do. What do you choose? Staying steady, being able to self-regulate, may be the most important overarching mental skill that you can develop to achieve your very best in sport. And in many ways, MMTS 2.0 and this book, are offering you myriad ways to do just this, strengthen your ability to choose to engage, concentrate, and stay engaged with the moment regardless of how you feel. And doing so based on your values. Sometimes it is important to take the nap or go to the party. We are empowering you to live your values.

At the onset of my academic career, I (Amy) explored how 38 elite rowers coped with competitive pressure. When asked about one of their most difficult experiences dealing with competitive pressure, strikingly about 50% of the elite rowers reported when in either in a World Championship, Olympic races, or during selection for one of these teams they wanted to give up, to quit in a race! At the time, I found this extremely surprising. Why would such high level athletes want to quit in the middle of a six-minute race when they had prepared years for the opportunity to race for the US team?

We have found that often people have the misconception that elite and professional athletes have it all together and know how to self-regulate, to have poise. Yet these athletes were reporting something quite different. They were reporting that in the worst moments, they were void of self-regulation. And after a few decades of working with high level athletes, it has become abundantly clear to Josh and I that

© Springer International Publishing AG 2017
A. Baltzell, J. Summers, *The Power of Mindfulness*,
https://doi.org/10.1007/978-3-319-70410-4_12

most athletes, at all levels, struggle with knowing how to self-regulate. They would self-regulate, if they could. So when a coach yells, *don't think, next play!*, our guess is that almost every athlete would do so if they had the mental and emotional regulation skill to get their heads back in the game. Yet many athletes dearly need ways to combat intense self-criticism, low confidence, and the desire to quit.

In the study of rowers, upon reflection, it has become clear to me (Amy) that the rowers' desire to quit was not a function of having low levels of care about the results. Instead the intense urge to quit was a reaction to the intense performance distress that comes along with the fear of not meeting performance expectations in critical performance moments (e.g., falling behind in the middle of an Olympic 2000-meter race) and having no idea how to handle the distress. In that study, one athlete recalled how she was feeling in the middle of World Championship race in which she had lost any ability to self-regulate. Isabelle stated,

> I would have done anything, I would have screamed, jumped to get out of the boat... it doesn't feel like I could do anything... You are getting to a certain point where you can't, all the tricks are out of the bag. It's like, Jesus, there's nothing left! (Baltzell 1999, p. 101)

Self-regulation in such an instance would be to tolerate the intense, distraction of hopelessness and still focus all possible energy on making the boat move as fast as possible. In rowing, that is the metaphorical *next play*.

Yet, if you don't cultivate self-regulation, if you don't have strategies to handle such moments, you too might become victim to such thoughts and emotions that are created and charged by fear. In another interview in that same study, Jessie directly talks about her intense urge to quit:

> I just want to get the hell out of this boat and I don't want to be here... there is nothing I could have done that could have got me out of that boat faster and just on the plane and out of there.... Physically I was still rowing and finishing the race but mentally I could care less. (Baltzell 1999, p. 101)

In this chapter, we focus on how the power of body awareness can help get your awareness and attention placed back, in the present moment. In some ways, this doesn't make sense. You are, of course, *literally* always in the present moment. There is nowhere else to be! And yet our attention and thinking can easily get caught up in the past and future. When you bring your attention to physical sensations, in that moment, you are choosing to bring your attention back to physical experience of present moment awareness. And for that moment, both your mind and body are situated in the present. In such a moment, you have more of a chance to release your regrets about the past and worries about the future.

Why does this matter? Being able to pull our attention back into the present moment is absolutely essential to be able to do anything in regards to handling our distress. If you are not able to pull your mind back to the present, your mind remains lost in fear of the future or lost in the regret of the past and you then are victim to your well-learned reactions. If you are not present and making choices about how to respond, you will simply respond based on decisions you have made in the past, when in a similar state. And if these reactions – like giving up in a race when you fall behind – are well trained, you have no hope of creating an alternative response to such distress. Getting in your body is not necessarily enjoyable. It can be wonderful and, in distressful moments, it can be painful. Yet, getting present through your body can also be a performance life jacket. You can get present, see what is happening around you and make the best choice about how to move forward.

Imagine Jessie above, the athlete that was bombarded and overtaken by the desire to escape the World Championship rowing race. Her thinking mind was lost in the fantasized relief of being on a plane flying away from the venue. Her body was left rowing in the way Jessie typically would row when in a panicked state. Because her mind was so focused on escape fantasies, Jessie lost the chance to be in her body and notice how it was feeling and thus the information happening around her that could offer sublte cues to optimize boat speed. Information on how to race more wisely was being received, but the focus on the future, prevented her from being aware and utilizing the critical present-moment information.

Jessie's performance was only as good as it could be, with Jessie in a checked-out, reactive, overwhelmed, fear-state. With practicing body awareness, as an anchor to the present, she could have cultivated awareness to the information was she missing out on. Maybe she could have established better rhythm. Maybe she could have noticed a competitor lagging and been inspired to make a move. She will never know because she was not mentally present to have such awareness and, in turn, to make new choices.

From the start of this book (and the MMTS 2.0 program), we have been encouraging you to work with the body through the practice of mindfulness meditation, beginning with noticing the physical sensation of breathing. In the formal meditation practice, focusing on the breath can feel random and not important. Yet, focusing on the breath is quite intentional and has clear purpose. Focusing on the breath brings your mind's awareness and body experience to the present moment. Focusing on the breath is not focusing on all aspects of the present moment experience, but it is an access point back to the present. Because rationally and literally, you can only be aware of your lived experience of breathing in the exact moment that you are aware of the breath. Can you physically feel breath in any other moment than this moment?

And once aware of being in the body, with your attention shining in that direction, you can more easily opt to open up to the present and notice other body sensations, sounds, emotions, thoughts, and notice what is happening around you. You also in that moment of being back awake, back to the present moment, can opt to intentionally use your thinking mind to figure out how to best proceed with the information that is streaming in, moment-to-moment.

Information with Physical, Body Awareness

Being aware of the breath is one way to practice being present. In everyday life, you can easily zoom in, with your awareness, to become aware of other physical sensations of physical experience. Awareness of body sensations can offer a path to being present to other aspects of experience, including emotions, thoughts, and overall sense of wellness. If you do not do this, you lose out on important information that can re-direct your choices and behavior. Consider the example of Leo, below.

Leo. In a recent initial meeting with Leo, a professional runner, the reason for our work together (with Amy) was not quite clear. When I asked why Leo had made the appointment, his response was vague and noting he just wanted to learn something about sport psychology. One question and response, below, sounds quite typical.

AB: *How are you feeling?*
Pro Runner: *I feel great!*

Yet about fifteen minutes into session, with some discussion about what it was really like to practice and compete, it became clear that something was getting in the way of Leo running well. Essentially he would burn out and slow down prior to finishing most practices and competition. So, I asked again,

AB: *How are you feeling?*

And I received a very different answer,

Pro Runner: *I don't ever really honestly check-in with myself.... Well, I feel totally exhausted. Totally exhausted!*

With this response, the session could really begin. Instead of pretending everything was OK, Leo got present in his body and had access to information that was important to attend to. In that session he made a number of decisions about how he would train differently for the next month or two to physically recover from pushing his body too hard, for too long. We concluded the session with Leo asking himself each day: *What am I feeling, physically? What do I need, today (to help me perform better, over time)?* We invite you to ask yourself the same question and see what wisdom or insight arises.

Concentration with Physical, Body Awareness

Mindfulness meditation practices often start with focus on the breath. And concentration meditations also often start with your attention placed on your breath. One reason for this, as we have been discussing, is the benefit of getting both your body and mind awareness situated in the present. In addition, the focus on the sensations of breathing is, at once, a concentration practice. If you visit the meditation cycle, and look at it through the lens of concentration, this is a concentration practice! There is practice over and over again starting with concentration (i.e., on the breath) and then of the mind wandering, awareness of the wandering mind and then intentionally bringing attention back to the breath.

To offer a whole picture of the meditation cycle, as well, we encourage you to note that the value of the *relax* aspect of the cycle. The important choice to relax happens right after you notice that your mind has wandered. To intentionally relax practice bringing some acceptance and, if possible slight relaxation, to the body before you bring your attention back to the focus of the meditation. When you notice distraction and opt to intentionally relax, you are strengthening your muscle of poise. You are creating an ability to have more internal balance in the face of distress. The whole meditation cycle represents all aspects of what it means to meditate. The meditation cycle also reflects how both concentration and internal balance (equanimity) are practiced and strengthened.

Each time your mind wanders and you are able to bring the attention back to the breath, your muscle of attention is strengthened. As you strengthen this muscle of attention, you can bring this strengthened ability to the athletic field. Rick Hanson and Richard Mendius (2009) wrote a valuable book on the impact of meditation on the body. They emphasize that the benefit of mindfulness is having attentional control:

> Being mindful simply means having good control over your attention: you can place your attention wherever you want and it stays there; when you want to shift it to something else, you can. When your attention is steady, so is your mind: not rattled or hijacked by whatever pops into awareness, but stably present, grounded, and unshakeable. Attention is like a spotlight, and what it illuminates streams into your mind and shapes your brain. Consequently, developing greater control over your attention is perhaps the single most powerful way to reshape your brain and thus your mind (p. 177).

Focusing on the physical sensation of breathing is the core practice of both concentration and mindful meditation practice. Both lead to the strengthening of concentration.

Body Awareness for Emotional Regulation

Body awareness practices have also been associated with helping with emotional regulation. When the focus is on some part of the physical body – from doing body scans, focusing on the breath to walking meditations – it can help shift the focus away from ruminating and back into the present moment through physical sensations. Everyone has heard from someone who cares about you when you are upset, "Just relax and take a deep breath!" And sometimes this is a perfect way to reset, to calm the system down. Yet sometimes this can backfire, particularly in sports in which breathing is an important part of performance. If you are, for example, feeling quite a bit of performance anxiety and you focus on your breathing, you might become more distressed as you notice a short, quick breathing pattern. Another way to get present, without having to bring full attention to your breathing, is instead through bringing awareness to your feet.

We have found that the following *Soles of the Feet* exercise has been a favorite by a number of MMTS 2.0 participants. They reported that it was a practical, easily applicable mediation to sport, particularly when they were upset. Focusing on the sensation of walking has been found to be an effective way to calm the mind when feeling emotionally overwhelmed, a way to cope with emotional difficulty for the general population. Of course you don't always want to turn down the emotional intensity. Sometimes intense emotions, even if negative emotions, can be helpful. Sometimes you need the emotional intensity of fear, or anger or frustration to fuel performance.

Yet, other times the energy is so high, so intense, that the negative emotion becomes distracting and unhelpful. If you think of a water faucet, imagine the water turned on full blast. Our emotional intensity can be similar. Intentionally shifting your attention from anger or frustration to the sensation of the soles of your feet can be a way to significantly turn down the intensity of emotions while staying in the present moment. This exercise can be integrated into most sports, if you have walking between points, shifts, or plays. Or it can be used as you are walking to your venue (e.g., the swimmer on the way to the pool deck).

Soles of the Feet: Walking Meditation (ten-minutes)[1]

Soles of the Feet is a mindfulness-based body intervention, a walking meditation. This exercise offers a direct strategy to handle emotional difficulty via body awareness, and more specifically awareness of sensations in the soles of your feet. If you are trying this on your own, we encourage you to try it now! You don't have to be distressed to try this walking meditation. In fact, it would be much better to try this a few times, many times, before heading into a stressful, competitive situation where you need to put it to use. The walking meditation often is used as an alternative to a formal sitting mindfulness practice. Essentially the exercise is about bringing your attention to the sensations that arise as you walk. You can walk as slowly as you like, or walk at your typical pace. You might even want to experiment with walking at a very slow pace, a moderate, and a bit too fast pace. Through trying out varying speeds, you can figure out the right speed for you. You want to go slowly enough that you can keep your attention on the changing sensations of the bottom of your feet as you walk.

If you are doing this on your own, it is probably easiest to read through the exercise and practice as best you can, based on what you remember, versus trying to read the exercise as you practice. Each time you practice it, you will remember more of the prompts. And the specific prompts are not the important aspect of the practice.

What matters is that you try walking for five to ten minutes, and with the intention of keeping your attention on the sensations that arise in your feet. Notice the sensations changing as you walk. Also notice how you are emotionally feeling before and after the exercise. And most importantly bring a curiosity and light-heartedness to trying this activity. It can feel a bit odd at first. Or, if you allow it, it can be an interesting, mindful movement. It is a meditation in motion that can help reduce distress symptoms. You can walk in a circle, in a line back and forth or you can just go for a slow walk. Enjoy!

---

[1] This exercise was adapted from the Mindful Self-compassion teacher trainer manual.

This exercise is an anchoring practice, a way to bring yourself (your awareness) back to what is happening in the present moment through your awareness of your body.

- Begin by noticing how you are feeling in the moment. There is no need to change anything.
- In a standing position bring awareness to how your feet feel, especially how they feel pressing against the floor. You can notice the different parts of your feet including your arches, the balls of feet, each of your toes. If you like, you can move the toes around. Notice warmth, coolness, tingling, pressure, and the changing and shifting of these sensations.
- Begin to notice the sensation of the soles of your feet touching the floor.
- When the mind has wandered, just feel the soles of your feet again.
- To better feel sensation in the soles of your feet, try gently rocking forward and backward on your feet. Next try gently rocking side-to-side. If you like and it is comfortable try making little circles with your knees, feeling the changing sensations of the soles of your feet.
- Now begin walking, slowly. Notice the changing sensations in the soles of your feet. Notice the sensation of lifting a foot. Notice the sensation of stepping forward and then placing the foot on the floor. Now doing the same with the other foot. And then one foot after another.
- As you walk, perhaps appreciating how small the surface area of your feet is, and how your feet support your entire body. If you wish, allow a moment of gratitude for the hard work that your feet do for you which is usually taken for granted.
- Continuing to walk, slowly, feeling the soles of your feet.
- Now returning to standing again, and expand your awareness of your entire body, letting yourself feel whatever you are feeling and letting yourself be just as you are.
- There is no need to change anything. Keep practicing until you feel more relaxed. When you are ready to stop, stop walking and take a moment to notice any thoughts that are arising. Welcome them. You can choose to respond wisely.
- Ask yourself, *What do I need right now?*

When you are ready, you are welcome to open your eyes.

Debrief

Take a few minutes to write in your journal about your experience:

- What was that like for you?
- Was there a difference in how you felt between when you started and when you finished?

The Soles of the Feet exercise has been integrated into the MMTS 2.0 program to offer you a way to calm down your mind and body when you have a need to step out of a reactive mode of being.

A tennis player in one of our MMTS 2.0 studies noted the value of this exercise when he was feeling intense anxiety over close matches and frustrations with opponents who were cheating (calling balls out when they were in, and in when they were out). After practicing the Soles of the Feet exercise a few times, he was able to adapt the exercise and bring it right into his match. When distracted with high emotional reactivity, he would focus on the soles of his feet as he walked from the net, back to the baseline. It was a way for him to center himself before initiating the next point.

- How could you integrate the idea of this exercise into your practice or competition?
- What else do you do to help calm your mind when thoughts are wandering, racing, or you feel intense frustration?
- If you think back to a recent difficult moment when your emotions were running too high, what could you have thought, said, or done to give yourself what you needed so you could regulate your emotions and get back into performing your best?

Chapter 13
The Power of Upgraded Performance, Intentional Engagement: (MMTS 2.0, Module 6)

> *It is not the strongest of the species that survives, nor the most intelligent that survives. It is the one that is most adaptable to change.*
>
> *Charles Darwin*

Ultimately MMTS 2.0 is designed to help you upgrade your performance (i.e., practice and competition) through helping you make better use of your attention and concentration when playing your sport. We hope to empower and inspire you to:

1. Give less power to distractions, upset (i.e., not allowing natural fear or dread get in the way of you focusing your attention on performing as well as you can, each moment).
2. Have less (unhelpful) reactivity to such upset (i.e., though the practices we offer in no way promise to stop such difficult emotions. Instead, you will be empowered to be less of a victim to them because you will learn to tolerate them and have the freedom to focus you attention where you want to place it!).
3. Lock-in your attention while adapting and adjust to what is occurring around you (i.e., you will be able to pay attention to your sport instead of to the uninvited thoughts and feelings surging through your mind and body).

The focus of this chapter is primarily about number three above, locking in your attention and being able to adjust to what shows up when practicing or competing. We will offer you ways to think about and implement a mental approach that helps you adapt and adjust to whatever shows up, good or bad, helpful or unhelpful, surprising or expected, including internal states as well as variations and unexpected occurrences in your practice and sport environment. We believe that this approach allows you to truly flourish in sport. As you free yourself from the bondage of past regrets, future fears and assumptions of what you will experience, you move into a new realm of faster learning and improved performance. The quality of your internal experience improves, as does your ability to take on whatever comes your way.

© Springer International Publishing AG 2017
A. Baltzell, J. Summers, *The Power of Mindfulness*,
https://doi.org/10.1007/978-3-319-70410-4_13

Panoramic Specificity

As performers we have to be able to shift awareness at all times in order to adjust to what is going on around us and have spontaneity and creativity in the movement. We need to be playing the music, following the conductor, hearing our sound and how it fits into our section, following our section leader, listening to other parts of the orchestra and how it fits in with our part of the music, adjusting to the space we are playing in and connecting to the audience all at the same time.
  - Naomi Steckman, professional classical musician

Ultimately all performers want to have great flexibility and a wide scope of awareness when training and performing. There are always specific, predictable cues to focus on. Yet athletes tend to perform their best when they can *also* pick out new, unexpected, fresh sport relevant information in their environment that might nudge them to slightly adjust or adapt to the new (i.e., unexpected, surprising) information. Panoramic specificity is the term we use to represent this ability to be fully and effectively present to internal and external experience, in a broad and narrow way, as needed. With panoramic specificity, you both focus on what you choose to focus on and, at once, hold awareness of what is happening in the context of that concentration in case you need to adjust based on internal and external signs, cues, or points of data. For example, you could be having a great practice and all of a sudden thunder and lightning starts to explode in the sky. At this point you have to make some wise choices based on the new information: run to shelter!

Cultivating panoramic specificity is an expected benefit from the mindfulness practices. Panoramic specificity means your ability to be at once fully focused on a particular task (often well-planned and practiced) and, at the same time, open to all possible sport-relevant cues in both the environment and your body. When you strengthen your panoramic specificity there is more openness to flowing and emerging possibilities and an increase in your potential for creative, spontaneous adaptability.

Italian Kickboxer, Gregario Di Leo.

Italian kick-boxer, Gregario Di Leo, was a world champion many times over. To succeed, Di Leo had to be fully present, every split second. Though a wandering mind and fear is totally normal for high level performers who chronically endure high levels of performance expectations, Di Leo had to stay locked into the present moment when fighting. He had to attend to both the core points of focus for kickboxing and remain ready to respond to unexpected slight variations of a kick, a move to an attack, which he could only notice if he kept openness to what was happening broadly in his experience.

If he allowed his attention to get *tangled up* in fears of not winning or lost in regret of wishing he responded slightly differently a moment before, he put himself in danger. It could easily result in missing ever-so-subtle cues in the moment that could have devastating results both in terms of his physical safety and the ever-important results of high-pressured matches. In order to prevail Di Leo had to be consistently present to his opponent's subtle, positional shifts while at the same time tuned into his own body. He had to maintain a concurrent awareness of his balance, his positioning, while protecting his vulnerabilities. And at all times, he had to be ready to take advantage of openings for well-placed attacks.

There are many ways to think about what Di Leo did psychologically that supported him in being so consistently successful within World and European championships. You might assume that he had to have effective focus, resilient drive, and extraordinary fitness. All of these are true. But there is one additional factor that Di Leo needed, and that all great performers need in order to give themselves the ultimate edge. Di Leo was *mindful* in the fullest sense. Di Leo needed to be fully aware of the totality of what was occurring (kickboxing relevant) both within and around him each and every possible moment.

We have been offering explanations and practices of mindfulness throughout this book, yet we will take another round of considering what it means practically. *Mindful* is a word that you hear almost everywhere you go. A friend might say, "Please be mindful when parking my car." Or a coach might advise, "Be mindful of number 27 in the offensive zone!" And in these contexts, the word seems to mean something along the lines of "*be careful*" or "*pay attention*". These definitions are representative of an important aspect of mindfulness (i.e., awareness of a particularly important and predictable aspect of performance) however; these examples do not convey the fuller meaning of the word *mindfulness*.

Though it is important, for example, for the player above to be aware of his opponent, number 27, he would have many other factors to hold in his awareness, *simultaneously*. The athlete may need to be aware of his entire team and opponents moving on the field, assess how to position and move his own body and to regulate his emotional state, such as dissipating fear or over-excitement. Being mindful includes taking in many data points of information and being able to wisely and swiftly make the strategic choices that will lead to success, all the while fully engaging in the heat of battle.

Consider your own sport or performance realm. What are the typical things that you know that you need to focus on to perform well? For the runner it could be keeping their head up, for a pitcher it might be seeing the target or tuning into an aspect of the physical sensations that are associated with a good throw or catch. But clearly this is not all a runner or baseball pitcher needs to hold in their awareness. They need to be able to focus on one or two key prompts that will cue them into the present moment to perform well, yet they need to hold in the background of their awareness all that is occurring within the boundaries of their competitive environment that could impact their moment-to-moment experience. They need to hold in their awareness anything that they would potentially need to adapt or adjust to for optimal performance (e.g., the long distance runner may need to be aware of subtle opportunities to run a few less inches around a new turn).

Open-Awareness Meditation (ten-minutes)

In this next practice, we ask that you set aside ten minutes and practice in an environment that offers low sound distractions (including text messages and/or people walking through the door). This practice will include many elements of traditional mindfulness meditation. In this round, we are going to ask you focus for two minutes on different aspects of your experience while meditating. (Please find a comfortable position, eyes closed or gaze softened and lowered.)

Please spend two minutes on each point of focus below:

1. **Noticing breath (two-minutes).**

Noticing breath is a traditional place to begin with practicing mindfulness meditation. You can notice the physical sensation of breathing. You also can, if you prefer, simply notice the space that includes your heart and breath, together.

2. **Labeling of thoughts and feelings (two-minutes).**

In this practice, we encourage you to do what feels right for you, which holds true for any of these practices. It sometimes can be helpful to practice with the labeling, noting experience that is arising (i.e., *thinking, planning*, or *this is what anxiety feels like*). And other times, you might have a preference to do no intentional thinking, and only engage in the task of noticing, bringing a warmth and curiosity to the thoughts and emotions that are arising (or sometimes tolerance, as best you can).

3. **Elements of self-compassion (bringing warmth to experience) (two-minutes).**

It can be helpful to practice offering kindness to yourself, along with the intention to be balanced and healthy. There is no need to be distressed to offer kindness to yourself! Yet, in performance settings, you have to wisely think about when to offer such kindness to yourself. For example, at the end of a difficult lift pushing yourself as hard as possible is a good thing, if you are healthy without injury concern. This is not a time to call for a state of ease or contentment. Yet, it is equally possible that offering a bit of kindness to yourself is invaluable to help put you in a poised focused state of mind. We hope you understand that there is no harm, only benefit, in offering yourself kindness in your formal meditation practice. You just need to use it skillfully when competing.

4. **Body awareness/Distress tolerance.**

In this practice, we encourage you to bring your attention fully to your body, noticing feelings like pressure, coolness, warmth, pulsing, movement, and tingling. We have encouraged you to notice such sensations for a number of reasons. One reason is the great value you can gain from the practice of intentionally placing and keeping your attention where you choose to place it. In addition, bringing your mind and awareness to physical sensation can be a great way to intentionally bring your mind back, away from a wandering mind, to the present moment experience (very helpful for sport performance!). This practice can both be a source of soothing (by virtue of drawing your attention away from distracting thoughts and emotions) as well as a way to strengthen your concentration via focusing intentionally on what is emerging moment-to-moment in your awareness. And when you bring such awareness to the athletic field, you are empowered with incoming information to adapt and adjust as necessary for enhancing sport performance.

5. **Traditional open-awareness mindfulness meditation – Awareness of all thoughts, feelings, and sensations.**

The open-awareness practice is both challenging and a gold mine. When you can truly learn how to open your awareness to all experience – liked and disliked – you train yourself to have the tolerance to broaden your awareness. You no longer have to avoid your current reality to protect yourself. Your awareness is the background to whatever you are focusing on. When you can do this on the athletic field, paired with concentrating on task relevant cues, you train your capacity to strengthen you *panoramic specificity.*

We ask that you focus on each of the mindfulness points of focus below for two minutes: including your (1) Breath, (2) Thoughts and feelings (you can label these if you prefer), (3) Self-compassion (Please note: if you are in a good place, you can opt to simply feel the warmth of your hands on your knees while you send good intentions to yourself), (4) Body-awareness, and (5) Open-awareness. Now, please set your timer to chime gently in two-minute intervals and begin!

Debrief

Take a few minutes to reflect in your journal what that practice was like for you:

- What is it like to practice different aspects of presence and then bring it all together?
- Did you like the interval meditation training? If so, great! If not, then just chalk this up as an exploration and return to the practice(s) you like.
- What would it be like to bring such presence to sport? When would it be most helpful to have this type of awareness in practice or performance? Intentionally shifting from point of focus to point of focus.

This practice is about learning to accept whatever is going on so you can be more ready to adapt and adjust to relevant incoming information. Have you ever had a performance where your mind quieted down and you could compete better than usual? You were not thinking about what to do next, you just knew and acted? You were better able to respond to what was happening? Though meditation can't stop your uninvited thinking, over time with a mindfulness meditation practice, your thinking mind will quiet down, more often and more easily. And the times that your thinking mind just won't shut off, you can become progressively more comfortable with the busy mind at work and more able to turn your attention away from the chatter. Such mind activity can become simply a backdrop to performance, instead of a distraction, so you can use your mind and attention most efficiently.

Mindfulness, Ellen Langer Style

"Wherever you put the mind, the body will follow." Ellen Langer
(Fienberg 2010)

Ellen Langer, a Harvard social psychology researcher, brings a different understanding to mindfulness, one that is very helpful. Langer's approach to mindfulness is invaluable once your monkey mind has settled down, when you have learned to be less reactive to the mind when highly activated (e.g., *I really can't do this!*), or when you have an absence of distress. We find her approach very helpful when conceptually thinking about what an athlete can "do", in their effort to leverage mindfulness to help improve sport performance.

She (2012) defines mindfulness simply as, a "process of actively making novel distinctions about objects in one's awareness" (Langer, Cohen & Djikic, p. 1114). Though simple, this is a big idea! Essentially she directs us to wake up and be present to what really is going on, not living your lives based on your assumptions of how you think things should be, or go, based on past memories and decisions of similar situations (e.g., *We always lose to this team, so we will probably lose again today.*) One of the biggest opportunities to improve performance is to maximize your awareness to novel stimuli, that are task relevant. Why? Well first, let's think about the value of trusting what you do know.

It is important to trust well-learned skills and strategies because you can't think through everything. For example, it is a waste of energy to think about how to tie your shoe. You already know how to do this, automatically, without having to waste your energy to think through the step-by-step task. However, it remains critically important to notice new or unexpected occurrences. To explain, we start with a twenty-first century example – the driverless car.

The Driverless Car

The driverless car will soon be a common occurrence on our roads. Such vehicles are programmed to be able to drive you wherever you would like to go. Just speak out loud where you want to go and it will get you there. Right? Well, driverless cars can *almost* get you there, on automatic pilot. Yet, the creators of this ingenious invention also require that a driver be present *just in case* something goes wrong, to respond freshly to the unexpected. The pre-programming may work quite well for 99.5% of the myriad challenges of navigating the road; yet going on a trip across town is not 100% accurate because *the programming is based on what has occurred in the past.* Even the genius inventors cannot plan for the unexpected that cannot be anticipated. Thus, there needs to be someone alive, present, and awake to make quick adjustments when necessary. The pre-programmed machine is not enough.

Flash back to sport. You spend a lot of time practicing so your skills and application can be automatic. Yet, to perform your best, you also must be *aware* of what is happening around you. With this awareness, you have access to the necessary information for your mind and body to opt to slightly or dramatically adjust to the cues in the environment. In sport, you can turn on your automatic pilot for much of your world of performance. In fact, you must. And this is a good thing! For example, the tennis player cannot be questioning his grip throughout a three-hour grueling match. Instead he must trust his well trained and practiced feel of his grip and have this be one of the many points of automaticity in his play. He must trust his training. Yet, just like the driverless cars, playing on autopilot in any sport is also not enough.

To learn to perform your best you must intend and prime your mind to notice novelty so you can take in the unexpected, necessary information to adapt and adjust to whatever is showing up. *Noticing novel stimuli* is about noticing what is different in your environment that is worthy of your attention to make slight modifications to improve performance. Be your own shotgun driver!

Imagine a rower racing down the course. She doesn't need to think about the well-engrained rowing stroke style. In such a kinesthetic domain, she doesn't want to disrupt the non-conscious expression of the kinetic chain of energy. In general, it is not a good idea to call attention to this process because it might disrupt what is working quite well, what is well trained and automatic. But you do have to notice slight variations in what is happening within you and outside of you, and then trust the non-conscious subtle adjustment. So, for example, if there is an unexpected wind gust the rower will need to notice this such that her system can make the appropriate adjustments to row as efficiently and fast down the course as possible. In contrast, the rower might become aware of her energy waning, and consciously re-focus her attention in a way that might help her make the most of what her body can offer during the remainder of the race. Sometimes the adjustment will be sub-conscious and others quite intentional adaptations or adjustments. Regardless of how it is used (i.e., conscious or sub-conscious) you need to be present – to be aware – to take in the necessary unexpected information.

Often in sport psychology we encourage athletes to recall a past great performance and try to replicate it. We use mental skills, such as visualization and self-talk words or phrases, to re-create mind states and points of focus to help prompt excellent performances. This approach is useful, yet it is not enough. We help athletes use *past* experiences to help them get ready for *future* sport performances. Though helpful, this exclusive focus on *past* experience can serve to strengthen a driver-less car approach to performance. In Ellen Langer's words we may be helping athletes strengthen a mindless approach, *"We act like automatons who have been programmed to act according to the sense our behavior made in the past, rather than the present"* (Langer 2000, p.220).

To get the most out of your mind, you can do both. Use prompts or reminders to help create an optimal mind state and focus your attention where it needs to go. At once, be open to making subtle changes in response to whatever shows up. Be the shotgun of the driver-less car for your own performance. Generally, you will perform your best when you both trust your skills and are at once open to slightly adapting and adjusting to what you encounter as you practice and perform.

Jeffrey, the World-Class Fencer. I (Amy) have recently worked with one of the top fencers in the world. He too was caught up in the trap of deciding future match results, prior to his bouts. This worked when competing against fencers he "knew" he could beat. In almost all instances, he beat them. Yet he was fencing like the driverless car, a mindless fencer! He knew how he fenced against his competitors and would strive to replicate past bouts against these same competitors. His mindless assumptions served some benefit by strengthening his confidence in his ability to beat the opponents he believed he should beat.

Though, there was a problem. He also would expect to lose, and live out these expectations, when he faced those few competitors who had statistics that would indicate he should lose to them. His mindless strategy did not work there. Before we started our work together he typically would "*know*" in advance the results of those matches. He would predictably lose to those athletes. Why? He decided he would lose and fenced to lose, his mind was filled with past moves he had made against these fencers and the points and bouts he had lost.

His mindless assumptions about who is better became loosened when I asked him, "*Do you fence at the exact same level as you did six months ago?*" He laughed, and quickly replied, *Of course not! I am a 1000 times better.* And then I asked, *Then can you assume that they, your competitors, will fence the same way and expect the same results when they fence you?* And after a pause, he stated, *You are right, of course not.* At this moment Jeffrey began to be freed up to be more present to what was happening in his bouts. He became open to adapting and adjusting to what he encountered on the fencing strip, regardless of whom he was fencing.

> Every performance is unique.

Langerian mindfulness reminds you to intentionally notice what you are experiencing. In the *now,* in practice or performance, nothing is ever exactly the same (though sometimes it feels like that). Nothing is static. The combination of your skills, physical capacity, knowledge, mind-state, level of energy, the competitive scene (the venue and your competition) are dynamic, ever changing. Where best to place your attention, or where to shift it, may subtly or significantly differ from what was needed in the past, from moments ago to last year.

Langer, Russel and Eisenkraft (2009) designed an insightful study of orchestra musicians. They discovered the value of focusing on subtle differences in the moment instead of relying on re-creating a past best performance. They invited sixty professional orchestra musicians to play in two conditions with an audience watching:

1. "Play in the *finest manner you can, offering subtle new nuances to your performance"*
2. *"Think about the finest performance of this piece that you can remember, and try to play it. (p. 127)*

"These orchestra players were prompted to draw on novel distinctions within a *boundaried, task-specific focus* related to creating excellent music" (Baltzell & McCarthy, 2016, p. 160). Instead of re-creating a *past* best performance they created a new one that was intentionally excellent but different. From a traditional sport psychology perspective, re-creating a past best performance would be expected to prompt the best performance. Surprisingly, it didn't! Instead, intentionally creating subtle new nuances was more enjoyable for the musicians to play and, concurrently, created better quality music, based both on the musicians' and audience's assessment.

Antonio

Antonio is a world-class track athlete. In one of my (Amy's) sessions with him, he shared with me a strategy that helped him get in the right mindset to compete in international competition. Antonio offers a strategy that ingeniously offers a Langerian mindfulness approach to nudging a fully present awareness to adapt and adjust when under high pressure,

> I first took a few steps back and then stepped forward onto the line, where we start. I intentionally focused in on some random object and did not think about anything else for a few moments. I did this in an effort to become 100% ready. The first time I tried this, I stared at a random electrical box. I told myself to be aware of what it looked like. After this thought, I began to notice colors in ways I had not noticed before. I noticed the shape, thickness and vibrant colors of the many wires in the box. (Baltzell & McCarthy, 2016, p. 164).

Antonio's innovative practical strategy to get ready to perform is a fantastic example of Langerian mindfulness in action. His strategy inspired us to integrate this concept into the MMTS 2.0 intervention.

Preparing to Adapt and Adjust

In this next practice, we invite you to intentionally notice novelty both in your experience of breathing and then of a physical object.

Noticing Novelty of Breath (five-minutes)
We invite you to take about five minutes and practice intentionally noticing novelty while engaging in a mindful breathing practice. Take this time to experiment with noticing new sensations or experience while noticing your breathing. Just like the orchestra musicians playing their music in subtly different ways that no one else would notice, we ask you to notice the slight variations or differences in the experience of breathing. Ready, begin.

Noticing Novelty of Physical Object (five-minutes)
Next, we woud like you to bring this fresh awareness to a physical object. Intentionally looking at an object can also be a great way to practice noticing what might be new or fresh. Just as Antonio, the track athlete above, noticed unexpected (or never before observed) colors and shapes in the electric box.

For this practice, we ask that you observe a physical object, your hand. Notice the variation in color, shape, and surface. Spend a few minutes looking to see things that you have never noticed before. You might notice lines. You might notice variations in the color of your nails. You might notice variation in the color of your skin. Perhaps consider the difference in the texture of your palm compared to the back of your hand. Ready, go!

Debrief

This practice is designed to prompt you to notice novelty, newness, and freshness all around you. With such noticing you can be freed up to be more engaged with what you are doing.

- How might noticing novelty connect to how you practice? To your performance? We have known countless athletes who tend to go through the motion in practice, just because they have gone through the same drills, the same exercise so many times. They feel like they can go on automatic pilot and just "*get through*" the training. Yet, if you stop and think about it, how much learning have they missed in those moments of being turned off?
- How could you apply this idea to your next practice? How could you engage with it in a more alive, present way?
- What specific area of practice or performance has become boring, repetitive? Would you be willing to try to notice subtle differences in an effort to learn and improve? To get back engaged and present?

We hope that this practice inspires you to bring an intentional awareness to practice or performance, an awareness that is both accepting and open to seeing the freshness of what is unfolding.

Preparing to Engage

We would like you to try creating such a present, open, ready for a fresh performance experience through the next brief imagery exercise. The goal is to get you in a fully present state, ready to practice or perform. We will start with you creating a go-to thought, one that can prompt you back to presence and have you check-in with yourself, to know your starting point. And with these tools in hand, we you encourage to engage in a brief imagery exercise.

Your Go-to Thoughts for Performance

Please identify one or two phrases or words that you can bring to mind that remind you what you most need to focus on to improve in your *next* practice or to performance. Bring to mind a sport appropriate point of focus (i.e., a verbal cue). Some examples might be, *Head up* (for a sprinter), *See the target* (for a pitcher), and *Smooth* (for a swimmer). You also can plan to bring to mind a thought that would be soothing if you anticipate the next practice or performance to be a distressful *(e.g., It is OK to feel like this: Others feel like this too; I don't have to feel confident to play well)*. Do you have one in mind? Take a moment to bring one to mind.

Know your Starting Point

Next, tune into how you are feeling *right now*. Of course you would feel differently if you were just about to start a practice or compete. But try this exercise, based on how you are feeling in *this moment*. Take as much time as you need between each sentence below to bring to mind the answer per question, before you move to the next.

Note how you are feeling physically, emotionally right now, including that which is not perfect. Take a moment to accept yourself just as you are (e.g., *It is OK to feel just like this.*) Next, note your strengths as an athlete. What is good about how you are, just as you are? For example, you might think about your determination or love for what you are doing (e.g., *I am determined; I am passionate about this*). What can you bring to mind to create the best approach for today? Think of a word or image that will help you live out your inspired sport value. Perhaps you remind yourself of why competing matters to you (e.g., *This is my life long dream*). Or perhaps bring to mind what you most need to hear to prompt a present and courageous state of mind. You might need to bring to mind a word or phrase of kindness (i.e., *I will be OK, no matter what; It is OK to feel like this, I can still perform well; I don't have to be confident, I just need to focus in on playing*).

Prepare to Adapt, Adjust and Create

Once you have your word or phrases ready, we encourage you try this brief imagery, to help prime you to be more present and ready to go! But before you go, a phrase you can bring to mind to help you get ready to perform. Your list of tools:

- Performance word or phrase for focus

- (e.g., *I see the ball; Next Play*)_____
- Notice, Accept How I am Feeling:
- (e.g., *I am psyched and ready!; I just wish I could go take a nap, I am so tired*)

  _____

- Kindness to yourself (If you need it): (e.g., *This is what anxiety feels like: it is OK to feel like this; I don't have to be confident to play well*) _____

  _____

If you are getting ready to compete make a note of the environment you will be playing in. Perhaps bring to mind others who will be there. Teammates? Competitors? Bring to mind the space (i.e., particular field, venue). Take your time to bring all of this to mind. When you consider the sport environment (whether for practice or competition) – the field, the gym, the court or the pool – you might only hear sounds. You might see it all from the vantage point of you seeing through your eyes or you might see the scene from the outside, like a video camera would see. There is no right way. Just bringing to mind any aspect of the venue that feels comfortable and what comes easily for you is the right way. Now bring to mind one or two of the phrases you created above that would be most helpful to you, to get you in a present, fresh state of mind to engage in your practice or performance. This is just like the track athlete who took a few minutes to focus on the novelty of the electrical box, he was getting himself into a present, accepting, tuning-into-novelty state of mind.

Visualize a Present, Accepting, Tuning-into-novelty State of Mind (5-minutes)

Once you have read through this, we encourage you to bring to mind the few cue words or phrases you created above. Shut your eyes and imagine yourself ready and prepared at your practice or competition venue. You are in a state that accepts your physical and mental state, just as they are. You are ready to commit to, live out, your inspired sport value. Bring to mind your sport inspired-value. Maybe also bring to mind a word of kindness for courage. Notice where to focus your awareness. Bring the intention of noticing what is fresh and new, trusting that you will have the wisdom skills to naturally adapt and adjust to what is showing up.

Take a few minutes to review these prompts and then bring to mind the part of the exercise that most resonates with you. Maybe first take a few deep breaths at your own depth and rate that is comfortable for you. Try closing your eyes or softening your gaze and visualize all of the above that is compelling to you. Allow yourself to feel ready, accepting, and present. You might take a moment or two to look at your hand or notice what is novel in your breath, as a way to invite a present moment focus to novelty, to freshness. Briefly close your eyes, imagine yourself in this state in your performance realm, ready to compete....begin!

Debrief

Take a few minutes to write about what you just experienced, learned.

- Was there a phrase that most resonated with you?
- Were you able to capture any sense of your competition venue? Sounds? Images? Movements? Maybe you just saw yourself from an external view? Or perhaps you sensed being in your body? Part of any of this is common, few people have imagery experiences of all of their senses.
- Were you able to bring a phrase of acceptance to yourself? Maybe you are not feeling 100% powerful in your mind or body. Were you able to accept this?
- What did you learn that you could bring with you to your next practice?

Which of these ideas have had the most meaning for you? What might you try to bring to your pre-practice or pre-game routine to help cultivate a holistically mindful approach (accepting and being open to novelty) to your training and performance? How can any of these ideas be applied to your sport? And beyond?

Flow

We would like to end our offerings of the MMTS 2.0 program concepts and practices through discussion of flow. Why? We believe that when you work to cultivate a mindful and self-compassionate approach to preparing your mind to perform, that entering the flow state becomes much more available to you.

But, first, what is flow and who captured such a state by words and research? Flow is an idea that was initially brought to the world of psychology by Mihaly Csikszentmihalyi (1975, 2014), who has been a thought leader in sport psychology and positive psychology. He defines flow as "a particular kind of experience that is so engrossing and enjoyable that it becomes autotelic, that is, worth doing for its own sake even though it may have no consequence outside itself" (1999, p. 824). When you are in flow in sport, it can create a satisfying and sometimes even ecstatic type of engagement.

His research was based on thousands of people fully engaged in doing something that they loved, from rock-climbers, athletes, and artists to surgeons and just regular people gardening and reading. Being in flow requires that you commit to what you are doing and stretch your ability in an effort to do the best that you can, moment-to-moment, with your attention on the task at hand. It is not enough to be skilled. Purposeful and focused engagement is an essential aspect of the flow experience. Being in flow has more to do less with how you are performing and more to do with the quality of your *internal* experience. Though typically when it occurs you also are engaged in a top-notch practice or performance, and sometimes peak performance. Flow involves *awareness* and invested attention on the task at hand or, as

Csikszentmihalyi (2014) founder of the term refers to as "total involvement" (p. 136).

We contend that a mindful, self-compassionate approach can help nudge you toward flow experiences in practice and performance. Of course, you cannot guarantee that you can create a full flow-state experience. But you can certainly intentionally create micro-flow (i.e., fleeting) experiences that, we think, can more often bloom into full flow states. Research in sport is indicating a strong connection between flow and mindfulness (e.g., Kaufman et al. 2009).

How does this work?

If you are willing to be stretch yourself, intentionally place all of your attentional capacity on what it takes to perform well, you set yourself up to more likely get into the flow state. Both being mindful and the flow state involve an initial, intentional engagement with present-moment experience followed by a commitment to stay engaged with the experience of choice (i.e., whether watching your breath or keeping pace in a marathon race). Such an effort might result only in being mindful, which is about intentionally staying present to your choice of focus no matter how you feel or what thoughts arise. However, the intentional investment of attention on a particular task is also requisite to get into the flow state. Of course, there are no guarantees of ensuring such an experience arising.

The flow state is often is associated with the best performance. Often in the literature, flow is considered an elusive, magical state. We contend that you can achieve flow more easily with a mindful self-compassionate approach to training and performance. Once you are able to accept the constraints of your skill level you can opt to fully invest your attention in the present moment, on factors that will help you perform moment-to-moment. Flow or not, this is the best psychological recipe to set yourself up for optimize learning and performance.

Part III
Research and Future Directions

Chapter 14
Lessons from the Field: MMTS 2.0 Instructors' Insights Gained

This chapter is based on reflections of all of the instructors who have offered MMTS 2.0 and provides suggestions and insights about running MMTS 2.0 with a group or team of your choice. (The list of MMTS 2.0 instructors, with their background in mindfulness meditation and self-compassion training are listed in Appendix H). Prior to writing this book, we had mentored each of the other instructors (meaning via in person, Skype or Zoom sessions, talking through each module) prior to their teaching MMTS 2.0. We hope that this chapter provides a similar support to you. We have grouped their responses together with our own suggestions by theme. We hope that this chapter will answer most of your questions as you embark on teaching MMTS 2.0.

Recommendations for Preparing to Run MMTS 2.0

Normalize Experience of Meditation

It is challenging to practice meditation. Expect that the athletes will struggle the most with thinking that they are *bad meditators* and that meditation is not for them. This is typical reaction. It can be very helpful to normalize this reaction up front. You might even discuss the challenge for you, as you started your own practice.

You can anticipate a lot of expectation and judgment from the participants about how one "should" meditate. There is shared, mainstream idea that meditation should be relaxing and you should have a quiet mind, all the time. You know that this is not true, yet this is what most people new to meditation will expect. We offer you the mediation cycle a few times throughout the book. It can be very helpful to start with discussing the meditation cycle, when you first introduce mindfulness meditation, and emphasizing how *all* parts of the meditation cycle are meditating. The focus of the meditation, the mind wandering, noticing mind wandering, accepting mind wandering, relaxing, and re-attending to the focus of the meditation are all part of meditating. It can be very helpful to normalize the fact that everyone's mind wander.

Anticipate Athletes' Critical Judgment of Their Meditation Abilities

No matter how much you try to emphasize that it is OK to have unintentional thinking arise when meditating, you can expect that the participants will get into a judgmental and evaluation mode about how their meditation is going. Expect the question: *Am I doing this right?* And expect them to feel like they are doing it wrong.

Remind them that there is no right or wrong level of activity in their minds, but instead the meditation practice is about becoming aware and accepting what is showing up. This point needs to be offered over and over again.

> They will often be critical of themselves being critical! It is essential to normalize that this is a typical response to learning meditation. In addition, offering personal examples of accepting naturally occurring judging thoughts can be quite helpful.

For example, you are encouraged to remind them that that when they start meditating they might begin with the intention to focus on their breath. Inevitably, at some point, their minds will wander. In that moment of noticing, new meditators will often have thoughts like, *I am bad at this; I will never be able to do this; My mind is racing and I can't stop it; I am really bad at this!; This should not be happening.* It is a very normal thing to have such uninvited thoughts. When we talk about non-judgment, we are not suggesting that you should never have judging thoughts! You must make judgments, sometimes. This non-judging suggestion comes in both when we are not having "judging" thoughts and when we are. It is our relationship, our ability to be accepting or tolerant of such unwanted thoughts, that is the key to practicing with a non-judging mind state. You can learn to stop judging your judging, automatic thoughts! Also, a great value in learning to accept uninvited judging thoughts: When you can accept your initial, uninvited "judging", you can become more discerning and make better judgments.

Importance of Group Size

For those instructors that had some variation in the size of their group, session to session, it became clear that a group size ranging from six to eight participants would be ideal. A few of us had experiences with larger sessions (up to 20) and smaller (as small as 3). When the group is smaller, about eight or under, it allows for athletes to talk and ask the questions that they need to get the most out of the group. Sebastian described the importance of being able to "cater to struggles" . There can be benefits to larger groups in terms of energy, yet when too big, all the questions in the room cannot be addressed in the relatively short intervention format.

Predictably there will be many questions about the ideas offered in the program by the participants. Participants will have many questions about how to implement the ideas for themselves, in their sport or performance realm. They will ask questions about their internal experience, resources, and the demands of the performance environment. If possible, it is ideal to keep the group small enough to be able to address questions that emerge. Though, if not possible, we also have found that often the questions that are being asked are questions that are held by many of the participants. As long as you make sure to hold the ten minutes for discussion after each practice, the pressing questions can be addressed.

30-Minute Versus Longer Sessions?

We designed MMTS 2.0 to run over six-hours, to be offered in twelve thirty-minute sessions or six one-hour sessions. A few of the instructors have run the program in such varying length formats. For example, Ian noted,

> I taught golf teams separately. I taught two 30-minute sessions each week. That was awesome. It never felt overwhelming or too much (information) in one-day. We had a good balance of discussion about their application and introducing and practicing new skills.

For the Army Rangers, Ian offered seven sessions instead, which he broke into 45 to 60 minute sessions. He noted that, perhaps because of their discipline, "It was easy for them to stay locked into that block of time." He found that both ways worked for him, as the instructor, and his group of performers. Ian noted,

> I was impressed with how well they both worked. I liked that in the longer sessions, it was cool to be able to do a meditation, discuss, and then do another one (meditation). However, I could imagine the longer duration being more of a challenge for many of the college teams I work with.

Either format works (six-one hour or twelve-thirty minute sessions). Yet, practically, the ability to run a program consistently for a sport team is contingent on how the coach values the program as well as how they are able schedule the time and space to run the program. We recommend that you go with what the coach wants and what they deem will work for their team. Regardless of thirty-minute to one-hour session format, the most important aspect of making sure that MMTS 2.0 is successful is to confirm time and space with the coach, group leader(s), and participants prior to beginning.

Connection with Gatekeeper: Involve the Coach(es)

If you are working with a team, invite the coach(es) to participate. We have found that when coaches opt to participate that the program runs much more smoothly. And, conversely, when they do not it is very difficult to confirm consistent times to meet and adherence to the program is less consistent. When the coach sets the schedule and opts to participate, in all cases thus far, the schedule remains set and there is much higher athlete participation (i.e., they show up each session). The participation rate for attendance mirrors that of practice, the athletes show up without question when the coach does too.

However, if the coach attends then the sessions must *count* as a practice time for NCAA schools. The MMTS 2.0 sessions would then be considered mandatory and countable hour of sport participation. Therefore, the choice to hold MMTS 2.0 training in their practice time often demonstrates greater buy in to the program, but can be challenging at many times of the year. While working with the coach(es) to determine the optimal time and approach, an alternative to consider when all mandatory sport hours are already allotted is to allow the team members to choose to engage in the training voluntarily at a predetermined time. In these cases the coaches would not be able to attend but could be trained in a separate coach(es) session each week.

Know Your Athletes, Their Sport, & Team Dynamics

Consider your audience. Spend time with the head coach and players before you start offering the program. Relationship building is essential. If possible, get to know administrators as well. One of the instructors was asked to meet seven times with the head coach and staff prior to getting a green light to start the program. This may not be necessary (or possible in most cases), but it highlights the importance to get to know the sport culture that you are stepping into. Anecdotally, running MMTS 2.0 has been more successful when the instructor had previously established rapport and trust with their group.

Thus, if the group is new to you, you will need to focus on rapport building. MMTS 2.0 will bring most athletes out of their comfort zone, so it is important that they can trust you to make it tolerable and safe for them in the difficult or challenging moments. Ian, Sebastian, and Rob all noted that it was important that they each knew their athletes and/or sport well.

For the German site (Sebastian's), there was some difficulty in translating the term of self-compassion to an appropriate German phrase. We expect that this is symbolic of the need to know your group, sport, coaches, and team culture and adjust and adapt as necessary to ensure that the program resonates with your group. It is also pertinent to get to know the athletes and the sport so both in the teaching and discussion segments you can offer examples that resonate, ones that are sport specific. Specifically, you can help tailor the ideas of mindfulness and self-compassion to your athletes, to help them apply the lessons learned to their own sport reactions, responses, and behaviors. Connecting the training to task-relevant and team-specific examples is a powerful way to help demonstrate how athletes can take mindfulness off the cushion and into their sport.

Attune Yourself: Do the MMTS 2.0 Meditations

The instructors agreed that it was very important to get comfortable with each of the exercises. Even though all of them had had previous mindfulness meditation experience, having attended a range of related workshops and retreats, they found that it was important to practice meditation. Ian noted, "I did 10 or 15 minutes of meditation (Self-compassion, or LKM) before participants entered the room." Others' practice was more closely tied to the given module. Some instructors used the meditation practice of the day to prepare them to teach. For example, Rob stated,

> I wanted to be attuned to myself when doing meditation. I wanted to make sure that I was experiencing the meditation. I tried to use an embodied teaching style to help participants engage more wisely with the program. I practiced the exercises myself to live and embody.

Some of the instructors would audio-record each of the activities that they were going to lead and practiced with the recording. Others worked with a colleague, who was attending the sessions, and they took turns leading one another other through the meditations. All of them would practice meditation prior to leading each session. As best you can, do whatever you need to do to get yourself into a poised, focused teaching mind state. All of us studied each module, knowing the rhythm of the session. We prepared ourselves via studying, meditating, and thinking about how we could tailor the sessions to the needs of our athletes.

Attend Mindfulness-Based Workshops

We all attended a number of mindfulness-based workshops and thus exposed ourselves to different mindfulness teachers. We found this helpful to witness and experience different leaders' styles. This helped both with having a deeper understanding of mindfulness as well as experiencing (not just knowing) that offering the training and meditations can be done successfully in a variety of personal styles. It doesn't have to be one way. Ian notes,

> Ideally, work with different meditation teachers and expose yourself to various different styles so you don't get stuck trying to teach like someone else, but rather can bring your own unique voice and style into the structure that MMTS 2.0 provides. That balance brings it to life and makes it rigorous at the same time.

It is important to teach it in a way that resonates for you, not just mimicking someone else's style. There are many resources to learn ways of teaching mindfulness, from on-line free meditations, webinars, and in-person workshops, which can provide a wide exposure to teachers and styles. If you cover the core ideas, have your own meditation practice and teach from the heart, you will be setting yourself up to offer a good program.

Make Transfer to the Athletic Realm Clear and Up Front

Making the connection between the mindfulness and self-compassion exercises and performance for your group is essential. Though this seems logical and obvious, offering this clear connection (i.e., application to life) does not happen in most mainstream mindfulness-based interventions. Even before you begin your first session, consider the sport that you will be offering the program: consider the typical challenges and need for concentration, engagement, and coping with distraction (to distress) in that sport and be prepared to offer examples of how the ideas of MMTS 2.0 can translate *directly* to the given sport. The more clearly you can explain the potential benefit to performance, transfer to athletic realm, the more quickly you will get buy-in into the program.

Yet, do not feel like to you have to be an expert in their sport. Ian's experience with a group of Army Best Ranger competitors speaks to this. He had little to no understanding of the grueling competition these soldiers were preparing for, but spent time with them learning about the demands of both training and competition, watching prior competition videos, and asking them about how the MMTS 2.0 lessons translated into their performance domain. Allowing them to teach him how mindfulness was critical to their performance may have provided the added benefits of enhancing both their autonomy and commitment to the program.

Teacher-Practitioner Model

Make the program your own. If you call the program you run MMTS 2.0, it is important to stay true to sharing the core ideas and activities in the program (at least 90% of what we offer). But whether you run all six sessions as outlined in the appendix or opt to use only part of the program and name it something else, take ownership of what you are offering. For example, Ian noted that he used his own sport stories and examples (in making the ideas come alive – from theory to meaningful application to the sport). He used his own style and tailored the program to the needs of his athletes. Ian noted adjusting the rhythm and emphasis for a men's collegiate team, a women's collegiate team, and the Army Ranger team.

Adapting to the needs of the group and the individual is essential. The athletes (or performers) need to feel met along the way. I (Amy) recall one athlete who was concerned about offering himself self-compassion when he did not need it. We spent almost all of a ten-minute discussion segment on this one concern. I confirmed that he was wise. How to best attend to our distress varies. It is like the need to turn up or down the flow through a water spigot: sometimes you need to turn up the intensity (to help with performance) and sometimes you need to turn it down. Having the tool of self-compassion on hand is invaluable, but it is not meant to be used in all instances! If you need to turn down the aversive impact of performance distress, self-compassion is a gift. You need self-compassion when your negative self-talk, harsh internal critic, or negative emotions are running so strongly that you are distracted from being present and making the most of what is in front of you. This athlete was right. Sometimes you don't need to offer yourself kindness. And sometimes you do. It depends. And having the option and skill to use it can be invaluable.

Trevor suggests using examples of professional athletes who use a mindfulness approach to help them with performance. Retired NBA superstar Kobe Bryant offers a quote that Trevor used which resonated with the athletes. "When my 'obnoxious roommate' knocks on the door in my head, I've found it's better just to let him in. If you try to tune him out, he just bangs louder. If you let him in, he sits down, watches TV and shuts up." Trevor's inspiration of using examples of professional athletes and Kobe Bryant's quote came from a presentation on the delivery and effectiveness of the MAC program (Wolanin and Gross 2017, August). When he discussed concepts of acceptance and explaining how thought suppression can amplify performance distress, the athletes were able to use Kobe's quote to draw a connection to their own performance. Additionally, Trevor found that sharing examples of how professional athletes adopted a mindfulness approach also contributed to the athletes' quick buy-in of the program.

Read the Chapters Ahead of Time

This book can be of great support to you. Read the chapters that are relevant to each module ahead of time. Trevor stated, "I had the chance to read the chapters ahead of time to prepare for teaching each module of MMTS. It made me more confident going into each session and I felt like I was able to answer any questions that the athletes had."

Tips from Instructors About Running MMTS 2.0

Meeting Athletes Where They Are: Moving to Presence

Typically, competitive athletes are in a high stress environment. Rob noted, as did other instructors, the challenge of the players' schedules and how it would impact their state of mind as they entered the sessions, "Players would come in late, (with a range of energy levels, from) deflated to having extremely high energy." Rob noted that his intention was to help them develop a wise relationship to their own experience and be more present with themselves. Rob encouraged his athletes to make some mental space for what they were learning. The phrase he used that resonated with his attendees: "Stop shoving ten pounds into five pound bag." MMTS 2.0 can offer the participants a way for them to provide themselves a little ease which can ultimately help with performance. Sometimes ease is better than more pressure, more information.

The intention of the program is first to help the athletes bring awareness to their experience. Whether collegiate, elite, or a professional athlete or performer, Rob reflected, "It is typical for their minds to be going a thousand different places and it is hard to just get to the exhale." Athletes are often future oriented, which can cause anxiety. Or they can be equally past-oriented, filled with regret for making a mistake, losing, suffering an injury to a decision a coach made. The challenge in teaching MMTS 2.0 is to help them into the present, with one breath at a time.

This won't mean stopping the highly active mind or emotional responses. But, instead, the settling into the present moment can offer information through the awareness. For example, when athletes are able to create some space (with so much going on) they are able to bring into their awareness what they most need. They could realize things like, *I need to sleep, I need to go to the trainer,* or *I need to have a conversation with friend.* Without creating this space, the precise thing that they need to do to improve performance, improve the quality of their experience or to reduce their distress is simply unknown, thus ignored.

Encourage Physical Comfort

Regardless of when MMTS 2.0 is taught, it will be an additional demand in the lives of the participants and they will have physical needs that they should be encouraged to meet. We have offered the program in early morning, mid-afternoon, early evening, and evening time slots. We recommend doing all that you can to make the experience as physically comfortable and nurturing as possible. Encourage the participants to attend to their physical needs, which can include eating, drinking water, icing body parts that need it, or simply putting their legs up, if needed. This creates a more at-ease environment that invites self-care. In essence, the external environment you help create for the participants should mirror the internal environment that you are helping them nurture within themselves. They can notice discomfort and make choices to offer themselves ease.

Consider Space, Time-of-Day, and Logistics

As best you can, provide a safe space. If you run the hour program, book your space for two hours – including a thirty-minute cushion before and after the program. That way, if athletes like, they can come a bit early or stay late to ask questions, settle in, or savor what they are learning. Some of the most poignant, teachable moments have been when the athletes engage with the instructor in a brief five or ten (or thirty) minute discussion before or after the given module. Rob encourages you to have a dedicated space. "It is hard to land the plane, when people are coming in right on top of you. Create a safe container for the work."

When to offer the program? Given the many pros and cons of each possible time slot in the day, it is a toss-up. The end of practice could be beneficial: Just like the meditation portion of a yoga class comes at the end of the physical portion of the typical yoga class, engaging in MMTS 2.0 post-practice may add a similar benefit. This time segment offers the athletes a chance to let things settle after high energy, high challenge practices. On the other hand, Ian emphasized the benefit of running the sessions before practice,

> I ran all of my sessions prior to practice and one of our teams now does five minutes of meditation prior to every practice. I like the ability to center oneself and be present before beginning practice so they can maximize their time and reps. I prefer this, when possible because student-athletes are more alert, less distracted, and it allows them to immediately put lessons learned into action.

Practically, the best time will be when the coach can schedule six or twelve consecutive, secured meeting times!

Embody the Practice: Model It

When teaching the ideas of mindfulness and self-compassion, perhaps one of the most important tasks as the instructor is to hold a clear intention to model these ideas. For example, if you don't present an idea clearly or you make some other mistake, being willing to notice it, talk about how it made you feel and what you most need to do for yourself to move on – and do it – offers one of many ways you can model the program in action. Bob noted the importance of "having a presence in the room to model what it means to be present here and now".

Bob talked about the need to "actively use techniques that are used in MMTS" to address challenges and unexpected opportunities that arise when working with a group. He noticed the benefit to the athletes when the instructor both used the MMTS practices and modeled being present.

Adjust as Needed

It is important to know that no matter how well prepared you are, you will need to be able to adjust along the way. You will find that you will be called to make changes based on the needs or schedules of the group. Sebastian noted: "Adapting and adjusting was key. Athletes' schedules required dispersing the six weekly sessions over four months instead of two. I had to add several one-on-one sessions to make up for missed group sessions when players were travelling to tournaments." In the end, meeting athletes where they were in their high-performance career will enhance the program's efficacy.

It is essential that you get a read on your athletes or group and adjust to how they are feeling and responding. For example, all of the exercises are slated for a ten-minute segment. You may opt to have some of the exercises or meditations run a bit shorter or longer. And sometimes, due to critical conversations, you may have to wisely leave a practice or topic for the next session. Meeting the athletes or participants by listening to what they want to focus on, noticing their resistance or great interest and honoring them is essential for MMTS 2.0 to be optimized.

> Rob encourages you to:
> Be prepared to constantly adjust. Some will come late, some will leave early.
> It never goes as planned.

Bob reflects, "Once in the room, with the team, whatever plan you have made is great and being able to commit to what works for the athletes, you must adjust. Inevitably there will be different reactions for different teams (e.g., political issues; internal team factors). Being able to acknowledge what is happening (is essential) to be aligned with the team."

I (Amy) recall asking a group of athletes how they felt about doing a concentration exercise (the breathing ladder). One athlete noted that she opted to simply stop doing the activity in the middle of the exercise. At first I hesitated in how best to respond. I had to adapt. Of course I wanted her to want to practice, but I had to accept the reality. She did not. I congratulated her for honoring herself, knowing what she most needed in that moment. And this is true of self-care – an essential aspect of self-compassion.

Sometimes you need to stop and take a break even when all of those around you are surprised and inconvenienced by your choice. I thanked her for trying the activity and opting to do what was best for her in the moment. The athlete's initial comment could have de-railed the session – a team leader clearly opting out. Instead, by agreeing with her and noticing, genuinely, the importance of self-care, the session continued in a good direction. Those who wanted to stay engaged could opt to do so and no one was pressured to participate in any particular activity.

We have to model and support being mindful and compassionate to ourselves and others throughout the program to optimize the intent and benefit of MMTS 2.0. Though it is not always clear how to facilitate the discussion, having the intention to help cultivate mindfulness and self-compassion in the participants – with the goal to help with performance – offers the aspirational ideal for the facilitators.

Helping Athletes Transfer Ideas to the Field, to Their Lives

Teaching the ideas of the program and the meditation practices are challenging. Yet, helping the individual athlete transfer the ideas from the program and the lessons learned through the meditation practices to their lives outside the classroom space is of utmost importance. One way to do this is offer to do very brief intervention with a member of a MMTS group, just as the issue arises. Often if you can help one athlete in the room – for example transfer the ideas from the practice of meditation to having control over their urge to throw a racquet or skip out on studying for exams – can impact everyone else in the room, in a constructive way. Bob summarizes this by encouraging instructors to, "Be willing to do loose interventions with athletes. Help them figure out how they are going to use new skill, how they can take it out of the room and use it on their own through out the week. The transfer piece is essential. Whether to academics, to the athletic field."

Modify Length of Recommended Practice, Out of Session

It may be important to figure out how to help increase independent practice on the part of your team or group. So far the research on MMTS indicates that the athlete participants have a relatively low compliance to their meditation practice, outside of the instructor-led session. Trevor experimented with recommending using short practices. His athletes were interested. He reflects, "What I think would be very helpful if we can get the athletes to practice just one to three minuets a day. For some, starting with ten minutes may be very difficult. In their very hectic schedule they might be more likely to engage in a brief, non-formal mindfulness practice, like walking to practice. If you can get them to practice the meditation cycle and commit to it, it might make a big difference. That way they don't have to sit and do a formal meditation." After offering the short practice option, his athletes actually increased their listening to the 10-minute audio recording.

Discussion Segment of MMTS 2.0.

MMTS 2.0 is broken up into roughly twelve thirty-minute sessions of ten minutes of information, ten minutes of mindfulness and self-compassion-based practices/meditations, and ten minutes of discussion. Two of the six-hours of the program is dedicated to discussion. This portion of the program is designed to give you space to tailor the focus to the needs of the group, on any given day. Ian noted, "I found it [the discussion segment] provided a clear foundation and by not trying to oversell anything, instead I could let the athletes' experiences speak for themselves."

The discussion is similar to running a one-on-one session with an athlete as a sport psychology practitioner/counselor. The questions, comments, and reflections of the group direct the conversation's content and tone. We were surprised many times by what the athletes were getting out of the session and the personal questions that would be posed. We would do our best each moment to follow and offer support, no matter what.

Ian noted, "I loved the discussion piece and allowed them to take over the application. When they used it and how they applied it. It was up to them to make direct link into their performance." Though the skills were the same per session, the actual application of the ideas by the athletes was very different. The athletes were able to tailor the application of the ideas on their own and, at once, be supported by both the instructor and the other athletes in the group. Sebastian discussed how the power of having these discussions allows you to both process the activity you just did and notice how the participants experience the same thing quite differently. And it is this moment of personalizing the material that brings it alive for the athletes: they figure out how sitting in meditation can help them respond differently to a bad call by a referee, missing a pass, to learning to respond differently to persistent internal harsh self-criticism.

Be Prepared for Resistance

The more familiar you are with the ideas of mindfulness and self-compassion, the more normal these ideas seem to you. Yet for many collegiate and elite athletes, the application of mindfulness and self-compassion is not yet mainstream (if you check out our sport psychology textbooks, there is very little attention on mindfulness and none on self-compassion). For novel concepts that are not part of the typical approach to mental toughness training, be prepared for resistance to the meditation practices. Sebastian notes, "Be prepared that some of the athletes will have trouble grasping concepts compared the ease with which many athletes can easily understand, say, psychological skills training."

We recommend for any group that you (as best you can) practice a non-judgment and non-expectance approach. Once rapport was built, the instructors were consistently surprised and impressed by how open their groups and teams were engaged in the program. You offer the best that you can and trust that understanding will build through practice and discussion.

What Instructors Liked About MMTS 2.0 Design

Clear Format and Structure/Balance of Didactic and Practice

The instructors seemed to like that the program was clearly laid out. The program is set up to offer ten minutes of each: 1) Content, 2) Practice, and 3) Discussion (10–10-10). Ian noted,

> I really benefited and so did the whole group from the clear format, structure. Having the lay out for all six sections helped me and helped the athletes who participated. They knew what was coming.

The instructors reported that some players wanted more experience and more talking about their experience in the program. And other athletes noted that they would like more didactic and more neuroscience based teaching. Certainly more time could be spent on any of these areas, but the time constraints for most competitive athletes is a motivator for us to keep the program in its current design and length.

Walking Meditation (Soles of the Feet Exercise)

Many of the athletes liked the walking meditation. They liked the idea of getting the benefit from a mindfulness meditation practice in a more active format. Some athletes reported that having a way to physically calm themselves was helpful, other than focusing on their breath. Sometimes focusing on the breath can be more problematic than helpful when the athlete's breathing is disrupted by distress.

When teaching this meditation practice, we suggest that you try it two or three times, at varying paces. In one session, I (Amy) responded to an athlete who noted that the pace that I had led was simply too slow: he felt like he was going to fall over. So, in an effort to follow what the athletes wanted, we tried the activity as a group again at a much quicker pace. A second athlete then commented that the second pace was too fast. So we tried it one more time, inviting each athlete to pick their own area to walk at their own pace. After the activity, we were able to talk about the value of tailoring this practice (and all of activities) to each athlete, whenever possible. We then had a chance to talk about where in practice and competition they could use the walking meditation. This meditation practice can easily be adapted into an active, intentional practice to get centered, getting grounded in one's body, while in the midst of competition (e.g., focusing on the soles of your feet as a tennis player from the point of picking up a ball at the net to turning to take the next serve at the baseline).

Breathing Ladder and Pyramid
The athlete participants consistently noted that they liked these concentration meditations. The focused concentration practices were more enjoyable and more engaging than the open mindfulness meditation practices for most of the participants. This is not surprising. These excises are naturally engaging and give metrics (i.e., you know if you count and how many times) that can be used to measure improvement — an act practiced regularly by most competitive athletes. You can also set these concentration practices to instigate more attention by making it a bit competitive between participants with prompts like, *Let's see who doesn't lose track of their counting and breath* or *Let's see who doesn't have to start over*. In addition, such concentration exercises are less provocative. The goal is to focus on the count and breath and to intentionally *not* pay attention to other experiences that emerge (i.e., distressful unintentional thinking). With these concentration practices, athletes will experience some break from their critical minds. Emphasizing the benefit of *strengthening concentration* is important to do in this exercise.

In for Me, Out for You (Loving Kindness Meditation)
When athletes are taught to be mentally tough, the traditional way, and turn away from knowing their true thoughts and feelings, they lose out on information that could help them move to higher ground. This loving kindness based meditation offers a way for the participants to actively offer themselves what they might need most in the given moment (e.g., they can breathe in peace, ease, safety, confidence) and then they also can practice generosity toward someone else (e.g., they can breathe out to a teammate sending them steadiness, courage, to ease). One of the instructors reported how when an athlete was able to offer herself kindness when struggling with a sick mother that she was able to truly face what was going on. And through this activity she became clear on some actions she needed to take to offer her mother the support that she needed (and the support she needed for herself). Bob noted that it "Helped with greater communication. It gave everyone a common language to talk about what is challenging to them and how to work with it. In sport, (he summarizes) this is not generally allowed."

MMTS 2.0 Audio Files

In the studies of MMTS 2.0, the scripts in the Appendix of this text were audiotaped and posted online for the athletes to access. When running the program, we encourage you to do the same. Some of the badminton athletes reported using these mindfulness meditation audio-files in preparation for matches. Sebastian found that some of these same athletes also reported using the mindfulness audios for falling asleep or general relaxation. The scripts that are in the appendix were designed for the tennis team study. We encourage you to modify the language so it is tailored to fit your group or team.

Conceptual Ideas in Action

Normalizing Distress

Athletes often experience distress due to pressure, expectations, self-judgment, coach feedback to audience response to their performance. Yet, in very few instances does anyone help normalize this universal experience of performance dukkha. Bob stated, "The most important aspect of program is normalizing distress. This is the piece of common humanity. You are not alone. This was transformative. It allowed people to be more authentic and honest about what they needed and could access out of the program. Being willing to use self-disclosure in an appropriate way. It sets up the environment that it is OK to talk about (sport distress) and do activities that will help the participants cope with it."

Value of Self-Compassion: Root of Courage

The idea of bringing self-compassion to sport to help optimize performance is a relatively new idea. Encouraging athletes to notice moments of sport suffering and to offer themselves some soothing through an image, a phrase or a behavior was, to some participants, a radically new idea. Most athletes are encouraged to ignore signs of distress and to *just focus on the next point* or *next play*. Using self-compassion for sport distress to **turn-up courage** was a new way for the sport psychology practitioners to help their athletes to be more mentally tough. Group after group of athletes resonated with the idea of self-compassion, after they learned how it could be applied to sport. Sebastian noted that, *The idea of self-compassion hit home*. Being able to discuss harsh internal self-talk on another level was found useful and beneficial. Trevor reported that sharing the connection of self-compassion to courage reflected the most poignant moments in his teaching MMTS. He recalls one of the athletes in his program stating, "I never knew I could have so much courage through caring for myself."

Ian also found that both the collegiate golfers and Army Rangers greatly benefited from being introduced to the idea of self-compassion. He was able to offer a clear pathway to his athletes/performers for them to use it in performance:

> I was amazed at how powerfully self-compassion resonated across the board. The phrase self-compassion can sound soft and be easily dismissed by high performers, but when I introduced it as the *root of courage*, the skill that leads to increased learning and the willingness to push the comfort zone and grow…there was incredible buy in. They shared very openly about their self-critic and the power of self-compassion for overcoming obstacles and getting back to the task at hand, both in meditation and in sport.

Self-compassion was introduced as the root of courage. Offering oneself self-compassion is a way to accept mistakes and to continue to learn and master the given craft. Ian noted,

Ian also offered the program to Army Rangers. He noted that the top performers talked about how powerful applying self-compassion would be within their competition. These competitions include very little sleep over three days of grueling physical activity (swimming, running, marching, climbing, weight lifting and carrying, night orienteering, and much more). Mistakes are bound to happen. For example,

> "Buy-in was incredible. That was the single most powerful thing that they took from it (MMTS 2.0), applying self-compassion."

they receive scores for marksmanship (target shooting) and knot tying while experiencing extreme muscle fatigue. Their ability to fully accept themselves in the moment is critical so that they do not get mentally derailed from the task at hand. The Army Rangers noted the benefit of implementing self-compassion in their competition as a way for them to address potential distractions before it became problematic. Rob also reported that the idea of self-compassion may have been the most important aspect of MMTS 2.0. When we asked Rob what was the most poignant moment teaching, he quickly replied,

> I get goose bumps thinking about the impact of self-compassion on the athletes and coaches: the self-compassion piece is woven throughout the whole program. There is cueing of kindness and warmth to one's own experience throughout the program…At first (one of the) coach(es) was worried that we were letting people off the hook. But the expectations (of the athletes' effort, their performance) remained the same. Learning how to use self-compassion, the athletes learned how to shift with how they were dealing with mistakes and they were more willing to take some chances.[35]

The collegiate basketball players essentially developed a strong sense of poise, they were more steady when dealing with errors and willing to take more risks in practice and games.

What Do you Need to Hear, Most?

In module four, there is a self-compassion exercise in which the athlete is asked to recall, through a visualization prompt, a difficult memory in sport. Prior to starting the exercise, they are asked to come up with a phrase: *What they most needed to hear in that past difficult moment.* They are instructed to come up with the phrase and prepare to offer it to themselves prior to engaging in the activity. Rob reflected, *What did you most need to hear was a mind blower. It offers athletes a way to handle possible mistakes.* We have found that athletes often internalize many different coaches and stakeholders in their development, and often such voices are harsh.

Labeling

The concept of labeling (i.e., offering a word or phrase to note the arising of thought, emotion, sound, or physical sensation) is new and unfamiliar to many athletes. In all of the groups, some athletes struggled with the labeling exercise (i.e., noticing unwelcome thoughts, feelings, and/or body sensations and creating some space between the experience and awareness via naming the experience). Do expect pushback from athletes but to still continue the labeling exercises. Some of the discomfort with the activity is simply learning to become aware of uninvited, unwelcome thoughts and feelings.

A consistent challenge that emerged in one group included the question of what to do when your mind is racing and full of thoughts. *How do you label such a flood of thinking?* Well, it depends. For formal meditation (e.g., during sitting mindful meditation), the practice of labeling can be simply to note the thoughts that arise and intentionally label them as "thinking," silently. It may be a ten-minute meditation of you bringing to mind the word "thinking", over and over again, as the mind receives uninvited thought after uninvited thought.

When in life (i.e., off the proverbial meditation mat), say before or during practice, you may still note "thinking" or you might just notice the pattern of flooding thoughts, accept it (or just tolerate, depending how difficult it is), and then intentionally bring your attention back to what you are doing in practice. So, practically, you want to encourage the athlete, when in sport practice or performance, to notice their distracting, uninvited thoughts and then intentionally shift away from them to points of focus that will help with performance. This is not an act of avoiding, but instead, an act of acceptance and choice.

In many ways the moment of labeling a thought is the point in the meditation cycle that trains your mind to learn how to respond differently during practice or performance, when you become aware of the mind wandering. You don't just stay in that moment of noticing the mind wandering while meditating. Instead, you shift your attention back to what you had intended to focus on for the meditation. For the labeling meditation, it is back to noticing the next thought that arises and holding it

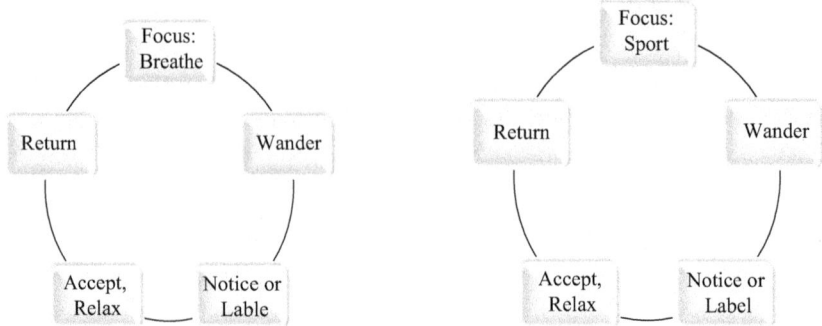

Fig. 14.1 Connection between meditation and performance

with interest, awareness. (For other meditation, the focus of the meditation may be the soles of your feet; your breath; the sound).

The same holds true for applying the idea of mindfulness to training or performance. Once aware of the wandering, distracted mind of uninvited thoughts, you can label them or bring awareness to them and then intentionally re-focus and get back to the business of your sport practice. This connection – meditation to performance – is critical to establish and continue to emphasize throughout the MMTS 2.0 program Fig. 14.1.

Non-Judgmental Approach

It is hard to explain this idea of a non-judgmental approach, so we offer you a brief overview of our understanding of how to explain this approach. The idea of non-judgmental approach does not mean having no judgment (we all judge, a lot!). And the non-judgmental approach means a very different thing when meditating and when living our lives off the meditation cushion. Let's be realistic, we all must make judgments throughout the day.

For formal meditation, the idea is to practice accepting all that shows up in your meditation experience, including judgments! It could sound something like this, *My coach doesn't believe in me and that means that I will not start this season; I will never be skilled enough to be in the lineup for the travel team.* These both are judgments. In a meditation practice, the idea would be to be aware of such thoughts and accept them (not judge them!). And if thoughts show up, *I should not think like that!*, you can practice accepting or tolerating such judgy thoughts as well.

In contrast, the practical application of a non-judgmental approach to our experience when practicing or competing is to learn to first be aware of what is showing up (e.g., *my coach really does not believe in me!),* accepting that this thought is arising and then decide to do something about it (i.e., the judgment might offer some insight into necessary action) or not. It might mean that you need to try harder in practice, you need to talk to the coach, or you need do nothing more than allow the thought to come and go.

Helping athletes understand how the idea of non-judgment applies to both formal meditation practice and on the athletic field and how to use it wisely is an important part of the program. Again, this will have to be touched on throughout the program to gain traction for the participants. When awareness of how to work with internal judgments strengthens, it can have powerful ramifications for helping athletes learn not to take each judgmental thought that arises so seriously. In summary:

- Judgments happen: They are normal, human and necessary.
- When practicing mindfulness-based meditation the practice includes allowing all to emerge including thoughts, feelings, physical sensations (even uninvited thoughts of judgments) and to attend to it all with interest.
- Judgments are necessary for making good choices through the day.
- In normal living, you can be aware of the mindful space where you can allow all information to be considered (including uninvited judging thoughts) before you make wise choices (i.e., judgments) about how to move forward.

Open Awareness Versus Concentration Meditations

There is a continuum within meditation approaches, from single pointed awareness (and blocking everything else out) to open awareness where all lived experience, everything, is in play. We intentionally start MMTS 2.0 with a concentration practice, of focusing on the breath. Both types of practices are helpful. Our experience has been that athletes tend to like the concentration practice. It is easier emotionally to do. With the single pointed focus, there is a clear goal (e.g., only notice the sensation of breathing). Athletes have a clear task, something to focus on, and can experience the positive feelings that accompany succeeding at a clear, short-term goal.

In contrast, the open mindfulness meditation practices can be more difficult to understand. How do you really sit in your awareness and observe thoughts that arise? And how do you know what to notice? And what do I do with the crazy monkey mind activity that is on fire in my mind? In sum, the open-awareness is a lot for the players to sit with, including awareness of sound, thoughts, physical sensations, and feelings. Yet the open awareness practice mimics what happens in practice and performance; the athlete is bombarded by information.

The formal mindfulness meditation practice helps athletes learn to be aware and tolerant of what really is showing up in their awareness. And in learning to be in this space, they realize that instead of automatically reacting to thoughts and feelings that show up (e.g., the strong urge to quit in the last 500 meters of a 5 K race), they can choose to respond wisely to what shows up.

Building Internal Capacity

Though we have written in detail about the value that the instructors found in the self-compassion portion of the program, we are emphasizing a benefit that can come from the intention to offer oneself self-compassion. Rob conceptualized the value of self-compassion well; he noted that the practice of self-compassion can help the athlete build internal capacity. Instead of the athlete looking for external validation and support (which often they do not or cannot get in key moments) they instead can learn to take back the power and offer themselves what they most need. Rob phrased it like this: *I may not get what I need but I can give myself what I need.*

Internal Capacity from Self-Compassion:

I may not get what I need but I can give myself what I need.

Building this internal capacity is woven through the program and directly emphasized in session four, when the athletes are asked to practice by offering themselves, retrospectively, what they most needed to hear in a past difficult sport moment. This activity offered the athlete the chance to direct self-compassion toward themselves and practice receiving such kindness, directed toward their own experience. Rob stated, "I was blown away by their courage (to bring up difficulty) and then come up with something to provide self-compassion for themselves."

The instructor can be quite helpful in providing space and support to create a *go-to phrase* when the memory of the difficulty arises in sport. As the athlete prepares to offer themselves phrases of self-compassion, while recalling moments they felt like giving up, you can offer them specific phrases that they can bring to mind. Such phrases could include: *The team needs me.* Or in moments when the athlete reports feeling overwhelmed, you might suggest: *It's not as bad as you think.* It doesn't matter how powerful or relevant the re-frame sounds to you or the others in the group, what matters is whether or not the words of kindness resonate with the athlete. They must believe that the thought or phrase could be soothing in such predictably threatening moments. Give them time to figure out the phrase that might work best for them.

Summary

MMTS 2.0 integrates some relatively new ideas with core Sport Psychology concepts. The topics, from an academic perspective, include concentration, mindfulness meditation practices, Buddhist mindfulness, Langerian mindfulness, flow, and self-compassion. Predictably you will feel stronger in some of these areas than others, as have all of the instructors who have offered MMTS 2.0. It is important to spend time getting familiar with the ideas both conceptually and developing some nimbleness with discussing how these concepts apply to specific athlete concerns and how they can help with performance. This is the art of sport and performance psychology. And this program adds the new challenge of integrating some of these newer ideas to sport performance. One instructor often questioned himself, "Sometimes it felt daunting to me to feel like I was doing it right. Am I inadequate here? How can I deliver it better?" We offer this quote to normalize the challenge of offering something new. The initial data on the program is indicating that the program works. Thank you reading this and best of luck running MMTS 2.0!

Chapter 15
The Road Ahead: Next Steps for Using Mindfulness in Sport

We hope that you have had some insights and found valuable practices that work for *you*. The goal of MMTS 2.0 and of this book is to offer a range of ideas, practices, and examples that will inspire you and offer you pathways toward enhanced:

- **Poise** (i.e., being able to handle a wide range of emotions),
- **Focus** on where you want to place your attention (driven by what you most value), and
- **Adaptability** to what is showing up, in the present, for improved opportunities to learn and perform better.

In this final chapter we hope to offer you *our* top list of take-aways from this book. If you opt to use a mindful-self-compassionate approach to leverage better performance and improve the quality of your internal experience, we offer you the following big ideas. Here's our top ten, *what-we-most-hope-that-you-will-take-with-you* list.

You Do Not Have to Meditate to Be Mindful

Us declaring that you don't have to meditate seems like an unlikely first take-away from a book that is committed to sharing the details of a program that is using mindfulness meditation to help cultivate a mindful approach to performance. Yet we have found that sometimes just the idea of mindfulness and how mindfulness can be applied to the performance world can be enough to help nudge you into a much improved mind-state for preparing for, engaging, and recovering from practice and performance. For some people the information about mindfulness and self-compassion, the educational piece of MMTS 2.0 and introduction to the meditation practices, is all that it takes to help them tolerate negative emotions, bring their minds back from distraction, and get their mind and attention back on performance.

© Springer International Publishing AG 2017
A. Baltzell, J. Summers, *The Power of Mindfulness*,
https://doi.org/10.1007/978-3-319-70410-4_15

If you have read this book through to this point and never meditate another moment, you still have the information that:

- It is possible to notice uninvited thoughts and feelings and opt not to believe or react to them.
- You can have a busy mind and still opt to focus your attention on performance.
- You know the value of being present to what really is happening (Langerian mindfulness) versus performing like a robot (i.e., you have your mind made up what the outcome will be before you begin). Noticing novelty and nimbly adjusting is freeing and a performance accelerator.
- You don't have to react to the emotions you are having. Instead you can opt to respond to uninvited harsh thoughts and emotions *differently* than you have in the past.

If you opt to start meditating, wonderful! Current research is indicating that just a few minutes a day, for just a few times a week, can offer great benefits to training your brain to respond in a calmer more balanced way to threat and challenge.

You Don't Have to Be Confident

Most of us have been told countless times, *Just be confident, believe in yourself!* and, at the same time, had fear, dread, or simply a lack of confidence course through our bodies. Though confidence is great – and truly optimal to experience – it is possible to play well no matter how you feel (or what you are thinking). You cannot control your thoughts or your emotions in the moment. However, with a mindful and self-compassionate approach you can feel a wide range of emotions and still perform well if you are willing to:

- Face or notice the thoughts and emotions that are showing up. Just a brief reminder, *This is how anxiety feels* or *It is normal to feel like this* can be enough. You don't want to dwell, stick to such feelings. You can opt to allow them to show up and disappear without agreeing or getting caught up in them.
- Tolerate (accept or befriend) any feelings you are having (i.e., *It is OK to feel this way),* and
- Commit to keeping your attention (as much as possible) on tasks or points of focus that predictably can help with performing.

So the days you are feeling off, when it might feel like it is not your game or not your day, you have the choice. You can give into uninvited, unhelpful thoughts and feelings (and create a poor performance) or you can opt to notice the distracting, critical thoughts, and uncomfortable feelings as part of the normal part of being an athlete, or just a human being. You can choose to endure the unease of playing with low confidence and still be in the game!

Plan for Predictably Difficult Moments (What will you Need?)

Part of a mindful self-compassionate approach includes being aware of expected patterns of thoughts and feelings that you typically experience. When such familiar thought-feeling combos are occurring (e.g., surge of fear paired with *I can never win this one!)* it can result in a performance derailment. Sometimes, in such instances, all you can do is tolerate the wave of fear and bring our attention back to the field, the play, or our competitor in front of us. And yet, this is so hard to do!

If you have such typical patterns (like difficult feelings and thoughts right before a game starts) you can use this information to your advantage. *In advance* you can cultivate some wisdom when you identify such anticipated thought-feeling patterns *(I'll never be able to beat him!).* This is how it can work: Bring to mind a predictably challenging moment. Plan now, what you might most need to hear when that thought shows up. It might be simple yet powerful, like, *I am prepared, I still get to play, no matter what* or an image of a past memory or flash of an image of how you want to play. You can plan to soothe yourself a bit in such predictable moments so you can get back in the game, no matter how you feel.

All this is to say that with mindfulness – instead of avoiding typical thought patterns or emotions that show up – you can hold unpleasant thoughts and emotions in your awareness and be empowered to respond differently (better!). Once aware of them, it is wise to intentionally shift your attention to whatever will help you perform, in that moment. Before such a challenging moment occurs, in a quiet, non-pressured moment of reflection (i.e., right now) you can decide how you want to handle such predictably challenging moments in the future.

Self-Compassion: What Do you Most Need, Right Now?

We have offered the idea of self-compassion throughout this book, integrated both in the mindfulness-based practices as well as an integral consideration when considering how to help you optimize sport performance. Clearly, we all are not suffering all of the time – or even most of the time. We hope not! Yet, in the moments when you are experiencing personal suffering, a great question to ask yourself is: *What do I most need, right now?* And after you have asked this question, wait. See what answer shows up. And then do something about it, take action, and give yourself what you need.

The answer might be that you need to call someone who loves you, you may need to go for a walk, light a candle, drink a cup of tea, or go for a long, hard run. Learning to tune into yourself, to tune into what you most need, is a beautiful practice of self-care (especially when suffering), which leads to courage.

When you are able to give yourself what you need, you then are freed up to engage with what matters most to you. And in sport, this can mean going to practice and giving 100% effort even in front of a coach who doesn't believe in you to taking a risk to see how fast you can race when the stakes are high. You can offer yourself kindness – when it is needed – to serve as a catalyst for courage. And you can still be hard on yourself if it helps with performance! You can use the skill of self-compassion wisely, as you choose.

Benefits of a Mindfulness Approach in Performance

Less Reactivity A mindfulness approach offers many benefits. The first is to be more aware of what is happening (and not hide from or get too wrapped up in whatever that is). Because of this poised approach to staying present to what is happening (from barely tolerating to accepting and maybe even befriending) you will be less reactive. You can tolerate a bad call, sit on the bench a bit longer, choose to train when feeling exhausted. And in this ability to hold (i.e., to rest in the space between stimulus and response), to be mindful of what is happening, you have more information to decide how you want to handle the situation (instead of just thoughtlessly and mal-adaptively reacting).

More Concentration Cultivating a mindfulness approach is interesting. There is empirical evidence that practicing mindfulness helps you concentrate more effectively. We like to think of it from a different vantage point that, instead, a mindfulness approach helps you from getting caught up in the past (e.g., regret), the future (e.g., anxiety), or lost in mind wandering (e.g., day dreaming). A mindfulness approach helps you from getting lost in distractions and because of this your ability to concentrate improves.

Being mindful is about being present and having more influence of directing your attention and concentration where you opt to focus. Just like in a meditation practice, you can opt to focus on the breath, your bodily sensations, or sound. You may have noticed that with such practice when you intentionally want to place your attention on one of these points of focus, that you are better at noticing your mind wandering and bringing your attention back to the place you intended to hold it. And with practice and time, you might find that your mind wanders less. So whether mindfulness is helping you from getting lost in the distraction of mind activity or simply strengthening your capacity to concentrate, these both result in having more power to strengthen your attention. And as we noted, USOC Sport Psychologist Peter Haberl (2016) is known to say, "Attention is the psychological currency of performance."

Enhanced Adaptability to Whatever Shows Up One of the more exciting, and sport relevant benefits of a mindful approach is being able to be more nimble and adaptable to what is showing up. And this adjustability is essential for performance. Imagine for a moment that you are on a playing field housed in a snow globe that has been shaken up (i.e., imagine being in a snow globe!). You would not be able to see the signs or cues in your environment to adapt and adjust to what is showing up right in front of your eyes (i.e., the snow would be in your eyes!).

Fig. 15.1 How performance can improve with mindfulness

As you are able to accept and not follow the distracting stories that can pulse through your mind (e.g., *the coach hates me, I always lose here, this is so boring*) the metaphorical snowflakes start to settle down. Once your thoughts settle down, including your attachment to your thoughts, you can shift your attention to what is going on in the field. When you pair this with the Langerian curiosity to what is novel and new, you then can trust your well-trained skills and strategies, and adapt and adjust much more nimbly to what you can finally see. George Mumford's book, *The Mindful Athlete* is a wonderful resource for more information about creating poise in sport performance Fig. 15.1.

If you Decide to Meditate

There are many resources to learn about how to meditate. We encourage you to pursue the resources that you find compelling. Whether it is a meditation phone app (e.g., head space) to an excellent applied book on meditation practices (e.g., Ronald Siegel, *The Mindfulness Solution*) there are a few tips that may serve you in your exploration of integrating meditation into your weekly routine:

- It is normal to have an active mind when meditating. Really. It is not about stopping the thoughts. Meditation practice is about being present and accepting to whatever shows up, and in this case a busy, active mind.
- Meditation is *not* about stopping any feelings from arising. Instead the meditation practice is a formal way to learn to have a changed relationship (accepting with kindness) to whatever emotions show up.
- Any kind of meditation practice can be helpful.
- Any length of practice can be helpful (a few minutes to hours a day!).
- Practicing at the same time of day, in the same place, with a few physical reminders to practice can be helpful (e.g., a meditation cushion, a low table with a candle).
- Try to set up your meditation practice so it is compelling for you to continue. If you are deeply suffering or just irritated, you might opt to stick with the same meditation practice or try a different practice.
- There are many types of meditation practices to choose from including loving kindness, mindfulness, to concentration meditations.
- It can be valuable to do the same meditation practice consistently and can be equally valuable to vary the practice in style, length, or frequency. It depends on what works for you.

- In the space of a meditation practice, it is encouraged to allow thoughts to come and go, just as you let physical sensations or sounds come and go. You are the witness in formal meditation practice. However, you can gain useful insights when you notice the content of recurring thoughts and emotions that show up. You may receive insights or information that you can wisely act on once you stand up from your formal meditation practice into your daily life and performance.

Tuning into Joy and Choice

We have offered primarily the benefits of mindfulness and self-compassion to help with tolerance of negative emotions and concentration. Yet this is only part of the story. A mindfulness approach also allows you to be present to all of the good that is unfolding before your eyes. Being mindful allows you to take in the love of your teammates to experiencing what it feels like to be passionate about your sport of choice. Also, a mindful approach can loosen you up from feeling like you are stuck doing the same, repetitive routine. Because when you wake up to this very moment, you have many choices of what to do, what to notice, how to apply our energy. You are not the programmed computer. You are alive and have the opportunity to feel the entire range of what it is to be human on and off of the athletic field. You can, metaphorically, be both the the driverless car and open to novelty.

When practicing or competing, there is great value in being able to rely on skills and strategies you have developed. In many ways you pre-program your body and mind to be the driverless car – to know how to perform, what to do, no matter what. When you are able to accept uninvited thoughts and emotions that are not helpful to performance and stay present to what is a happening you can allow your training and skills to take over. You can then allow much of yourself to go into an almost automatic pilot, much like the driverless car. You can just do it, which can be very helpful up to a point.

Once engaged with a quiet mind and allowing your training to take over, it remains essential to be open and notice novelty. You must stay present to signs and signals that indicate you need to slightly modify or adjust. The beautiful balance between trusting your training and leveraging awareness, adjusting when necessary (even if just subtly so), allows you to create optimal learning and performance.

Prompting Flow, Being in the Zone

We contend that cultivating a mindful performance approach is important to set yourself up for best performance. When your mind is settled, or when you are not giving distracting thoughts and feelings power, you are able to be more present to what you are doing. When you pair this with intentionally paying attention to what is fresh, new, unexpected – so you can adapt and adjust as necessary (while relying on your well trained skills) – you are offering yourself even more of a chance to up your performance. There is some building evidence that when you are more mindful you are more likely to get into the flow state.

Current Research on MMTS 2.0

Thus far, collegiate teams (basketball, golf, tennis, and soccer), an Olympic team (badminton), and Army Rangers have gone through the MMTS 2.0 training – including almost ten sport coaches along with their teams. We offer this brief section to give you a sense of the empirical data we have gathered thus far on the efficacy of the program. In all studies of athletes who participated in MMTS, mindfulness scores (comparing athletes at the start of the study to the end of the study) improved, statistically significant positive improvements. In terms of self-compassion, most of the teams that participated in MMTS 2.0 also had statistically significant positive jumps in self-compassion.

We also have interviewed athletes who completed the program, and they have anecdotal reflections that sum up the value of participating in MMTS 2.0. The following quotes include a sampling of what we are discovering in our research (all of the following quotes are from the collegiate tennis player group (Baltzell research laboratory data, manuscripts in preparation):

- **Normalizing unpleasant feelings:** "I remember the feeling of being frustrated and I connected to mindfulness and I became aware of it and like [the instructor] said you cannot get rid of it at that moment and it made me feel better that it's normal."
- **Ability to overcome negative thinking and emotions:** "It is an example of not necessarily getting angry but just feeling really crappy and down and out. And being able to separate myself from that feeling and having the whole downward spiral and be like 'hey, let's be realistic.' So that was super helpful because it's a mindset and if you have the right mindset then you can practically achieve anything. I ended up coming back and playing really well that day."
- **Increased commitment to sport relevant focus:** "I gain confidence in my focus. I can keep my focus on the task better than I used to before so, it's kind of comforting to know that. I also know that even when I know that I'm feeling bad and I'm feeling off, I still know that if I focus on the right thing then I can still win, I can still play well."

Conclusion and the Beginning

In sport, mindlessness can mean being consumed by fear, thinking only of the outcome of the game, match or race, ruminating about a missed shot, or allowing your mind to be easily distracted from focusing on physically performing your best in the moment. You can have all of these experiences and be mindful. It comes down to being 1. Aware of these experiences, and 2. How you opt to respond to them.

The reactivity to such negativity, this *mindlessness reaction,* is such a conditioned habit that you might not notice how pervasive it really is. And even when you are aware, most athletes and performers don't know what to do about it. In our program and in this book, we hope that now you have some practical ideas of how to handle distracting thoughts about the future or past, and are empowered to get engaged with the moment in the way you see fit.

In truth, mindfulness is quite easy to experience for a few moments but hard to sustain over time. Even though it really *is* simple to be aware of just *this* moment, people rarely live their lives through this simplicity. Most lives are spent in states of *mindlessness.* By this it doesn't mean that you don't have a mind, but rather you might not be fully aware of where your mind is moment to moment or how to handle it. All too often people disregard what is actually happening right in front of them: their minds are somewhere else, lost in thoughts about the future or the past, and not aware and fully present to what's actually occurring in the here and now.

For example, you could think about how your coach was harsh at practice or how you shouldn't have made that stupid mistake. Both examples are representative of being lost in the past, as long as you remain caught up in the drama of what happened. Or equally mindless, you can be obsessed with how you will place, how fast your competitors run, how strong they are, how much training they have had to how much international experience they have had. Such thoughts are equally mindless if you allow yourself to remain caught up in the worries of the future, once you are aware that they are happening (e.g., moving from mind wandering to aware your mind is wandering, just like in meditation).

Now you have a choice. You now are empowered with the knowledge that, if you decide to, you can bring a mindful approach to whatever you are doing, whether going for a weight workout, a practice, or getting ready for an important competition. You can opt to allow thoughts and feelings to come and go (and yes, sometimes tolerate when they are sticking with you) and still choose to pay attention to what you personally value. You now also can choose to notice when you are suffering (e.g., anxiety, fear, regret, comparison to others) and choose to offer yourself what you most need in that moment (e.g., taking a nap, talking with someone who loves and understands you, to bringing to mind your inspirational value to keep pushing even though your strong preference is to curl up into a ball). And, equally important you also can be aware of and tune into what is working, what is right. When you are mindless, you can easily miss the subtle cues and information that marks what feels just right in a particular move or strategy in motion. Being more mindful does not always mean being in touch with misery! Being more mindful means being more alive – noticing what is not working and what is working.

You now have choice.

Whether you decide to never meditate for one more moment of your life, you are changed. Because now you know that with awareness and choice, you have great power over your ability to stay engaged, learn, and to produce your best possible performance (within the constraints of reality). Our hope is that MMTS 2.0 is a catalyst to strengthen presence, poise, and engagement for your sport performance and life.

Wishing you well.

Appendices

Appendix A: Mindfulness Meditation Training in Sport (MMTS) 2.0 Protocol

We designed MMTS 2.0 to be run in an instructor-led format for a total of six-hours over a period of six weeks (Though in some instances it has taken up to almost three months to teach MMTS 2.0 due to scheduling challenges in the high-pressure world of competitive athletics). In this Appendix A, we provide the MMTS 2.0 six-module program protocol, including main ideas offered in each session and exercises for each module. The basic structure of the program includes the following:

- Six one-hour modules, each offered in two thirty-minute sessions (in the case that you would like to offer the program in thirty minute segments versus one hour).
- One-hour per week or two half-hour segments per week
- Each instructor-led thirty-minute segment includes

    - ten-minutes of instruction (basic content in table below);
    - ten-minutes of practicing mindfulness-based exercises, and then;
    - ten-minutes of discussion or de-brief of the exercises with an emphasis on lessons learned that can be applied to practice or performance.

- Recommended daily, self-led mindfulness practice throughout the program for participants. Audio-files are provided to all participants before the start of the program. For MMTS 2.0 facilitators, we encourage you to create audio-files of the meditation using your own voice and posting on sound-cloud or some other internet audio site that is easily accessible by your program participants. The baseline for the scripts for the MMTS 2.0 daily ten-minute independent meditation practice can be found in Appendix B and Appendix C.

© Springer International Publishing AG 2017   163
A. Baltzell, J. Summers, *The Power of Mindfulness*,
https://doi.org/10.1007/978-3-319-70410-4

We recommend that those who instruct MMTS 2.0 have some experience with a personal meditation practice. It would be very difficult to teach the ideas and practices of the program if an instructor had never practiced some form of meditation. This sentiment is also shared with Jon Kabat-Zinn (2003), "Mindfulness, from our point of view, cannot be taught to others in an authentic way without the instructor's practicing it in his or her own life" (p. 149). Before and while leading the program, we encourage you to engage in some mindfulness meditation practice most days, if possible. If you have skipped the main text and jumped directly to this Appendix, we recommend that you read Chap. 14, which offers insights and suggestions for MMTS 2.0 instructors about what to consider before and during the time of offering the program.

You can repeat the exercises offered at the end of the chapter you are working on or you can elect to listen on-line to a range of self-compassion and mindfulness-based meditation practices. What is most important is that you discover mindfulness-based or self-compassion practices that work for you! Sometimes it can work well to repeat the same practice every day or sometimes it can work best to vary your meditation practice. For now, we encourage you to try the practices we offer and then opt to explore others and discover what works best for you.

Though we do want to encourage MMTS 2.0 participants to engage in meditation. Some simply will not opt practice on their own. That is OK! We have found that some athletes take to the meditation practice like ducks to water and others make radical strides in performance without practicing meditation. Simply understanding the value of being mindful, truly present and accepting, as well as being able to offer self-compassion when it is needed can have a powerful impact on performance. There is much to be learned if the athlete only participates in the group-led practices as well as the educational segments and discussions. Though, of course, we encourage the practice of a formal meditation practice given the myriad benefits.

Module 1

Module 1 (Part A): Introduction to Mindfulness (30 minutes)

Introduction to Mindfulness (Integrated with Self-Compassion)

Module one is designed to introduce participants to the experience of mindful-awareness and an understanding of how these ideas can contribute to optimizing sport performance. The first session introduces the idea of mindfulness (integrated with self-compassion) (Review Chaps 1, 2, 3 and 5 before teaching this module). In this module do your best to offer clear connections between mindfulness/self-compassion with sport practice and performance and introduce the basic mindful meditation practices. When teaching, the instructors choose anecdotes that offer ways of demonstrating some of the main benefits of bringing mindfulness to performance:

- **Poise:** You can offer an example of an athlete feeling intense frustration or anxiety and noting how being aware of such an experience and opting to 1) accept the feelings, 2) and stay focused on task relevant cues can be cultivated with mindfulness training (e.g., the runner who is getting passed in a race, feeling the urge to stop, noticing the feeling and opts to keep competing in a gritty, determined way).
- **Concentration:** You can offer an example of an athlete who is either lost in the past (regretting a play) or lost in the future (anxious about the outcome of a game), having them notice what they are doing (i.e., getting lost in thought) and then intentionally re-focusing on what they are doing in practice or competition.
- **Adapt and Adjust:** You can offer an example of going into a venue or against a well-known opponent and having the athlete notice their assumptions of how they know it will go (win or lose) and then how getting back noticing some in-the-moment unexpected information (e.g., their opponent isn't playing the way he usually does and there is a new possibility of how to beat him) and making good use of the information for a potential different outcome.

Regardless of how you do it, it is essential that you offer the connection between both the ideas in MMTS 2.0 and the connection between formal meditation and sport practice and competition. If the athlete does not understand the potential, direct benefit for themselves, they will most likely not engage in the program in a meaningful, useful way.

Offering the definitions of mindfulness from both Kabat-Zinn and Langer is important (You can review Chaps. 1, 2, 3 and 13). When offering these definitions, make sure, again to make direct links to sport performance. Explain why being in the present moment is better than lost in regret and/or fear. Also note how noticing novelty can be beneficial to sport performance.

The first session (module 1, part A) of the program is focused on offering an introduction to mindfulness and examples of how a mindful approach can be helpful in sport so that the participants have an understanding of how cultivating mindfulness can help with performance. Provide an example for the sport you are working with when explaining the connection between mindfulness and performance (e.g., Basketball player – star – misses a few shots and thinks to himself, "It is just one of those games." Shrugs and gives up. With awareness and acceptance – mindfulness – the athlete is given freedom to choose a different response from his habitual reaction).

Practices and exercises	Rationale and explanation
Introduction	Set the stage of how mindfulness and self-compassion can help with improving performance in sport practice and performance (for coaches and athletes). Introducing mindfulness from the Kabat-Zinn and Langer perspectives. Offer a few sport examples that are sport appropriate to your group that demonstrate how mindfulness can help with practice and/or performance.
Offering purpose of MMTS 2.0	**Clearly introduce purpose of MMTS 2.0:** **1. Poise: Increase athlete's ability to cope with the experience of negative thoughts and emotions** that may be present due to competitive pressure. Emphasize that you are not trying to stop the emotions and thoughts from flooding in but, instead, help the athletes change their relationship with aversive emotions, thoughts, and sensations. We hope athlete will learn to observe and accept them without being dominated by them.
	2. Concentration: Emphasizing the importance of concentration is offered across the entire MMTS 2.0 training via guiding participants to notice distractions and bring attention back to the present moment. The formal meditation practices translate perfectly to sport practice and competition/performance. Hanson and Mendius (2009), leaders in linking mindfulness meditation to positive changes in brain structure, write that formal meditation practice directly increases one's ability to control their attention. They write, "Having good control over your attention: You can place your attention wherever you want and it stays there: When you want to shift it to something else, you can." (p. 177)
	3. Adapt & Adjust. When more mindful, you are able to be more present and you can intentionally adjust during practice and performance (i.e., more aware of sport relevant novel stimuli).
Definition of mindfulness	1) "Paying attention in a particular way: on purpose, in the present moment, and nonjudgmentally" (Kabat-Zinn, 1994, p. 4).
	2). Openness to novelty (not assuming it will be like it has always been in the past) (Langer 1989).
The structure of the program	ten-minutes of information ten-minutes of practice ten-minutes of discussion
Overview of daily mindful meditation practice (10 min total)	Share with the participants the basics of a meditation practice. Please review the initial chapters, particularly Chap. 5 about ways to introduce beginning a formal meditation practice.
	This is a great time to introduce the *meditation cycle*. We have found that it is particularly helpful to emphasize that it is *normal* for your mind to wander. Many athletes report feeling badly at meditating when they first start.
	Also, emphasize that *all parts* of the meditation cycle are all part of meditating. Meaning the focus of the meditation (e.g., focus on sound); mind wandering; awareness of mind wandering, relaxing and re-focusing on the intended meditation practice are all part of what it is to meditate! In this example, it is not just focus on sound (but meditating also includes the mind wandering, noticing wandering, relax, refocus back.)
Mindful breathing exercise (10 min.)	Participants are guided through a basic mindfulness meditation based breathing exercise. Participants are prompted to get comfortable, close their eyes, and bring their attention to their breath, noticing the physical sensation that is most dominant as they breath in and out. When they notice their minds wandering, they are encouraged to notice, relax, and bring their attention back to their breath (Refer to Appendix D)

(continued)

Practices and exercises	Rationale and explanation
Debrief (10 min.)	You can normalize here how it is common for the mind to wander. It is common to decide that you are bad at the practice. And it is common for the mind to be very busy. Questions? Experience? How could this practice connect to sport performance? Facilitator offers example of parallel of meditation practice and practicing or competing. The practice of noticing the mind wandering and bringing the focus back to the breath in meditation: The practice of noticing the mind wandering and bringing the focus back to what you are doing in practice or competition.
Reminder to practice	Encouragement to practice daily with provided audio-files that you provide!
	When to practice? 4–6 times per week for the duration of the ten-minute audio-file. Experiment with the best place to practice, morning or night.

Module 1 (Part B): Brief Introduction to Self-Compassion (30 minutes)

Module 1 offers a brief introduction to self-compassion and discussion of how kindness to self can help when addressing performance distress (i.e., performance anxiety).

Practices and exercises	Rationale and explanation
Brief check-in	How is it going?
Define self-compassion and offer examples in sport performance where it is helpful. Theme: Self-compassion cultivates courage (10 min.)	When you suffer, care for yourself as you would care for someone you truly love. Emphasize the importance of bringing self-kindness to self when suffering. Self-compassion includes self-kindness, a sense of common humanity, and mindfulness.
	Examples of self-compassion in sport offered. Comparison between self-compassion and self-confidence offered. You don't need to be self-confident, but rather have the courage to focus on task relevant sport cues. This is an important message in the program, which should be woven throughout the discussions.
Breathing with kindness (10 min)	Ten-minute breathing exercise while emphasizing intentional kindness to self. The meditation practice for this section is adapted from the affectionate breathing activity of the mindful-self compassion program (See Appendix E).
Discussion of practice (10 min.)	How was that for you? Were the first and second practice different? Simply noticing breath versus intentionally bringing to mind some kindness to self? How might this practice connect to sport or performance? Facilitator offers connection to sport examples. Also you might discuss how it is unusual in the sport realm to offer kindness to self, but when an athlete is struggling (e.g., anxiety) offering oneself kindness can be a way to amp up one's courage to stay engaged.
Reminder to practice	Encouragement to practice daily with provided audio-files.
	When to practice? 4–6 times per week for the duration of the ten-minute audio-file.

Module 2

Module 2 (Part A): Tolerating Sport Distress (30 minutes)

Labeling of Experience to Help Athletes Build Awareness of the Choice
to Respond Versus React

The second module is devoted to addressing initial challenges encountered by participants, the universality of the wandering mind, and the fruitlessness of trying to stop the
mind from wandering. Recognizing their "stories" (e.g., I am not good enough) and the
way in which they allow such uninvited thoughts to influence how they perform.

Practices and exercises	Rationale and explanation
Brief check-in	How is it going?
Brief review of the concepts of mindfulness and connection to sport practice or performance	"Paying attention in a particular way: On purpose, in the present moment, and nonjudgmentally" (Kabat-Zinn 1994, p. 4).
	Present moment awareness with an interest and/or acceptance of what is happening – In a balanced way (not ignoring, not tangled up in, not assuming it will be as it always was).
	Openness to novelty (not assuming it will be like it has always been in the past) (Ellen Langer).
	Facilitator offers a sport relevant example.
Stimulus and response (10 min Total)	Facilitator explains the difference between automatic reactions to things (e.g., giving up when you start to lose) versus being willing to tolerate the negative emotion in the "space" between the stimulus (e.g., anxiety, fear, self-doubt) and then the intentional response (deciding how you choose to respond, not just re-acting as one has in the past – If the reactions are harmful to performance). (Review Chap. 8)
Mindful of sound practice (5 min.) and body sensation practice with labeling (5 min)	Facilitator leads group through 5 minutes of mindful meditation focused on sound only. Encourage no intentional judgment, just noticing. Just being the observer. This is a good opportunity to practice with accepting judgments that do unintentionally arise.
	In the second 5-minute segment, facilitator prompts participants to shift attention to the body and "label" physical sensations (e.g., heat, warmth, coolness, tingling, pressure).
	From this point forward in the program, offer self-compassion cues. For this exercise you can say something like: "Bring a kindness, acceptance, warmth to self as you bring your attention back to your physical sensations, the point of focus."
Discussion (10 min.)	What was it like to try to keep your attention on what was arising? Without judgment. When you did notice judgment arising, were you able just to observe it or did you get caught up in thinking (on-purpose)? The first part of this practice is about awareness and being fully present. Practicing acceptance. This practice is inviting you to accept something that is relatively easy to accept (sounds, physical sensations). The second part of the practice is about beginning to create some space between what you are experiencing and how you bring awareness to it, through the labeling exercise. Facilitator offers example that is sport relevant (e.g., trying to keep one's attention on the play unfolding; noticing when the mind wanders; and intentionally bringing attention back to the play with less reactivity)

(continued)

Practices and exercises	Rationale and explanation
Reminder to practice	Questions about practice? Encouragement to practice daily with provided audio-files.
	When to practice? 4–6 times per week for duration of ten-minute audio-file.

Considerations for Facilitators:

- Model meditation. You can talk about your own practice. The challenges of practicing. Particularly in the beginning, it is invaluable to note how your mind wanders in your own practice. You can talk about how you are able to notice such mind wandering and ways that you "relax" in the meditation cycle. You might just naturally notice the wandering and re-focus back. But you might also notice a sense of relaxation in your body when you return, a bit of humor of how your mind is wandering again. The facilitator normalizing the meditation cycle can be very helpful to those new to a meditation practice.
- Remind group: It is hard to start something new. This is particularly true of high-level competitors. They are so used to being excellent at what they do! Josh says, *Do not despise humble beginnings; Have no contempt before investigation.* It can be very interesting to learn about how you respond to learning something new. Athletes and performers must constantly be learning something new. Maybe not as drastic as how to meditate, but always cues for change from teachers and coaches. This is a good, "safe" opportunity to notice what happens when you are trying to learn something and it doesn't go as you ideally think it should go.

Module 2 (Part B): Tolerating Sport Distress (30 minutes)

Invited Versus Uninvited Thoughts (Emotions, Physical Sensations)

The second part of module two is devoted to addressing a new way to approach negative or harsh thoughts that spontaneously arise and a new way in sport psychology to address them. It is one thing to notice changing sounds in the environment and another to witness self-criticism and fear.

Practices and exercises	Rationale and explanation
Brief check-in	How is it going?
Learning to accept the flow of uninvited thoughts	Explain what uninvited thoughts mean. Offer examples in sport. Note that secondary thoughts (uninvited thoughts) are normal. Uninvited thoughts that help with practice and performance: "I've got this!," "It feels right today."
	Uninvited thoughts that don't help with practice and performance: "I can't do it," "I can't beat her," "It doesn't feel right today."
	Explain the difference between changing unhelpful/uninvited thoughts versus *accepting* (if you can shift from unhelpful to helpful thinking, great; but if you can't learning to accept and not be controlled by uninvited thoughts can be freeing).

(continued)

(continued)

Practices and exercises	Rationale and explanation
Understanding thought suppression and importance of experiential acceptance (10 min total)	Explain how deliberate attempts to suppress thoughts and feelings can increase their occurrence and behavioral impact. You can offer stories of when athletes that tried to suppress thoughts and feelings, simply amped up their performance distress. To help explain this, you can reference essential ideas of Hayes (2004) (Acceptance and Commitment Therapy, ACT): (Review Chap. 8)
	a. Behavioral Avoidance: Experiential avoidance functions to provide an individual experiencing heightened negative affect *a means to short-term emotion regulation*. Offer sport example (e.g., opting not to go to practice because coach is too critical).
	b. Cognitive fusion to de-centering (with unhelpful thoughts/beliefs recurring…). Offer sport example (cognitive fusion: The thought occurs "I cannot win this! Athlete believes thought and gives up; De-centering: Athletes has thought "I cannot win this!". Athlete accepts thought arising and gets back to competing and trying to still win).
	In ACT, "It is the tendency to take these experiences (anxious thoughts) literally and then to fight against them that is viewed as harmful." (Hayes 2004, p. 651) From the Gardner and Moore (2007): The degree of experiential acceptance is critical to best performance through the following: "Accept internal experience as normal." "Willing to persist despite these experiences." "Maintains attention on the task at hand." "Remains behaviorally engaged in the task at hand."
The basic breath and Labeling of uninvited thoughts exercise (10 min)	Introduce the "spider web" metaphor as awareness to thought.
	Prompt: Rest in awareness until a thought arises, allow attention to rest there until another thought arises.
	1. Don't try to shift your attention. Just observe as it happens. Each time a thought arises, label it and don't intentionally think about it: Observe. Once thought has passed rest back in awareness until another thought arises.
	2. Don't try to change anything; unwelcome thoughts, feelings are very normal;
	3. Bring a kindness, acceptance, warmth to self as you bring your attention back to your breath;
	4. Like a snow globe, thoughts will settle when you are aware of them and don't try to make them go away. Just notice and label. With warmth.
	Summary: Benefit of practice for sport performance; Acceptance/ tolerance; De-centering; Less reactivity to difficulty; Builds awareness.

(continued)

Practices and exercises	Rationale and explanation
Discussion (10 min)	What thoughts emerged? How did you label them? How was it different when you labeled your experience? Were you able to be kind/gentle with self when you refocused on your awareness? What was it like to try to keep your attention on thoughts that were arising? This practice is about awareness and being fully present. Practicing acceptance.
	This practice is inviting you to accept thoughts, which may be the HARDEST (thoughts and emotion) to accept.
	Facilitator offers example of benefit of such practice that is sport relevant.
Reminder to practice	Questions about practice? Encouragement to practice daily with provided ten-minute audio-files.
	When to practice? 4–6 times per week for duration of ten-minute audio-file.

Module 3

Module 3 (Part A): Concentration (30 minutes)

Introduction to Concentration: When Things Are Going Well

This module is focused on defining concentration and discussing directly the importance of concentration to help optimize performance. The participants will understand this, but to make it clear discussing ways that they get distracted can be quite helpful.

Practices and exercises	Rationale and explanation
Brief check-in	How is it going?
Concentration defined	Offer the definition of concentration, *Intentionally focusing your attention*, and the four components of concentration: 1). Focusing on relevant environment cues; selective attention: Selecting what cues to attend to and disregard. 2) Maintaining attentional focus. 3) Situation awareness: The ability to understand what is going on around oneself (to size up a situation). 4) Shifting attentional focus when necessary. Provide a sport relevant example of each component so the value of training their concentration through mindfulness practice is more compelling.

(continued)

(continued)

Practices and exercises	Rationale and explanation
Application to sport (10 min total)	Facilitate discussion about what athletes experience when concentrating optimally in practice or performance.
	Facilitator offers an example. Prompts for discussion: When things are going well, what is good to concentrate on in practice? (e.g., When serving? Volleying?) Encourage them to personalize this. Though in the same sport, there may be different prompts for focus that are most helpful.
The breathing ladder (10 min.)	This is a concentration exercise. The practice is to keep count (when their mind wanders they often will lose count, where they are in the ladder). Normalize mind wandering and their plan to get back into the practice when they lose count. This is a great place to make a connection to sport when they lose focus, what do they do to get their attention back as quickly as possible?
	Introduce the "Breathing Ladder," which is a breathing and concentration exercise. (See full explanation in the body of the book). Counting 1 up to 10 One full breath (in and out) counts as one breath = 1; second full breath = 2 and so on Once you reach 10 then you count backwards to 1 If you miss a number or lose your place, return to 1 Facilitator reminds athletes that unwelcome thoughts, feelings are very normal; facilitator reminds athletes to bring a kindness, acceptance, and warmth to self as they bring their attention back to the breath.
	Offer snow globe metaphor: Thoughts will settle when you are aware of them and don't try to make them go away. Just notice. With warmth.
Discussion (10 min)	What thoughts emerged? How did you handle making a mistake on the count and starting over? How does this show up in sport for you? Examples? Facilitator makes clear connection between activity and sport practice or performance. (e.g., When you are distracted from a task on the court, and you notice it, you can choose to bring your attention immediately back to task relevant cues.)
Reminder to practice	Questions about practice? Encouragement to practice daily with provided ten-minute audio-files.
	When to practice? 4–6 times per week for duration of ten-minute audio-file.

Module 3 (Part B): Coping with Distraction & Tolerating Sport Distress (30 minutes)

Introduction to Concentration: When Things Are NOT Going Well

The second part of module three is devoted to addressing a new way to approach negative or harsh thoughts that spontaneously arise and a new way for sport psychology to address them. Instead of trying to come up with ways to challenge, dispute or change the thoughts, this section is about learning to accept (or tolerate) unwanted, uninvited thoughts and feelings.

Practices and exercises	Rationale and explanation
Brief check-in	How is it going?
Discuss distractions to performance (10 min.)	Invite general examples of times when things are not going well in sport or performance for participants. And then invite and also offer examples in sport when there is a problem with concentration for each of the categories below (refer to Chapter 9): Focusing on past/future Getting lost in stories of fear (not quick enough; haven't beaten her/him) Lost in feelings of exhaustion; lack of motivation Example: How about when you are angry and you want to throw a racquet? Where does your attention automatically go? Where would you optimally like to place your attention, instead?
Pyramid breathing (10 min.)	The purpose of using this practice is to introduce a concentration practice that is more challenging and likely prompt some minor emotional irritation.
	Introduce "Pyramid Breathing," which is a breathing and concentration exercise (see full description in main body of book). However, instead of counting a number for a full breath and moving directly up to ten, the pattern is as follows: 1-2-1; 1-2-3-2-1; 1-2-3-4-3-2-1;… until the middle number is ten…and then back down.
	Again, one full breath (in and out) counts as one breath = 1; second full breath = 2; and so on. And again, if you miss a number or lose your place, return to 1.
	Reminds athletes that unwelcome thoughts and feelings (e.g., frustration, irritation, self-criticism) are *normal*; Some prompts to offer: If you lose track, start over. Notice any feelings of frustration. Plan to bring a phrase of kindness to yourself – What would you need to hear in that moment to feel better about losing track, mind wandering? (i.e., It's OK, everyone loses focus.)
Discussion (10 min)	When your mind wanders in the exercise, bring a kindness, acceptance, and warmth to self as you bring your attention back to your breath. Bring to mind your phrase of kindness. Practice accepting – mind wandering (words of acceptance, if needed) – and focusing back on counting, just as you could on the athletic field (e.g., court for tennis study). This is a great chance to make a connection between the intent of the exercise and application to sport or performance. What is a typical frustration in sport? What would a good teammate say to you when you are frustrated? Coach? What would you say to a teammate in a similar situation? How could bringing this to mind help you re-focus on performance? If time, provide an example for the participants.
	What thoughts emerged? What did you experience while on task? When the mind wandered? How did you handle making a mistake on the count and starting over? Did you experiment with offering yourself a word or phrase of kindness? How does losing attention show up in sport for you? Examples? Facilitator makes clear connection between activity and breathing practice. (e.g., When you are angry, frustrated, anxious you can still choose to bring your attention back to task relevant cues without trying to make the feelings and thoughts go away. You also can offer yourself a word or phrase of acceptance and kindness that helps empower the athlete to refocus.)

(continued)

(continued)

Practices and exercises	Rationale and explanation
Bonus: Open awareness meditation practice (2 min.)	If you have time, this can be a great time to practice a brief, open-awareness meditation practice. Prompts to participants: Rest in awareness, accept/ tolerate all that occurs. Use labeling if helpful. If you notice getting lost/ actively engaged in thinking – Bring your attention back to your sensation of breathing for a few breaths; and then back to open awareness (of thought, emotion, physical sensation and sound). Bring a kind, friendly attention to all that is occurring.
Reminder to practice	Questions about practice? Encouragement to practice daily with provided ten-minute audio-files.
	When to practice? 4–6 times per week for duration of ten-minute audio-file.

Module 4

Module 4 (Part A): Self-Compassion & Mindfulness for Difficult Moments (30 minutes)

Self-Compassion for Difficult Moments in Sport: Create a Courageous Response to Challenge

This module offers a continued, more in-depth discussion of self-compassion. It is a good time in the program to clarify how and when to use self-compassion in a wise way. Self-compassion is particularly called for and helpful with negative emotions/anxiety (e.g., mistakes, threat, disappointment).

Make sure that you do not start the exercise *Sitting with Difficulty* until 100% of people in the room have some word of kindness that they can offer themselves. This may be the most challenging exercise in the program and you want to set it up so the participants understand the intent of the exercise and have the best chance at practicing tolerating sport- or performance-related difficulty.

Practices and exercises	Rationale and explanation
Start with brief compassionate breathing (2 min)	See previous guidelines
Brief check-in	How is it going?
Self-compassion defined and connection to coping with sport distress clearly made (10 min)	Review the idea of self-compassion and be prepared to offer a number of instances when performance distress arises your participants' sport.
	Offer the definition: "Self-compassion involves being touched by and open to one's own suffering, not avoiding or disconnecting from it, generating the desire to alleviate one's suffering" (Neff 2003, p. 87). 1. Self-compassion is not about going easy on yourself when you don't feel like doing something. Self-compassion is not about increasing pleasure/avoiding pain. Self-compassion is about wisely dealing with intense negative emotions, thoughts, physical sensations that if left alone would shut you down (I'm out of here; I don't care; I am overwhelmed) or cause a wide range of problems that come from ignoring how you are feeling. 2. Self-compassion is a way to become courageous in times when, if left alone, the performance distress would distract the performer from focusing on performance.
	Present self-compassion model by Kristen Neff and Chris Germer (2013) 1. Self-kindness: Offering warmth and unconditional acceptance to self in the face of difficulty. 2. Common humanity: Recognizing we all suffer. 3. Mindfulness: Paying attention with acceptance (tolerance). Offer example or two in sport of using self-compassion to cultivate courageous response to difficulty. It is important to note that self-compassion includes all three dimensions. It is not enough just to notice the suffering, but also important that there is an emphasis to do something about it! That is the self-kindness piece. Help the participants connect to what they most need in moments of difficulty to keep competing, to keep fighting.
	Offer concept: Pain X Resistance = Suffering The more they resist unwanted thoughts, feeling and sensations, the worse it gets, the more they are distracted by the unwanted experience(s). Offer sport or performance example.

(continued)

(continued)

Practices and exercises	Rationale and explanation
Negative mind state fire drill. Sitting with sport difficulty (10 min.)	The first step in the negative mind state fire drill is to identify a difficult moment in sport that the participant is willing to consider. You can have athletes pair up and talk about such a challenging moment. Pairing up helps athletes normalize sport difficulty with a teammate or friend (for full explanation, see *Negative Mind State Fire Drill* in the main body of the book)
	Before imagery begins, ask: What did you most need to hear in that moment, something that would be kind and soothing to you? Make sure all participants have a phrase to bring to mind before starting imagery session.
	Facilitator prompts: Close your eyes, get comfortable… Now bring to mind your past negative performance.
	And slowly – with silence between – offer these prompts: Notice how you were emotionally feeling. Where in your body do you feel the sensation most strongly? You are invited to keep your attention with the physical sensation. If the emotion is ever too strong at any time, go back to your breath or simply take a break from the exercise. Repeat: Notice how you were emotionally feeling. Where in your body do you feel the sensation most strongly? Bring to mind your statement (of self-kindness) 4 or 5 times throughout the activity. This activity is about accepting negative thoughts; learning how to be comfortable with the internal distress.
	The goal is to prevent the participants from or running away from the inevitable negative emotion in order to allocate maximum effort and concentration to the relevant task at hand. It can be helpful to explain this before you begin leading the activity.
Discussion (10 min)	What was that like to bring that distressful experience to mind? Were you able to bring a phrase of kindness to yourself in that moment? If you were able to, or not, can you imagine bringing to mind what you might most need in a future distressful experience in sport? What would that thought be? When might you bring it to mind?
	Offer sport examples of how important it is to stay present. When you avoid negative thoughts and feelings, you also are stepping out of the moment. When you do so, you have lost the chance to make the wisest decisions toward action and/or response.
Reminder to practice	Questions about practice? Encouragement to practice daily with provided ten-minute audio-files.
	When to practice? 4–6 times per week for duration of ten-minute audio-file.

Module 4 (Part B): Self-Compassion & Mindfulness for Self and Others (30 minutes)

Warmth toward Self and Others

This module offers a way to bring kindness to self and to send kindness to team-mates or others that the athlete cares about. The exercise Soles of your Feet, which follows in this section, can be a way to help soothe athletes if they have touched a past experience that is difficult to tolerate.

Practices and Exercises	Rationale and Explanation
Start with brief compassionate breathing (2 min)	See previous guidelines
Brief check-in	How is it going?
Address value of caring for self and others (e.g., teammates) when facing difficulty (10 min.)	When athletes are facing difficulty it can be invaluable to be kind to themself and others. Often times when they accept difficulty as normal (e.g., others feel great pressure and anxiety too) and they can then bring sport-appropriate kindness to themselves, their experience can shift to feeling more in control and engaged. Specifically, when they do so they then can gather enough courage to stay in the game (even when feeling such disempowering feelings as fear, anxiety, harsh-self-criticism). To stop avoiding or getting too caught up in difficulty, it can help to offer themselves/others some kindness or compassion; it helps them be able to tolerate difficulty and face the challenge at hand.
	It is essential for facilitator to offer at least one sport example (e.g., runner so filled with self-criticism, she stops trying and gets shot out the back of the pack).
One for me, one for you meditation (10 min.)	Using breath paired with wishing self and other well. In this practice, participants will be guided to breath-in what they wish most for themself and breath-out for what they most wish for someone else. This meditation is good to read from the script. Please refer to Appendix G.
Discussion (10 min.)	What was doing this practice like for you? What have you learned that you will you take with you, back to sport? How can you offer kindness to yourself, when it matters? Would you consider offering kindness to your teammates? In this way? In another way?
Reminder to practice	Questions about practice? Encouragement to practice daily with provided ten-minute audio-files.
	When to practice? 4–6 times per week for duration of ten-minute audio-file.

Module 5

Module 5 (Part A): Self-Regulation – Sport Values to Help Performance
(30 minutes)

This module helps athletes clarify their sport values, inspired values that will inspire
them to keep engaged in moment to moment experience whether they are enjoying
the challenge or not. The idea is that no matter how you feel (you don't have to be
confident), you can still make choices to adhere to personally cherished, inspirational values.

Practices and Exercises	Rationale and Explanation
Start with brief compassionate breathing (2 min.)	See previous guidelines
Brief check-in	How is it going?
Values explored (10 min.)	In this segment, you will help the participants figure out what values would help them keep going, whether they feel good or not. The following prompts are offered to guide the discussion: What do you value most as a player? Specific example: Fitness. If you value being fit, pushing hard physically is tolerable; if you don't value fitness, pushing physically hard is intolerable. Specific example: Being courageous. If you value courage, trying hard when you are losing is tolerable; if you don't value courage, trying hard when you are losing is intolerable.
	Distinguish between goals vs. values: Goals are achievable (winning) vs. values guide our action (e.g., trying hard, being loyal). Values are about how you want to be in the process of trying to achieve goals.
	Explore some core values in sport: Courage; loyalty; persistence. Performance values guide day-to-day actions and encourage athletes to live a values-directed life rather than an emotion-directed life.
	Provide sport examples.

(continued)

Practices and Exercises	Rationale and Explanation
Your end-of-your athletic (or performance) career celebration: How do you want to be remembered?	Prompt: Looking back on your (name sport) career (when over) – What would give you deep satisfaction, contentment – Regardless of win/loss record? End-of-your athletic (or performance) career celebration exercise. Prompts for the facilitator: How would you like your career as a University of X collegiate athlete to be remembered? You were someone who always.... (e.g., worked hard, kept trying…) (2–3 minutes of silence) Ideally, what values do you want to exhibit on the court (field, pool, etc.)?
	Invite athletes to discuss and/or write down values that represent how they want to be remembered in their sport. Make sure everyone has at least one value in mind before you move on. This also is a great time to offer a poignant example. (You could consider the example of the 24-hour runner Jenny in the text regarding inspired values). Prompt: What are some of the external obstacles to living your value in sport/competition (e.g., place on team; time constraints)? Prompt: What are some of the internal obstacles? (e.g., exhaustion, fear, frustration, harsh self-criticism) Could self-compassion help you live in accordance with your true values? More specifically, how would self-compassion help with typical internal obstacles (uninvited thoughts, emotions and physical sensations)? What could you bring to mind or do that would be soothing (or kind) when your inner critic is harsh? (Suggestions: "It is normal to feel like this"; "I can feel like this and still perform well"; "I am not perfect and that is OK; I don't have to be confident, I just have to focus in on what I am doing.").
Discussion (10 min)	What did you learn? What will you take with you? When could you bring this phrase of self-compassion to yourself in sport? What is a specific, predictable moment that an inspired value would be of value to you?
	Key take-aways: The ability to perform with poise and concentration in spite of difficult thoughts and emotions can be strengthened by incorporating self-compassion. Instead of trying to control emotions – fighting them – allow them to be there and you have the option to decide to focus on the task at hand, regardless of thoughts and feelings AND live your values that inspire you.
Reminder to practice	Questions about how the mindfulness meditation practice is going? Encouragement to practice daily with provided ten-minute audio-files.
	When to practice? 4–6 times per week for duration of ten-minute audio-file.

Module 5 (Part B): Self-Regulation – Body Awareness to Help Performance (30 minutes)

Participants have clarified their sport values – values that will inspire them to keep engaged in moment to moment experience whether they are enjoying the challenge or not. The idea is that no matter how you feel, you can still make choices to adhere to personally cherished inspirational values. A problem that will arise, that no matter how much they try to keep their minds on what they value, they might be in an emotionally overwhelmed space. There are many ways to address being overwhelmed. In this section we offer one way, through bringing awareness to body sensations, which can help anchor the participant in the present moment. We have had many athletes note that the exercise we offer below has been quite helpful.

Practices and exercises	Rationale and explanation
Start with brief compassionate breathing (2 min.)	See previous guidelines
Brief check-in	How is it going?
Using body awareness to handle emotional difficulty (10 min.)	Use the experience of working with the body as a way of grounding oneself in the moment in the face of difficulty. Body Awareness is: A way of cultivating mindful awareness – an anchoring practice (to the present moment). A way to get present – awareness of body functioning, moment to moment. An effective way to calm the mind when feeling emotionally overwhelmed. A tool to help turn down the intensity when the emotions and thoughts are unhelpful.
Soles of the feet (10 min.)	This exercise can be used when you have a need to step out of reactive mode (e.g., being intensely angry, fearful or full of dread).
	Prompt: Use the experience of working with the body as a way of grounding oneself in the moment in the face of difficulty. Please refer to Appendix F: Walking meditation practice, for the script. This is a practice that is good to read most of the script directly. You can tailor a bit to ensure that the word choice makes sense to you, the facilitator.
Discussion (10 min.)	When could you use this exercise in practice? In performance. What else do you do to help calm your mind when wandering/racing/too harsh/too angry?
Reminder to practice	Questions about practice? Encouragement to practice daily with provided ten-minute audio-files.
	When to practice? 4–6 times per week for duration of ten-minute audio-file.

Module 6

Module 6 (Part A): Preparing to Adapt & Adjust in Performance, Moment-to-Moment with Open Awareness (30 minutes)

This module focuses on using open awareness, to all that is occurring internally and externally, to help with performance. Open awareness includes awareness of thought, emotion, sound, and physical sensation both within the person and in their external environment. This final module offers a discussion of the role of open awareness (to all experience) and application to sport – the ultimate connection of mindfulness to sport performance.

Practices and exercises	Rationale and explanation
Start with brief compassionate breathing (2 min.)	See previous guidelines
Brief check-in	How is it going?
Open awareness and open awareness interval training introduction (10 min.)	Explanation of open awareness: Being able to accept all that occurs and eventually use this awareness is important in performance. Open-awareness serves as the background to sport-specific attentional cues. The athlete knows mainly what she should be attending to, but also must remain open to novelty. The athlete needs to be prepared to adapt and adjust to new, relevant information. Offer example(s) in sport when one needs to adapt and adjust to factors that are unfolding, unexpectedly. For example, noticing when opponents making an unexpected move, the physical conditions being different than expected to having unexpected emotions to new physical sensations (e.g., I feel I have more power than I thought I would at this point in the race).
	Prompt participants to practice a brief, mindfulness meditation practice utilizing the breath as the anchor to the present moment. During this time, the participant will practice becoming aware of any body sensations, thoughts, or feelings and, then, prompted to practice acceptance of thoughts, emotions and physical sensation without judgment. 1) Awareness of breath (2 min.) 2) Awareness of sound (2 min.) 3) Awareness of physical sensations (e.g., tingling, pressure, heat, coolness) (2 min.) 4) Awareness of thoughts/emotions – and labeling (2 min.) 5) Allowing awareness to go where it wants. Traditional open-awareness mindfulness. Mindfulness meditation – A including awareness of any thoughts, feelings, and physical sensations. (2 min.)

(continued)

(continued)

Practices and exercises	Rationale and explanation
Discussion (10 min.)	What is it like to be present or open to all experience (not focused on past or future)? What did you notice, that you have not noticed before? Did you notice experience changing? Sounds coming and going? Thoughts coming and going? What would it be like to bring such presence to sport? When would it be helpful to have this type of awareness? How does such awareness work with your need to concentrate?
Reminder to practice	Questions about practice? Encouragement to practice daily with provided ten-minute audio-files.
	When to practice? 4–6 times per week for duration of ten-minute audio-file.

Module 6 (Part B): Accepting, Adapting, Adjusting – Including Novelty (30 minutes)

This final section offers a discussion of the role the importance of noticing novelty and the application of such awareness to sport and performance. Using mindfulness to be present and accepting of what is occurring (internally or externally) and then being able to strengthen discernment of what is best to pay attention to is, together, the ultimate connection of mindfulness to sport performance.

Practices and exercises	Rationale and explanation
Start with brief compassionate breathing (2 min.)	See previous guidelines
Brief check-in	How is it going?
Mindfulness – The Ellen Langer approach (5 min.)	Offer the definition and explanation of Ellen Langer's approach to mindfulness. For Langer, "Mindfulness is the process of drawing novel distinctions. It does not matter whether what is noticed is important or trivial, as long as it is *new* to the viewer. Actively drawing these distinctions keeps us situated in the present. It also makes us more aware of the context and perspective of our actions than if we rely upon distinctions and categories drawn in the past" (Langer and Moldoveanu 2000, pp. 1–2).
	But applied to performance, it *does* matter what you pay attention to. It is critical that the attention is on novel stimulus that provides information to help you perform better.
	Langer's Orchestra study is an excellent example of experimenting with novelty. We encourage you to review this study. Essentially in her study orchestra musicians were asked to do the following: 1. "Recall best performance and play in that manner." 2. "Play in subtly different ways that only you would know." Musicians and audience preferred second condition (playing in novel way vs. trying to re-create a past experience). Musicians also found this approach much more enjoyable.

(continued)

Practices and exercises	Rationale and explanation
Breathing exercise, novelty (5 min. each)	Prompt: Notice new sensations, experiences when breathing – Each breath (5 min.); Focus on physical object (hand). Notice the variation in color, shape, and surface. (See chapter 13 for more detailded explanation).
Discussion (5 min.)	Application to sport? How would noticing new information help you have a better practice? How might it help with performance? Offer an example.
Prepare to Adapt, Adust, Engage. Imagery: visualize a present, accepting, tuning-into-novelty state of mind (5 min.)	Create your go-to thought, to help prepare to perform Noticing and accepting your current state of mind, experience (See Ch. 13 for more detailed explanation). Visualize: With eyes closed, after taking a few deep breaths, consider the following…. a. Know your starting point: Note just how you are feeling physically, emotionally – including that which is not perfect. Take a moment to accept yourself just as you are: Note your strengths today – What is good about how you are, just as you are? Consider where you will be practicing, performing next. Make note of the environment you will be playing in, who you will be playing, your teammates or competitors (upcoming performance, game or competition)? Prepare to adjust and adapt. See yourself ready to practice, perform.
	Prompt: What can you bring to mind to create the best approach *for today*… your inspired sport value? Your passion? A word or phrase of kindness? An image? b. *Now see yourself on the court (field, pool, pitch) – Getting ready to play to the best of your ability, just as you are….* Notice what may be different, novel…. Fresh…
Thank you!	Any comments about this practice? Take-aways from being part of the program? The most important thing that you learned from MMTS 2.0 that you can apply to performance or you life? Thank you!!

Appendix B: MMTS 2.0 Audio-file Script 1

Find a quiet comfortable place to sit. Sit in an upright, regal position – your head lifting upward over your spine. If it is comfortable for you, please place your feet flat on the floor, palms resting on your lap in the most comfortable position for you. Or, if you prefer, you are welcome to lie down. Allow your eyes to close or soften your gaze.

- Now bring your awareness to your breathing. All you need to do is breathe, at the pace and depth of breath that is most comfortable for you. You do not need to do anything but bring your awareness to your breathing. Throughout this practice I invite you to bring a sense of acceptance and warm-hearted interest to all of your experiences. Whether your mind is quiet or busy, your body at ease or sore, try bringing an openhearted, kind acceptance to whatever you experience. Though we may want things to change in the future or be different in the past, for now practice accepting things just as they are – for now, no need to do anything, or change anything. (pause)

- As you continue to place your awareness on your breath, you may notice a range of physical sensations – from warmth, coolness, tension, and vibrations to a sense of lightness or openness. You also may notice a particular sensation as you breathe, perhaps coolness as you breathe in or a sense of ease as you breathe out. Perhaps you feel your chest gently rising and falling. Notice, where do you feel your breath most strongly and easily? Rest your attention in the place that draws your attention as you breathe in and breathe out. (pause)

- As you breathe, you will notice that your mind wanders from time to time. Your mind may unintentionally drift to thoughts, feelings, worries, planning or just simply daydreaming. This is normal. As long as you are aware of what you are thinking, feeling, or sensing – you are successfully meditating, whether you have a quiet mind or wandering mind. (pause)

- When you notice your mind wandering, this is an important moment to help strengthen your poise. When you notice your mind wandering you can label what you are noticing. If it is a thought, you can just note "thought." Or if it is a feel-ing, you can just note "feeling." Or if you like you can note the type of feeling you are having, like "This is what irritation feels like," or "This is what calm and ease feels like," or even "This is what fear or anxiety feels like." You don't need to change anything, just note what is showing up. And then you have the oppor-tunity to gently bring your attention back to the focus of your choice. In this moment, I am asking you to focus on your breath. (pause)

- Throughout this practice, you will be asked to bring your attention back to your breath, body sensations, sounds, or thoughts. This practice of noticing your mind wandering and bringing your attention back to your choice of focus, like your breath right now, this practice will help you learn to focus your attention back on things that are important on the (insert performance environment; e.g., tennis court). Your mind wanders there too of course. As you practice re-focusing your attention here, you can bring that skill of strengthened poise and concentration to the (insert performance environment; e.g., tennis court). (pause)

- It does not matter how many times your mind wanders, just bring your attention back to your breath – with kindness each time you notice your mind wandering. And for this moment, just feel the breath. As best you can, bring kindness and compas-sion to your awareness, bringing gentle curiosity to your full experience. (pause)

- Shift your attention to sounds. Notice any sounds that arise. You might notice sounds coming, changing, and fading. Just bring your openhearted, friendly awareness to the sounds that are emerging. There is no right or wrong sound, it is just sound. Allow your awareness to rest with the sound that is most promi-nent. Notice as the sounds come and sounds fade. Notice how your awareness shifts from sound to sound. (pause)

- Shift your awareness to the physical sensations of your body. What do you notice? Perhaps you notice warmth or coolness, pressure, ease, or tension. Allow your awareness to freely move within your body. Noticing whatever physical sensations arise. Your awareness may naturally move from sensation to sensation within your body – just as it did with sound. Or your awareness may rest in a particular place in your body. Either way, just bring the same gentle, openhearted curiosity to whatever you physically sense. Just let it be as it is, whatever sensations are arising. (pause)

- If you would like to shift your body position, you are welcome to do so at any time. Just practice mindful awareness of your body as it shifts to a more comfortable, at-ease position. (pause)
- For a few moments, allow your awareness to open to all sounds, physical sensations, thoughts, emotions, and your breath. Allow your attention to rest wherever it likes. Allow awareness to move, just bringing an openhearted interest to all experience. Just as it is. Just for now, you only need to breathe. To be here right now. (pause)
- Whenever you are ready, slowly bring your attention back to the room and open your eyes.

Appendix C: MMTS 2.0 Audio-File Script 2

Find a comfortable quiet place to sit. Sitting in an upright position– your head lifting upward over your spine. If it is comfortable for you, please place your feet flat on the floor, palms resting on your lap in the most comfortable position for you. Or, if you prefer, you are welcome to lie down. Allow your eyes to close or soften your gaze.

- Now shift your awareness to the physical sensations of your body, what do you notice? Perhaps warmth or coolness, pressure, ease, or tension. Allow whatever physical sensations arise in your awareness. Your awareness may naturally move from sensation to sensation within your body, or your awareness may rest in a particular place in your body. And bring a gentle openhearted curiosity to whatever you physically sense, just let it be as it is, whatever sensations are arising. When you become aware of any discomfort or unwelcomed physical sensations in the body, that are not causing a potential harm, notice them and see if you can maintain a kind caring awareness of them without having to do anything more. Don't try and stop these physical sensations or try and make them go away. Just allow yourself to make some room for the discomfort or tension just noticing or maybe tolerating whatever you may be sensing. You may notice the sensation suddenly changes from moment to moment. See if you can make room for this discomfort, allow it to be there and be willing to stay with it for a bit. (pause)
- Now, I would like you to shift your attention from physical sensations in your body to noticing thoughts and emotion that may arise. Just as you did with your awareness of your breath and of your body, bring your warm friendly awareness to all thoughts and feelings that arise. In this particular practice we are not trying to stop our thinking, and not trying to avoid our thinking, but instead simply watching and being aware of thoughts and feelings as they arise. (pause)

- You can label these thoughts and feelings. You may note things like "planning," "remembering," or "worrying." If it is too much to label them specifically, you can just label them "thoughts" or "feelings." Whatever your thoughts and emotions, you can practice noticing and not getting lost in them. So, for example, you may notice yourself thinking, "This is what anxiety feels like." You can then observe the anxiety without engaging with it – you can allow it to stay without having to do anything else. You don't have to fix it, stop it, or change it. You may notice how thoughts and feelings come and go in your mind and body. You are not your thoughts or your feelings, if you allow them, they will come and go like waves upon the shore. (pause)
- If you ever notice that you are unable to stay with this practice because of a particularly uncomfortable physical sensation in your body or uncomfortable emotion – allow yourself to let go and shift your attention away from the physical or emotional discomfort back to your breath. Given what is happening, this is natural to feel just what you are feeling. Others also have discomfort in their bodies and have unwanted thoughts and emotions coming and going through their minds. In such moments, you may label the thought, "This is what anger feels like," "This is what disappointment feels like," or even "This is what joy feels like." Notice what is arising, what is most predominant. Notice the physical sensations – or the physical sensations associated with the emotion. Do you feel tight? Cold? Hot? Stuck? You may want to resist such sensations, but if you do resist, it can make it more painful. Notice the physical sensation and see if you can *soften* around it. Softening by offering yourself warmth, comfort, and kindness. Also you might notice and validate how hard it is to feel like this. You are safe now, you can safely allow the feeling to be there, just as it is. As you stay with the sensations, you may notice the sensations subtly change. You may even notice peace and comfort as they arise. Whenever you like, or when the sensations subside, you can just notice what that is like. Maybe notice what ease feels like also. (pause)
- As you practice this meditation, you can strengthen your ability to do the same on the (insert performance environment; e.g., tennis court). As unhelpful thoughts or emotions arise, you can notice them, accept them, and kindly bring your attention back to the task at hand – focusing on playing your best (insert specific sport; e.g., tennis) moment to moment. (pause)
- For a few moments, allow your awareness to open up to sound, physical sensation, thoughts, emotions, and your breath to all experience. Allow your attention to rest where it likes. Allow it to move. Bring to all experience an openhearted, interested presence. Just for now, needing only to breathe. To be here, right here, right now. (pause)

Whenever you are ready, you can open your eyes.

Appendix D: Mindful Breathing

Please find a quiet, comfortable place to sit or lie down. Position yourself in a way that you may be able to remain in one position for the whole exercise. This may mean sitting upright position or lying down with your arms and legs comfortably resting. Also, if at any point you have an urge to move. First, notice the urge. If you are having an unpleasant experience, allow yourself to mindfully adjust the position of you body. Allow your eyes to close or soften your gaze, whatever feels right to you, in this moment. Please bring your attention to your breath and keep that as your primary focus of attention. When you notice your awareness on other things – like thoughts, emotions, sounds – allow yourself to relax or accept the mind wandering (everyone's mind does) and kindly bring your attention back to your breathing. Some prompts of reminder:

- Simply notice your breath.
- Breathe at your pace and depth.
- Bring an interested, non-judgmental, kind attention to your breath.
- Notice the physical sensation associated with breathing and allow your awareness to rest there. As the sensation moves, allow your attention and awareness to move with it.
- It is OK to have thoughts, feelings, physical sensations arise. When they do, just notice bring your attention back to your breathing.

Appendix E: Breathing with Kindness[1]

Prior to starting this practice, find a quiet, comfortable place to sit or lie down. In this practice you will be offering kindness to yourself. As best you can, begin by taking note of what is most comfortable for your body. You are welcome to take a few moments to check in with yourself, and then position your body in the way that allows you to feel physical comfort and ease. You might opt to lie down or to sit in a gentle, upright position. You might think about allowing your shoulders to relax and adjusting in any way that works best for you.

- Begin with taking a few breaths. Allow the breaths to be a bit longer and deeper than usual.
- At the end of each out breath, allow your body to relax.
- Gently close your eyes or let your gaze soften, doing whatever is most comfortable for you.
- Place your hands palms down on your knees or legs. Feel the warmth of your hands. Allow that warmth to include a kindness toward your experience. You

---

[1] This practice is adapted from the Mindful Self-Compassion Teacher Trainer manual (2015).

might choose to put one, or both, hands over your heart or over the center of your chest. Whatever works for you, for now.

- For now, let go of the weight of your responsibilities and difficulties.
- Allow the warmth from your hands to offer you a sense of balance, of ease. This warmth can serve as a reminder to intentionally bring kind attention to your experience, to your body, to yourself.
- Bring this kind attention to your breath. Notice the experience of your body breathing, bringing awareness to your breath in an effortless way. You may most easily notice a coolness as you breathe in, you might notice the tingly sensation the tip of your nose or slight movement in your belly as you breathe in and out.
- Allow your attention to rest here, in the awareness of your body breathing.
- Your mind will naturally wander away from your awareness of breathing. It doesn't matter how many times your mind wanders. Focusing on the breath, noticing your mind wandering and bringing your attention back to the breath is all part of the mindfulness breathing meditation practice.
- Bringing awareness to the moment of awareness-of-wandering is a beautiful time to practice kindness. When you notice your mind wandering, bring awareness to this moment of wandering. In this moment, offer kindness toward yourself.
- *Before* your bring your awareness back to your breath, you might intentionally take a deeper breath and exhale to relax your body a bit more. If you would like, try that now. Or you notice any frustration or other difficult response and shine warmth and acceptance toward those reactions.
- After you have offered some kindness to the wandering, gently return your attention back to the awareness of your body breathing. When you shift back to your breath, guide your attention with kindness, gently.
- Lean into your breathing as you might incline toward whatever you love most, in a interested, warmhearted way. With curiosity and tenderness.
- Simply allow your body to breathe as you hold a warm, loving awareness of the breathing.
- There is nothing more to do, just your body breathing.
- Bring awareness to rise and fall of the breath, the rhythm of the body breathing. Of the whole body breathing.
- Now, take a moment to notice the calmness of your body, the relaxation of your body. Notice what arises when you intentionally incline kindness toward your experience.
- When you are ready, gently open your eyes.

Appendix F: Walking Meditation Practice[2]

Using an active meditation is a helpful, practical way to bring yourself, intentionally, into present state awareness. Bringing awareness to physical sensations can be very helpful in an effort to get present, a starting point to be able to attend to matters that are in need of your attention. Intentionally bringing awareness to walking is an ancient practice. Focusing on the sensations of walking, what you feel in your feet, can be an efficient, direct way to get more grounded, more balanced, in the moment.

You can use the practice of walking meditation to help get yourself grounded in the present when you are contending with difficult thoughts and emotions. You can use this active focus, with attention on the sensation of walking, to help make whatever is occurring more tolerable. When you can face and tolerate what is arising, you will be much more empowered to both stay with the sensations, instead of fighting them (which makes it worse), and be empowered to see what is happening so you can also opt to take action to give yourself what you might most need.

For this walking meditation, with attention on the soles of your feet:

- Take a moment to notice how you are feeling in this moment. Allow any thoughts, emotions, sounds and physical sensations to arise.
- All you need to do is bring awareness to this experience. In this practice, there is nothing else you need to ask of yourself. Nothing more to do.
- At your own pace, stand up. Bring your attention to your feet. Noticing how your feet feel against the floor. Notice the arches of your feet, the balls of your feet. Notice the sensations in your toes. Notice the changing sensations in your feeet. You might feel warmth, coolness, pressure, or tingling. Allowing attention to rest in the awareness of the sensations in your feet.
- Now shift your attention to the soles of your feet. Feel the contact to the floor beneath you.
- Maintaining your attention on the soles of your feet, gently rock forward and backward. Now try gently rocking side-to-side as you keep your attention on the soles of your feet.
- Your mind will wander. When this happens allow your body to relax and then gently bring your attention back to the soles of your feet.
- Begin to walk at a slower pace that is still comfortable for your body. Maintain attention on the soles of your feet. As you move forward notice how the sensations on the soles of your feet also shift and change.
- Notice each sole, of the left and right foot, as it lifts into the air. Notice each sole, of the left and right foot, as it is placed back on the group to support your body.
- Notice how your soles of your feet feel, step after slow step.
- As you walk you might notice the benefit you receive from this small yet such important part of your body. You might experience a sense of appreciation for the soles of your feet, appreciation of your feet, as you walk.

---

[2] *Ibid*

- As you continue to walk, keep your attention on the soles of your feet (for a few minutes longer).
- Return to where you started this practice and stand in place, once again.
- Broaden your awareness of your entire body. Allow yourself to feel any physical sensations and be aware of any thoughts or emotions that are arising.
- For this moment, allow yourself be just as you are without any need to do anything, change anything. If anything comes to mind that must be taken care of, trust that you can choose to handle the situation wisely.
- Before you complete the exercise, Ask yourself, "What do I need right now?" Allow your answer to emerge.

Appendix G: One for Me, One for You (Adapted)[3]

Prior to starting this practice, please find a quiet, comfortable place to sit or lie down. Place yourself in a position that you will be comfortable in for the next 10 minutes. If at any point you want to move, to allow for physical comfort, feel free to do so. Hold the intention of moving to offer kindness and comfort to your physical body as you engage in this practice.

Please start by siting or lying down in a comfortable position.

- Begin with taking a few breaths.
- At the end of each out breath, allow your body to relax a bit more.
- Gently close your eyes or let your gaze soften, doing whatever is most comfortable for you.
- Whatever works for you, in this moment.
- Please rest your hands on your legs (if you are sitting) or you might choose to put one, or both, hands over your heart or over the center of your chest. Feel the warmth of your hands. Let this warmth support an intention to bring a loving awareness to yourself and to this practice. You are welcome to move your hands at any time. Please do whatever works best for you.
- Taking a few breaths, a bit deeper and longer than your typical breath. With each exhale, allow your body to relax. Lean into the sensation of breathing, noticing breathing in and breathing out. (pause)
- Focus your attention on your in-breath. Offering a warmth, a kindness, toward the experience of breathing in.
- Consider what you wish most for yourself. Perhaps you might wish to be happy, to be safe, to be healthy. What you most wish for might arise in a word, an image, a phrase. Perhaps to be loved? Perhaps to accept yourself just as you are, in this moment?
- Each time you breathe in, bring to mind the phrase or image that reflects what you most wish for yourself. Or you can just feel this intention. Perhaps of love, kindness or acceptance focused inward (pause)

---

[3] *Ibid*

- Now, consider someone who you would like to offer some wish of kindness or love.
- Perhaps say their name to yourself. Imagine them here, with you. Bring to mind what you might most wish for them. You might bring to mind phrases like, may you be at ease; may you feel loved; may you be safe. Bring to mind a wish for this person.
- On the next outbreath, offer this wish for the other. Feel the sensation of breathing out.
- Each time you breath out, either bring this wish to mind or feel the intention of the wish for the other. Perhaps it is sending love? Or kindness? Or Acceptance? To this person each time you exhale (pause).
- If you like, you can begin to breath in for you and out for the other (pause)
- If you wish, you can focus on yourself, just on the other person or on both. Whatever you need need. (pause)
- Allow yourself to savor your positive intention, wish, toward yourself and the other (pause).
- Take a moment to notice how you are feeling, allowing yourself to feel just as it is (pause).
- When you are ready, slowing open up your eyes.

Appendix H: MMTS 2.0 Instructors

Amy Baltzell (MMTS 2.0 offered to DI men and women's collegiate tennis teams)

Amy has had a "most-days" mindfulness meditation practice for the past 8 years. She has attended a number of mindfulness trainings including: MBSR intensive, the "5-day"; Mindful Self-Compassion (MSC) 5-day intensive; 7-day MSC teacher training program; a course at the Insight Meditation Center (Cambridge, MA); a retreat with Jack Kornfield; a retreat with Tara Brach; and a 2-day Self-Compassion program with Christopher Germer.

Sebastian Brueckner (MMTS 2.0 offered to male German Olympic Badminton team members)

Sebastian has been engaged in informal mindfulness meditation training since 2011. He has exposed himself to different approaches to mindfulness meditation and attended several mindfulness workshops. Throughout his eight years of consulting and counseling athletes at one of Germany's Olympic Training Centers he has used mindfulness and self-regulation techniques in an attempt to create a holistic model of service provision that combines theoretical underpinnings from both areas and offers unique applied techniques and experiences.

Ian Connole (MMTS 2.0 offered to men's and women's DI collegiate golf teams and Best Army Ranger Competitors)

Ian was the Director of Sport Psychology for an NCAA Division I university where he taught mental skills to optimize performance and well being. He has engaged in a personal mindfulness meditation practice since 2011 and combines mindfulness-based practices with sport psychology interventions in his consulting. He learned mindfulness meditation under the tutelage of Bill Reger-Nash's 5-day holistic wellness courses and ongoing mentorship in addition to his formal graduate education.

Trevor Cote (MMTS 2.0 offered to a Division III men's soccer team)

Trevor has been informally practicing mindfulness meditation since 2013. He has studied and worked under (he writes) "the esteemed advisement of Amy Baltzell in her mindfulness and performance research lab, which included observing the delivery of MMTS 2.0". Additionally, he completed a 3-day Mindful Self-Compassion core skills training program led by Christopher Germer. Leader in studying MMTS 2.0., Baltzell research lab.

Rob (Robert) Dibernardo (MMTS 2.0 offered to DIII collegiate women's basketball team and coaching staff)

Rob has been engaged with an on-going private practice that started intermittently in 2001 and more seriously since 2009. In addition, he has completed two silent meditation retreats (Barre Center for Buddhist Studies: 4-Day & 5-Day intensives), two MBSR workshops (5-Day & 7-Day), 200RYT Yoga Teacher Training with silent meditation and several yoga/meditation retreats with Rolf Gates over the years.

Bob (Robert) Diehl (Assisted in offering MMTS 2.0 program to DI men and women's collegiate tennis teams and DIII collegiate women's basketball team and coaching staff.)

Bob has been engaged in on-going private practice of mindfulness and self-compassion based meditation practices since 2013. He integrates mindfulness based approaches to both his sport psychology practice and clinical training. Leader in studying MMTS 2.0., Baltzell research lab.

Josh Summers (MMTS offered to DI women's collegiate soccer team and coaching staff)

Josh has engaged in intensive vipassana meditation training since 2001, training primarily in over 25 weeklong retreats at the Insight Meditation Society as well as a 3-month retreat in Burma with the late master, Sayadaw U. Pandita.

References

Baltzell, A. (1999). *Psychological factors and resources related to rowers coping in elite competition* (unpublished doctoral dissertation). Boston University, Boston, MA.

Baltzell, A. L. (2016). Self-compassion, distress tolerance & mindfulness in performance. In A. L. Baltzell (Ed.), *Mindfulness and performance. Current perspectives in social and behavioral sciences* (pp. 53–77). New York: Cambridge University Press.

Baltzell, A. L., & Summers, J. (2016). The future of mindfulness and performance across disciplines. In A. L. Baltzell (Ed.), *Mindfulness and performance: Current perspectives in social and behavioral sciences* (pp. 515–541). New York: Cambridge University Press.

Baltzell, A. L., & McCarthy, J. (2016). Langerian mindfulness and optimal sport performance. In S. M. Fatemi (Ed.), *Critical mindfulness: Exploring Langerian models.* Springer.

Baltzell, A. L., Caraballo, N., Chipman, K., & Hayden, L. (2014). A qualitative study of the Mindfulness Meditation Training for Sport (MMTS): Division I female soccer players' experience. *Journal of Clinical Sport Psychology, 8,* 221–244.

Bodner, T., and Langer, E. J. (2001, June). *Individual differences in mindfulness: The mindfulness/mindlessness scale.* Poster presented at the thirteenth annual American Psychology Society Convention, Toronto, Ontario, Canada.

Csikszentmihalyi, M. (1975). *Beyond boredom and anxiety.* San Francisco: Jossey-Bass.

Csikszentmihalyi, M. (1999). If we are so rich, why aren't we happy? *American Psychologist, 54*(10), 821–827. https://doi.org/10.1037/0003-066X.54.10.821.

Csikszentmihalyi, M. (2014). *Flow and the foundations of positive psychology: The collected works of Mihaly Csikszentmihalyi.* Dordrecht: Springer.

Davidson, R. J., Kabat-Zinn, J., Schumacher, J., Rosenkranz, M., Muller, D., Santorelli, S., et al. (2003). Alterations in brain and immune function produced by mindfulness meditation. *Psychosomatic Medicine, 65,* 564–570. https://doi.org/10.1097/01.PSY.0000077505.67574.E3.

De Petrillo, L. A., Kaufman, K. A., Glass, C. R., & Arnkoff, D. B. (2009). Mindfulness for long distance runners: An open trial using Mindful Sport Performance Enhancement (MSPE). *Journal of Clinical Sport Psychology, 3,* 357–376.

Ferguson, L. J., Kowalski, K. C., Mack, D. E., & Sabiston, C. M. (2014). Exploring self-compassion and eudaimonic well-being in young women athletes. *Journal of Sport and Exercise Psychology, 36,* 203–216. https://doi.org/10.1123/jsep.2013-0096

Fienberg, C. (2010, October). The Mindfulness Chronicles On he psychology of possibility. Harvard Magazine. Retrieved from http://harvardmagazine.com/2010/09/
   the-mindfulness-chronicles?page=0,1

Gardner, F. L. (2016). Scientific advancements of mindfulness- and acceptance-based models in
   sport psychology: A decade in time, a seismic shift in philosophy and practice. In A. L. Baltzell
   (Ed.), *Mindfulness and performance* (pp. 127–152). New York: Cambridge University Press.

Gardner, F. L., & Moore, Z. E. (2004). A Mindfulness-Acceptance-Commitment (MAC) based
   approach to performance enhancement: Theoretical considerations. *Behavior Therapy, 35*,
   707–723. https://doi.org/10.1016/S0005-7894(04)80016-9.

Gardner, F. L., & Moore, Z. E. (2006). *Clinical sport psychology*. Champaign: Human Kinetics.

Gardner, F. L., & Moore, Z. E. (2007). *The psychology of enhancing human performance: The
   Mindfulness-Acceptance-Commitment (MAC) approach*. New York: Springer.

Gardner, F. L., & Moore, Z. E. (2012). Mindfulness and acceptance models in sport psychology:
   A decade of basic and applied scientific advancements. *Canadian Psychology, 53*(4), 309–318.
   https://doi.org/10.1037/a0030220.

Germer, C. K. (2009). *The mindful path to self-compassion: Freeing yourself from destructive
   thoughts and emotions*. New York: Guilford Press.

Germer, C. K., & Neff, K. D. (2013). Self-compassion in clinical practice. *Journal of Clinical
   Psychology, 69*(8), 856–867.

Germer, C., Neff, K., Becker, M., & Hickman, S. (2015). *The mindful self-compassion teaching
   training manual* (unpublished manuscript).

Haberl, P. (2016). Mindfulness and the Olympic athlete: A personal journey. In A. L. Baltzell
   (Ed.), *Mindfulness and Performance. Current perspectives in social and Behavioral sciences*
   (pp. 211–234). New York: Cambridge University Press.

Haigh, E. A. P., Moore, M. T., Kashdan, T. B., & Fresco, D. M. (2011). Examination of the factor
   structure and concurrent validity of the langer mindfulness/mindlessness scale. *Assessment,
   18*(1), 11–26.

Hanson, R., & Mendius, R. (2009). *Buddha's brain: The practical neuroscience of happiness, love,
   & wisdom*. Oakland: New Harbinger Publications.

Harris, S. (2014). *Waking up: A guide to spirituality without religion*. New York: Simon & Schuster.

Hayes, S. C. (2004). Acceptance and commitment therapy, relational frame theory, and the third
   wave of behavioral and cognitive therapies. *Behavior Therapies, 35*, 639–665. https://doi.
   org/10.1016/S0005-7894(04)80013-3.

Jackson, P., & Delehanty, H. (1995). *Sacred hoops: Spiritual lessons of a hardwood warrior*.
   New York: Hyperion.

John, S., Verma, S. K., & Khanna, G. L. (2011). The effect of mindfulness meditation on HPA-
   Axis in pre-competition stress in sports performance of elite shooters. *National Journal of
   Integrated Research in Medicine, 2*(3), 15–21.

Kabat-Zinn, J. (1994). *Wherever you go, there you are: Mindfulness meditation in everyday life*.
   New York: Hyperion.

Kabat-Zinn, J. (2003). Mindfulness-based interventions in context: Past, present, and future.
   Clinical Psychology: Science and Practice, 10(2), 144–156.

Kabat-Zinn, J. (2005). *Coming to our senses: Healing ourselves and the world through mindfulness*. New York: Hyperion.

Kabat-Zinn, J., Beall, B., & Rippe, J. (1985, June). *A systematic mental training program based
   on mindfulness meditation to optimize performance in collegiate and Olympic rowers*. Poster
   session presented at the World Congress in Sport Psychology, Copenhagen, Denmark.

Kaufman, K. A., Glass, C. R., & Arnkoff, D. B. (2009). Evaluation of Mindful Sport Performance
   Enhancement (MSPE): A new approach to promote flow in athletes. *Journal of Clinical Sports
   Psychology*, (4), 334–356.

Kaufman, K., Glass, C., & Pineau, T. (2016). Mindful sport performance enhancement (MSPE):
   Development and applications. In A. L. Baltzell (Ed.), *Mindfulness and performance:*

Current perspectives in social and Behavioral sciences (pp. 153–185). New York: Cambridge University Press.

Keng, S. L., Smoski, M. J., & Robins, C. J. (2011). Effects of mindfulness on psychological health: A review of empirical studies. *Clinical Psychology Review, 31*, 1041–1056. https://doi. org/10.1016/j.cpr.2011.04.006.

Langer, E. J. (1989). Minding matters: The consequences of mindlessness-mindfulness. *Advances in Experimental Social Psychology, 22*, 137–174.

Langer, E.J. (2000). Mindful Learning. Current Directions in Psychological Science 9, 6, 220-223.

Langer, E. J., & Moldoveanu, M. (2000). Mindfulness research and the future. *Journal of Social Issues, 56*, 129–139. https://doi.org/10.1111/0022-4537.00155.

Langer, E., Russel, T., & Eisenkraft, N. (2009). Orchestral performance and the footprint of mindfulness. *Psychology of Music, 37*(2), 125–136. https://doi.org/10.1177/0305735607086053

Langer, E. J., Cohen, M., & Djikic, M. (2012). Mindfulness as a psychological attractor: The effect on children. *Journal of Applied Social Psychology, 42*(5), 1114–1122.

Löwel, S. & Singer, W. (1992) Science 255 (published January 10, 1992) *"Selection of Intrinsic Horizontal Connections in the Visual Cortex by Correlated Neuronal Activity"*. United States: American Association for the Advancement of Science. *pp.* 209–212.

Manna, A., Raffone, A., Perrucci, M. G., Nardo, D., Ferretti, A., Tartaro, A., et al. (2010). Neural correlates of focused attention and cognitive monitoring in meditation. *Brain Research Bulletin, 82*, 46–56.

Moore, Z. (2016). Mindfulness, emotional regulation and performance. In A. L. Baltzell (Ed.), *Mindfulness and performance: Current perspectives in social and Behavioral sciences* (pp. 29–52). New York: Cambridge University Press.

Mosewich, A. D., Crocker, P. R. E., Kowalski, K., & DeLongis, A. (2013). Applying self-compassion in sport: An intervention with women athletes. *Journal of Sport & Exercise Psychology, 35*, 514–524.

Mumford, G. (2016). *The mindful athlete: Secrets to pure performance*. Berkeley: Parallax Press.

Neff, K. (2003). Self-compassion: An alternative conceptualization of a healthy attitude toward oneself. *Self and Identity, 2*(2), 85–101. https://doi.org/10.1080/15298860309032.

Neff, K. D., & Germer, C. K. (2013). A pilot study and randomized controlled trial of the mindful self-compassion program. *Journal of Clinical Psychology, 69*(1), 28–44.

Newman, K.M. (2016). *What Mindfulness is Missing*, syndicated from *Greater Good (Jul 05, 2016)*.

Pineau, T. R., Glass, C. R., & Kaufman, K. A. (2014). Mindfulness in sport performance. In A. Ie, C. T. Ngnoumen, & E. J. Langer (Eds.), *The Wiley Blackwell handbook of mindfulness* (Vol. II, pp. 1004–1033). Chichester: Wiley.

Reis, N. A., Kowalski, K. C., Ferguson, L. J., Sabiston, C. M., Sedgwick, W. A., & Crocker, P. R. E. (2015). Self-compassion and women athletes' responses to emotionally difficult sport situations: An evaluation of a brief induction. *Psychology of Sport and Exercise, 16*, 18–25. https:// doi.org/10.1016/j.psychsport.2014.08.011.

Sappington, R., & Longshore, K. (2015). Systematically reviewing the efficacy of mindfulness-based interventions for enhanced athletic performance. *Journal of Clinical Sport Psychology, 9*, 232–262.

Schwanhausser, L. (2009). Application of the Mindfulness-Acceptance-Commitment (MAC) protocol with an adolescent springboard diver: The case of Steve. *Journal of Clinical Sport Psychology, 3*, 377–395.

Sedlmeier, P., Eberth, J., Schwarz, M., Zimmermann, D., Haarig, F., Jaeger, S., & Kunze, S. (2012). The psychological effects of meditation: A metaanalysis. *Psychological Bulletin, 138*(6), 1139–1171. https://doi.org/10.1037/a0028168

Stankovic, D. & Baltzell, A.L. (in preparation). *Mindfulness meditation in sport: Improved sport performance of masters tennis players.*

Wolanin, A. T., & Gross, M. B. (2017, August). The mindfulness--acceptance--commitment approach. In C. Glass Chair (Ed.), *Mindfulness-based interventions in sport---empirical sup-*

port and effective implementation. Washington, D.C.: Symposium conducted at the meeting of the American Psychological Association.

Wegner, D. M. (1994). Ironic processes of mental control. *Psychological Review, 101*(1), 34–52. https://doi.org/10.1037/0033-295X.101.1.34.

Williams, J. M., Nideffer, R. M., Wilson, V. E., & Sagal, M. (2015). Concentration and strategies for controlling it. In J. M. Williams (Ed.), *Applied sport psychology: Personal growth to peak performance* (7th ed., pp. 304–328). Mountain View: Mayfield Publishing.